Jokey Horse-Jockey North-South Rapport:
Diagnostic-cum-Prognostic-Academic Perspectives on Who Truly Depends on Whom

Nkwazi Nkuzi Mhango

Langaa Research & Publishing CIG
Mankon, Bamenda

Publisher
Langaa RPCIG
Langaa Research & Publishing Common Initiative Group
P.O. Box 902 Mankon
Bamenda
North West Region
Cameroon
Langaagrp@gmail.com
www.langaa-rpcig.net

Distributed in and outside N. America by African Books Collective
orders@africanbookscollective.com
www.africanbookscollective.com

ISBN-10: 9956-550-36-1

ISBN-13: 978-9956-550-36-4

© Nkwazi Nkuzi Mhango 2018

All rights reserved.
No part of this book may be reproduced or transmitted in any form or by any means, mechanical or electronic, including photocopying and recording, or be stored in any information storage or retrieval system, without written permission from the publisher

Table of Contents

Acknowledgments... v
Foreword... vii
List of Abbreviations.. ix

Chapter One
North-South Link to Conflict, Poverty and Underdevelopment... 1
i) Introduction.. 1
ii) The Use of Interventionism as an Exploitative Strategy... 12
iii) Free Market as a Ruse to Penetrate and Exploit the Global South.................................. 22

Chapter Two
Nature of Exploitative Relationship..................... 25
i) The Economies of Dominance and Exploitation.. 32
ii) It Takes Two to Tango: Two-Part Liability......... 43
iii) The Role of Technology in the North-South Relationship.. 50
iv) Is It Democracy or Demicracy?........................... 58

Chapter Three
When Dependency Hampers Interdependency..... 69
i) Inevitable Interdependency Partnering and Partnership... 75
ii) Essentialised and Internalised Colonialism.......... 79
iii) Global Warming as a Unifying Force................. 85

Chapter Four
What Worked and What Did Not in the North-South Rapport... 91
i) Liberal Peace: A Quick Fix................................... 105
ii) Is aid a Panacea or a Mere Panegyric?................ 109
iii) New Economic Model and New Superstructure........... 115
iv) Meaningful and Practical Policy Change............ 119

Chapter Five
New Take That the Global South Needs to Embark on..**125**
i) Unreservedly Addressing Colonial Legacy.....................126
ii) Rethink Human Needs and Human Rights....................132

Chapter Six
Part two: Two Case Studies: Africa, the Role of Definition and Divisionism...............................**137**
Troubling Myth of Africa's [Under-] Development............**137**
i) Introduction...137
ii) Troubling the Predicament of [Under-] Development..139
iii) Doctrinaire Development...156
iv) Wake-up Call for Africa as a Specimen for the Latter..158
v) Conclusion...165

Chapter Seven
Case two: Violence, Power, Politics and (Anti-) Development in Africa...**169**
i) Introduction...169
ii) Proxy Recolonisation and Extension of Divide-and-Rule..174
iii) The role of Parties to Conflicts in Resolving the Conflict..178
iv) Ethnoconflicts and Resources.................................182
v) How the Former Reinventing New people and Creating Animosity in the Latter.....................186
vi) Assimilation Inhalation and Perpetuation....................193
vii) Conclusion: What Should Be Done? 195

References.. 201

Acknowledgments

I acknowledge the humungous contribution my wife, partner and the best friend ever, Nesaa, made in the preparations of this volume. Listening to dry academic stuff has never been amusing and easy, especially for the person whose profession is completely different. Our young children, Ng'ani, Nkuzi and Nkwazi Jr. too, had a lot to offer however unbeknownst to them. Nesaa used to take them for swimming lessons alone in summer while I was busy researching and writing.

More importantly, I acknowledge exceptionally sincere and bottomless support I got from my brother, friend and mentor, Professor Sean Byrne (Manitoba University) and with his wife Professor Jessica Senehi who have always stood by me. Jessica and Sean, I am proud of you really. My brother and friend professor Eliakim Sibanda did a lot to challenge my rationale. So, too, my brother, Professor Munyaradzi Mawere (Great Zimbabwe University) did a great job to keep on encouraging me to take the task up, apart from reviewing this book. Ndugu Willy M. Mutunga, PhD, former Kenya's Chief Justice and President of the Supreme Court has always been instrumental to me. Thanks brother.

As a tradition, I acknowledge my readers who became friends and part of my family thanks to reading my ideas and some commenting on them such as Sirili Akko (Arusha-Tanzania) and Salih Ibrahim Hassan aka Mr. Darfur, (Winnipeg MB), among others.

I, also, acknowledge PhD students of the Arthur V. Mauro Centre, St. Paul, University of Manitoba (2015), especially those who were interested in the Africa affairs, particularly my best friend Chuck Egerton for many discussions we had on Africa and what can be done to address conflicts, poverty and underdevelopment resulting from North-South exploitative Jokey Horse-Jockey North-South Rapport. Similarly, I acknowledge my friend Ray Loewen, president of the West Park Motor, Altona, MB, Canada who helped me in the coming book on Terrorism. Ray, you are great man.

Foreword

I must make a clean breast from the outset. I have personal as well as academic interests in the topic this volume deals with. My aim is to tweak or add up to the dialogue that has been going on for many years since the Global North invaded and occupied the Global South under colonialism and thereafter, up until now, under neocolonialism and jokey-horse-jockey rapport. Being one of billions of victims of the exploitative nature of the relationship between the duo, my experience and views can add up to see to it that the said relationship is deconstructed, reconstructed for the peace of the world. I, therefore, must state it clearly that one of the aims of this volume, apart from contributing the dialogue academically, seeks to propose some solutions to the problems revolving around the relationship between two unequal equals; if I may use the term. Hypothetically, I can comfortably argue that many conflicts the latter experiences have the hallmarks of colonialism and unfair relationship and coexistence all perpetrated by the former.

In tackling the problems resulting from this exploitative and somehow nugatory relationship namely conflict, poverty and underdevelopment, the book looks at *praxis* and theories seeking to decontaminate, demythologise, deconstruct, and reconstruct the relationship in order to usher equality, equity, justice and parity in.

List of Abbreviations

ACHPR	African Charter on Human and People's Rights
ACP	Africa Caribbean and Pacific
AFP	Agence France Presse
ANC	African National Congress
AU	African Union
BHN	Basic Human Needs
CAR	Central African Republic
CIA	Central Intelligence Agency
CNN	Cable News Network
CPI	Consumer Price Index
DRC	Democratic Republic of Congo
EFF	Economic Freedom Fighters
EU	European Union
FDI	Foreign Direct Investment
FRIDE	Fundación para las Relaciones Internacionales y el Diálogo Exterior
GBV	Gender Based Violence
GDP	Gross Domestic Product
GFI	Government Funded Investment
GLR	Great Lakes Region
GM	Genetically Modified
GNP	Gross National Product
HIPC	Heavily Indebted Poor Countries
HSBC	Hong Kong and Shanghai Banking Corporation
ICC	International Criminal Justice
ICIJ	International Consortium of Investigative Journalists
ICT	Information Communication Technology
IFI	International Financial Institutions
IGAD	Intergovernmental Authority for Development
IMF	International Monetary Fund
KFC	Kentucky Fried Chicken
MCC	Millennium Challenge Corporate
MDG	Millennium Development Goal

NATO	North Atlantic Treaty Organisation
ODA	Overseas Development Assistance
OECD	Organisation for Economic Co-operation and Development
OPEC	Organisation of the Petroleum Exporting Countries
PEV	Post-Election Violence
PhD	Doctor of Philosophy
QME	Qualitative Military Edge
RPBC	Rational Political Business Cycle Model
SDT	Self-determination Theory
SSA	Sub Saharan Africa
TMK	Traditional Medicinal Knowledge
UDHR	Universal Declaration of Human Rights
UK	United Kingdom
UN (O)	United Nations (Organisation)
UNESCO	United Nations Educational, Scientific and Cultural Organisation
UNITA	União Nacional para a Independência Total de Angola
USA	United States of America
USSR	Union of Soviet Socialist Republics
WMD	Weapons of Mass Destruction
WTO	World Trade Organisation

Chapter One

North-South Link to Conflict, Poverty and Underdevelopment

i) Introduction

> *In other words, the North-South conflict also means a cultural division of the world's societies. It is the division that was defined during the 18th and 19th centuries by opposing terms such as 'civilization' and 'savagery/barbarism'; later they were substituted by the binomials 'development' and 'underdevelopment', 'modernity' and 'tradition', 'domination' and 'dependency', 'metropolis' and 'periphery', 'globalism' and 'localism'* Krotz (1997: 239 cited in Oliveira 2011).

The above quote, apart from being self-explanatory, suffices to answer the question about the origin of the terms of the relationship between the Global North and Global South dwelling on economic matrices and synergies between the twosomes. Therefore, too, from the quote one can grasp the spirit and the intentions of the formulation of these two terms whose major aim, *inter alia*, is for one side to belittle, discriminate against, dwarf and exploit another while for the other is an insult. Due to its self-explanatory nature, the quote above delivers the message forthrightly. Hence, this volume will not dwell on redefining or elaborating more on such terms because the provided reading goes even deeper and further as far as the etymology of the terms are concerned. Importantly however, some of the terms found in the defining quote above will feature in this volume.

However, we can add something in that the creation, and partly, the conceptualisation of the terms, seems to be more stereotypical, xenophobic and fabricated than logical. All depends on the lenses one uses to view and analyse them. This is why this volume avoids of using such terms stereotypical and xenophobic terms by taking them easily and applying them blindly without underscoring the ambiguities and the toxicity hidden behind them. Primarily, the volume takes a deconstructionist slant of scholarship (Jobson 2010) in order to scrutinise; and thereby contribute to how these terms can be made right. For, failure to deconstruct and reconstruct the terms blatantly means condoning injustice, hoaxes, and exploitation hidden behind the terms. Arguably, in dealing with the issues this volume raises experiential and historical realities will play a great role in devising fair and feasible solutions to the problems resulting from the relationship between two halves of the world however socially constructed. Specifically in particular, this volume dwells on exploitative and unfair relationship between the Global North and the Global South. Subjectively and objectively, this relationship needs deconstruction and general overhaul in order to serve the parties to it equally and equitably; and thereby gain big. For the purpose of this tome, the meaning the Global North is a little bit mixed and confusing depending on the elements discussed. For, example, if we consider neoliberal economic policies the Global North or the West has always superimposed on the Global South, the difference is the same.

Notably, although the volume is about exploitative and unequal North-South relationship, on balance, much emphasis will be on Africa due to experiential and academic, if not, historical reasons. Equally so, Africa is the most affected area of the Global South that needs to be given high priority shall the relationship in question intend to be meaningfully constructive. Additionally, Africa is the subset that has more resources than other areas in the latter which makes it an attraction to economic bullying and exploitation.

Moreover, this volume will specifically dwell on three facets of the relationship between the Global North and the Global South namely conflict, poverty and underdevelopment all resulting from this relationship. Here the major aim is to prove that the relationship in point is wanting and unfair. Although, North-South relationship, in dealing with various things such as commerce, conflict and underdevelopment, has worked in some places, it is still somewhat inequitable; and thus enables the former to dominate; and thereby exploit the latter. Thus, this relationship becomes the cause of conflict as it revolves around struggle for resource control, which infringes on basic and unmet human needs not to mention inequality, poverty, underdevelopment and insecurity in the latter that has led to relative deprivation.

Further, this volume uses theories based on academic, experiential and historical realities to shed light on the ontological nature of the relationship between the two as an extension of colonialism embedded in how the two deal with commerce, conflict and development among others. By nature, therefore, this relationship gyrates around opposing and dichotomous binary or dualistic paradigm. Emphatically, the major aim of this volume, *inter alia*, is to earmark some problems resulting from the unequal and unfair relationship to which it will suggest some viable solutions based on a diagnostic-cum-prognostic approach. I think; through this diagnostic-cum-prognostic undertaking, this volume will be able to add up to the already-existing literature; and thereby the adding up to dialogical aspect on how the two halves can synchronise and tweak their relationship in order to bear fruits and bring meaningful justice to both sides. It does not make sense, chiefly for the victims, to stay side and look while they are suffering simply because some of the people from the former do not want to see and do justice for all. Importantly, for the latter, justice is not a matter of begging or pleading for it; but instead, it is about facing the former and seeking justice based on equitable and equal footings of the relationship between the two.

Furthermore, the book, diagnostically, earmarks the areas wherein the Global North superimposes its will on the Global South through neoliberal exploitation, exclusion and imposition (Coleman 2007). As well, the volume touches on the weakness of the latter in dealing with the former. The volume adduces much evidence from academic literature and experiential realities to show how systemic flaws on both sides have contributed immensely; and thus, perpetually sustained the exploitation of the latter by the former. Through this systemic manipulations and collective thievery, the former has gained immensely in terms of wealth and status while, to the contrary, the latter has comparatively lost hugely almost in everything noteworthy. So, too, the effects of this exploitation, if not addressed now, are likely to take a long time to overcome and redress shall the international system remain archaic, biased and parochial. Primarily, leaving the situation as it is will create more breeding grounds for three central themed facets namely conflict, poverty and underdevelopment. What's more, from this backdrop, North-favouring exploitation created antithetical duality in which one side is significantly affluent as oppose to the absolutely destitute and dejected counterpart. If anything, this duality is one of the reasons that pose challenges to academics, activists and politicians in both sides of this divide as it begs to do something about it. Denying or ignoring the existence and consequences of such a situation creates a chaotic and uneven world wherein harmony, peace and prosperity for all become seemingly impossible.

In academically, competently and judiciously addressing and tackling some issues, sometimes, it is empirical to declare one's interests. At an individual level, I must confess from the outset. I have personal as well as academic interests in the topic. Being a victim of the North-South exploitative relationship, my experience and views can add up to the dialogue to see to it that the said relationship is deconstructed and reconstructed for the justice of the latter and the peace of the world at large. I, thus, must state it clearly that the aim of this volume, apart from aiming at contributing to the dialogue academically, proposes some solutions to the problems as seen through my own eyes.

Theoretically, I comfortably argue that many conflicts, high poverty rates and underdevelopment the Global South has experienced for a long time have all hallmarks of colonialism, unfair relationship and coexistence as, for many years, unabatedly the Global North Mark has perpetrated them (Mearsheimer & Walt (2006, 2007). This is why this relationship needs the deconstruction and facelift for the benefits of all stakeholders and the peaceful, just and stable world in general.

Through using diagnostic and prognostic approach and analysis, it is easy to note and notice that the Global North has more causation of conflict, poverty and underdevelopment in the latter than solutions. Hence, it becomes easy to detect the problems; and thereby prescribe what should be done to do away with such a catch-22 situation the two are in if we face the truth that the two need each other so as to survive. Logically, the wealth the former enjoys and takes pride in has its roots from the latter. Therefore, prescribing the former to redress the latter becomes one of the solutions. For, due to the hegemonic nature of this relationship, the Global North uses its market-oriented neoliberal and scheming policies to control and intervene in commerce, conflict and development in the latter. However exploitative they are, the former regards its interventionist strategies as a panacea while in fact they are but a henbane that begs the latter to be a misanthrope as far as the former is concerned.

Additionally, after either suffocating and ignoring or sidelining the Global South, the Global North created a paternalistic and clientele system in which the latter is at the receiving end while the former is in the position of dictating everything as far as this fatal and toxic relationship is concerned. Agonizingly though, this imbalanced and exploitative relationship has existed for a long time leading to a great loss for the latter resulting from the great rip off by the former that has made a killing.

Tjposvold (2006) crisply argues that circumstantially "conflict is thought to arise from opposing interests involving scarce resources and goal divergence and frustration" (p. 88) in whatever conflicants lay a claim on. In this conflict, the scarcity is not about resources but justice that results to poverty in the latter. A.H Halsey cited in Mack and Lansley (1985: 49) as cited in Walker (1987) defines poverty as being poor based on relation with people as it is socially or cultural conceptualised. Those in the latter know too well what poverty means based on their either experiences or definitions from the former. Again, always poverty normally centres on material things while the truth is that poverty transcends material and immaterial things. This is why it is difficult to have a single internationally agreed definition of poverty. This is because of the relativity of poverty and the lenses one used in measuring or defining it. Despite lacking a water-tight definition, this volume concurs with Robb (2000) cited in Akindola (2009) who defines poverty denoting it to, *inter alia*, imply "vulnerability, physical and social isolation, insecurity, lack of self-respect, lack of access to information, distrust of state institutions and powerlessness can be as important to the poor as low income" (p. 123). Consequently, defining poverty to revolve around material things makes the concept narrow and materialistic so much that it is likely to exclude other important elements such as the moral wellbeing of those facing poverty, among others. Essentially, the definition of poverty revolves around economic rationale as opposed to natural rationale. You wonder; why a person who owns a piece of land in rural Africa should be categorised as impoverished simply because he or she is not a consumer of industrial products; and thereby contribute to the existence of capitalism. Some of those who define poverty count calories intakes and other things without underscoring the fact that the criteria used in measuring such intake lack agreement globally. Toye (2007) observes that the definition of poverty heavily revolves around consumption (or income). Such a definition[s] tends to ignore both the productive assets of the poor and a range of communal and social resources that the poor use to supplement their consumption; and thus being defined as underdeveloped.

As for underdevelopment, as well, the Global North defines the South by using only capitalistic and neoliberal yardsticks. Wealth is quantified but not *qualitified*. Lall (1975) simply defines it noting that it "equals dependence" (p. 805) based on capitalistic benchmark of income. I would argue that there is no way one can define underdevelopment without considering manmade-systemic inequalities resulting from ills such as slavery, colonialism and now neoliberalism embedded in globalism. Again, as it is on poverty, the definition of underdevelopment seems to be constricted, conjectural and deceptive. For, if we consider underdevelopment to equal dependence, the global North is likely to be underdeveloped because it heavily depends on Africa for many resources. With such a definition, the latter is ahead of the former for it has many precious resources that capitalistic and colonial definitions of wealth purposely tend to ignore in order to make Africa look like a pauper that needs saviours from the West. Essentially, this is the development of underdevelopment (Scott and Marshall 2009) wherein the former has made the latter to believe that it cannot do anything without necessarily getting a leg up from the former. However narrow this definition may sound, it is ambiguous. It depends on the lenses one uses and the culture one comes from. Dependence in some cultures, especially collectivistic ones, is wealth based on Social Capital Theory that "suggests that social capital, the network of relationships possessed by an individual or a social network and the set of resources embedded within it, strongly influence the extent to which interpersonal knowledge sharing occurs" (Bandura 1989 cited in Chiu, Hsu and Wang 2006: 1873).

However, the social capital is *vice versa* in individualistic culture in which society is not as important as it is for the collectivistic people. Many concepts are relative all depending on who defines what and why; and who expounds and for what intention[s] for what purpose[s] or reason[s]. Lall underscores this by equating underdevelopment and dependence as the former defines it. Arguably, one person may be underdeveloped in one thing and developed in another. Let us use Lall's lenses. Based on this definition the former is rich. For, it does not economically depend on the latter based on who begs and donates what. However, when it comes to running its economy, the former more heavily depends on the latter than the latter does on it. For, the latter has immense resources and the former has much money to be able to balance the equation shall it decide to do so. The rationale that applies to this volume is that the relationship between the Global North and the Global South is naturally conflictual, exploitative and unfair due to having different and opposing goals and interests not to mention power undercurrents. The differences from natural conflict trend are that the scarcity is manmade thanks to greed on one side and sheepishness for the other on the other.

In this theoretical analysis of conflict, poverty and underdevelopment, firstly, treats the relationship between the Global North and the Global South as conflict, conspiracy and stumbling block due to its nature of causing conflict, exploitation, inequality, insecurity, poverty and underdevelopment to one side namely the latter as it produces pride, wealth and security for the other side namely the former. You can see this in policies and practices between the duo.

Secondly, the relationship in question has caused a lot of conflicts, poverty and underdevelopment in the former; while it, as well, has produced wealth and development to the Global North. Applying such two dicta and rationales, we think; the matter in question deserves to be treated as so. In other words, conflict, poverty and underdevelopment in this volume, among others, have a different nature of being the sources of other many conflicts, exploitation and sufferings that have been going on for a long time. Tjposvold (*Ibid.*) goes on arguing that conflict can be seen as a subset, and perhaps, not such a critical one, independent of the major issues of coordination, exchange, support, and decision-making. Essentially, conflict, exploitation and underdevelopment resulting from the relationship between the two have all hallmarks of unfairness in that there is a conflict between two geographical and political entities that has resulted in many conflicts between the elites that form governments in many countries and the majority citizens not to mention poverty and underdevelopment resulting thereof too. Likewise, conflictual are the situations the two found themselves in as they are all manmade thanks to the former's hegemonic nature and latter's mediocre role.

Going back to basic human needs theory, despite the theory as the Western scholars expound and propound it, the Global North has never, practically and equitably, applied its rationale regarding dealing the Global South. It is as if the envisaged theory meant to apply on the former but not for the latter. This theory lacks inclusivity concerning the latter. The neglect of basic human needs in the latter has led to many conflicts, poverty and underdevelopment resulting due to uneven and unfair distribution of resources of which the latter supplies to the former. In this unfair relationship, the latter becomes a mere source of resources and a consumer through unfair and unjust trade sanctioned by neoliberal policies the former enacted and reinforced. We can argue under the relative deprivation theory that the former has, constantly and systematically, of course, denied justice to the latter that in itself is a good source of the three evils or incongruities discussed in this volume. Under the basic human needs theory, all humans have the same basic human needs they are duty-bound to fulfil. Maslow (1943 cited in Wan and Chiou 2006), under the hierarchy of human needs, did a good job by categorising the needs all humans equally as they revolve around five hierarchies namely self-actualisation, esteem, social, security and physiological needs. I argue that due to colonial nature of scholars from the former, the needs so propounded only make sense theoretically due to the lack of one important element of making them attainable and enjoyable namely, justice. Further, I argue that lack of justice is the major element the world is lacking; and it causes to chaos and wars that kill many people besides destroying a lot of property in the latter. Arguably, if basic human needs do not include justice, it means; all expounded and propounded needs will never be achieved or obtained in the latter, especially because there is no mechanism ingrained in the basic human needs theory itself. Therefore, I can boldly maintain that among basic human needs that every human needs is justice. Therefore, I propose the incorporation of justice to the hierarchy of needs. I know; there are thinkers who argue that the lack of justice cannot lead to death. Some view it as a moral thing than a legal requirement *vis-a-vis* enhancing basic human needs. If you look at this rationale in a short term approach, it is true; but if you look at it in a long term approach, the results become different, particularly if we consider millions of people injustices have already claimed all over the world. What makes us ignore this element is the fact that the consequences of the lack of justice either come slowly or take long time to surface. Farmer, Nizeye, Stulac and Keshavjee (2006) argue that when basic human needs are not met, those lacking them are likely to legally or illegally engage in violent acts due to the lack of trust between each other resulting from the difficulty for them to rationally and unbiasedly consider and view each other's needs (Staub 2006). I think this speaks to the lack of justice which results into conflicts in the latter. You can see this in the relationship between the Global North and the Global South in which many protracted conflicts in the latter massaged and left to thrive as the people suffer as it is currently in the case in the Democratic Republic of Congo (DRC). Due to prevalence of long-time systemic injustices resulting from perpetual exploitation, the latter seems to have many more conflicts than the former. For, injustices in the latter have caused poverty and underdevelopment that force people to seek alternative means of survival through destructive means of satisfying their long-time deprived basic human needs. Once again, this is why criminality such as bad governance, civil wars and corruption become the means for political opportunists to survive in the latter.

Although justice is always politicised, it is supposed to be treated seriously just as any other human rights that humans are supposed to practically and equally achieve and enjoy. Due to politicisation of everything, it has been possible and easy for the former to maintain systemic exploitation for a long time without facing any consequences. However, thanks to globalisation, things are now changing. The former that used to be immune of the sufferings the latter faces, is now facing immigration crisis after some of the victims of its policies in the latter decided to follow the goodies in the former. Mhango (2015) considers this movement of the people as an emancipatory if not a balance act for the duo to address their historical relationship built on exploitation and injustices. The arrival of *unwanted* illegal immigrants to the former will change the habit and habitation forcing the former to start thinking globally, collectively and gregariously instead of looking at conflict, poverty and underdevelopment as the problems of the latter. This is why Mhango (*Ibid.*) calls illegal immigrants *modern-time missionaries* reciprocating from the latter to the former just like the first colonial missionaries did when they invaded the latter to lay a foundation of the current unfair relationship. There is no way the economies of the countries in the former will remain in a great shape while there are intruders coming every day seeking the greener pastures.

The lack of justice can take away basic human needs which is revolve around debilitating effects resulting from North-South relationship regulated by capitalistic *diktat*, drive and market only. After dominating and excluding the latter, neoliberal policies among which are the market. However, it seems; neoliberalism has purposely overlooked it as a good cause and source of conflict, exploitation and underdevelopment in the latter by the former. One important question we need to ask is why the former relatively deprives the latter its basic human needs by exploiting it while it advocates human rights. What type of human rights are these and for whom? The answer is simple; the former wants to fulfil the basic human needs and even secondary human needs for its population by depriving the latter the same right and necessity.

Arguably, such an uneven and unfair relationship has fuelled violent conflicts that have always preoccupied the international community and thereby forgets or ignores production and other aspects of life that are amiss in the latter *vis-à-vis* poverty and underdevelopment. In a word, the conflicts in case and point seem to have been internalised by both sides to the extent that they look like a reality under the international system. This is why it has become a norm for the so-called international community to discretionary deal or sometimes, ignore the conflicts in the latter while the same acts differently when the ball is in the former's court. Such practices and conceptualisation have enabled such conflicts and other problems resulting from them to slink under the ladder thus causing the duo failing in adequately and timely seeing and addressing them by those claiming to have what it takes to address them.

Another important area in this relationship is power. The former has absolute power over the latter that has always been recipient almost in everything. For any relationship to make sense and do justice there must be the balance of power. If anything, as we will see later, power is one of important things the duo needs to, adequately, address in order to enable each other to listen to and treat each other with decorum. Here, there must be the power of balance (Campbell, Patel and Singh 2008) without which the *status quo* will always prevail at the detriment of the Global South.

Similarly, the duo seems to have accepted the gap and disparity between them as a natural setting-cum-thing while it actually is but a dubiously created-and-nurtured one. Much effort is dwell on trying to resolve violent conflicts by ignoring the North-South unequal relationship that, in essence, is a major cause of conflicts, poverty and underdevelopment in many countries in the Global South. There are some flaws in Global North's exploitative and prescriptive interventions in conflict, development, democracy, policymaking, executing, funding all projects resulting from its exploitative relationship under its illiberal-neoliberal policies-cum-strategies in post-war, poor and underdeveloped countries. The approaches that the former–under the dupery banner of international community–has taken under its *diktat* to conceal and massage the effects are negative ones. So, too, this seems to be overlooked as the major causations of the many problems in the latter. It is sad to note that even academics have fallen in this trap either thinking they are defending their countries or continent or serving what seems to be their sacred duties as they were handed down depending on how they were brought up. The living example is the fact that all organisations in the former that exploit the latter use academics to formulate their exploitative policies.

ii)   The Use of Interventionism as an Exploitative Strategy

The Global North has been always using many strategies in dominating and exploiting the Global South. I will explore some of these strategies; and propose how they can be deconstructed in order to bring about change and equality between the parties to this relationship.

Practically, as noted above, the Global North has been using interventionist approaches as a pretext or a scapegoat from its original intentions motivated by its self-interests, self-serving and self-preservation under neoliberal development and peace initiatives. Under the international relations theory, the state has the task of protecting its interests even if it means to go to war with another state or suppress its people. Practically, states in the former can go to war with the states in the latter without necessarily following international laws or seeking permission from international organs responsible such as the UN. Hauss (2010) argues that the "stakes of a conflict can be magnified by security dilemma in which the actions of one state to protect its own security actually serve to weaken its opponents" (p. 30). We must make a distinction here. Do not confuse the state to be homogeneous. For, the meaning and powers of the state differ from one state to another depending on where the said state is located. If the said state is in the former, it has a *carte blanche* to do as pleased shall the enemy be in the latter. If the said state is in the latter; and it faces the situation that puts its stakes in danger by another state from the latter, the offended or threatened state needs to seek permit from the former-controlled international community. If the said state facing the danger is in the former versus the state in the latter, the aggrieved state can proceed taking whatever action[s] it deems fit without necessarily seeking permission from the international community. Refer to how the United States (US) acted when it felt (not evidentially proved) that its interests were endangered by Iraq.

Practically, international laws and, of course justice, only make sense in the former in that one country or some countries in the former can launch war against any country or countries in the latter whenever their interests are *threatened* despite the fact that this right or situation cannot be reciprocated if the situation implies or says *vice versa*. Hauss (*Ibid.*) makes a good point, mainly, when we consider what happened to *rogue* states such as Iraq and Libya after the West conspired and cooperated with disgruntled local elites who wanted to settle scores in toppling the governments in these two countries. This happened because the Global North and local elites sought to safeguard their hidden interests but not the interests of the citizens. Due to the weakness of the international law, the duo got away with murder. Who would *bell the cats* when the adversaries are good-for-nothings? Therefore, we can vividly see that anarchic and deceitful nature of the international relations and systems–especially the one between the former and the latter–as the former created them after the First and the Second World Wars still serve its interests even at the expenses of other countries in the Global South in particular.

In other words, I can argue that the Global North has always depended on its fashion of the anarchic and dupery international system to commit structural violence based on its norms, *diktats* and unchecked and interventionistic strategies all geared against and towards the latter. This becomes eminent because under current anarchic international system, the Global North conspires with a few elites from the Global South to safeguard interests of the two conspirators of who the beneficiary is the former. Notably though, while the local elites in the latter get satisfied with rat-like-baits on the trap, the former takes a lion share of the loots resulting from this conspiracy. Verily, this becomes a very good causation of backwardness (as the former likes to define it), conflict, poverty and underdevelopment in the Global South. What is currently going on in Syria speaks volume whereby two powerful nations Russia and the US are waging a proxy war at the expenses of Syrian people not to mention Afghanistan and Iraq among others. Who is helping the former to address the real cause of such a problem instead of keeping mum for fear of retributions?

Under dependency theory, what is going on in the relationship in question is detrimental to the latter and an advantage to the former. Caraveli (2016) notes that the "core-periphery "divide underlines the imbalance between the duo which means the latter is the periphery and the core is the former. I can argue that North-South way of dealing with conflict and development is totally antithesis to dependency theory that, too, is an antithesis of modernisation theory the former uses as its neoliberal drive to exploiting the Global South. Ever since the time the Global North envisaged exploiting countries in the Global South–through colonialism, and thereafter, through neocolonialism–it has installed its stooges to run some countries for its own benefits as opposed to the interests of the citizens of these countries.

Simmel (1950 cited in Petrocelli, Piquero and Smith 2003) argues that Conflict theory is about power dynamics whereby "power of a given social group dictates social order in that powerful groups not only control the lawmakers, but also the law enforcement apparatus of the state" (p. 2). Likewise, the Global North–through using local elites–does not only control the lawmakers and apparatuses of the state but also the entire state, chiefly in some countries–if not all–in the Global South. By controlling the state, the former gets an upper hand in proxy-decision making in the latter. By affecting policymaking in the latter, the former swiftly exacerbates poverty and underdevelopment as it acquires much wealth from the losing latter. Through policymaking powers bestowed on them, corrupt local elites do is put their countries to liberal open free market for the former to plunder as pleased provided that they cling to power on the one hand; and safeguard the interests of the former. By so doing, they fully participate in exploiting their countries; and thereby usher in more poverty and underdevelopment that result in chaos and conflicts in many countries.

Fundamentally, even if we address power dynamics in the relationship between Global North and Global South as it is regulated by, and based on what Joana Macy cited in Burrowes (1996) defines as "power over" which–she says "reflects a bias that is characteristic of Western social science" (p. 83)–we can still detect defects and anomalies. This is because the former has power over the latter and the latter is under the former. The power dynamics in the relationship between the two lacks equity, equality and mutual reciprocity that is fundamental and vital in any meaningful relationship that is *sine qua non* in any relationship (Simmel 1950 cited in Komter 2007). Such a situation maintains, and, sometimes, causes poverty. On its side, poverty hampers development and fuels conflict. Hauss (2010) notes–as realists put it–that conflict is an inevitable feature of international political life because the international system is anarchic, mainly as regards to the relationship between the Global North and the Global South. On this, the DRC provides an ideal example in which the Central Intelligence Agency (CIA)–under the instructions of the White House in conjunction with Belgium–assassinated DRC's first Prime Minister Patrice Lumumba after disagreeing with the extension of colonialism soon after the DRC gained its political independence. Due to anarchical nature of the international system under which the Global North dictates everything, it has never forced the CIA and Belgium to redress the DRC or even face criminal charges. How would the international community have reacted if we can treat this crime *vice versa*? Whitehead, Gerard and Kuklick (2015) note that "after Lumumba's death the United States had propped up Mobutu who ruled Congo for thirty years" (p. 3). Mobutu's kleptomania ruined and plundered the country for such a long time without being brought to book up until he was booted out from power; and thereby died in exile in Morocco in 1997 (Mhango 2016). Ironically, despite obvious and viable greed that Mobutu displayed, the former supported this albatross. Again, was the former insane or stupid? The answer is clear that, concerning making quick bucks, the former has no rule except gains. Mac Ginty and Williams (2009) claim that Mobutu and Ferdinand Marco, former presidents of the DRC and Philippines respectively robbed their countries of approximately $ 50 billion (p. 36). Ironically, despite preaching rule of law and accountability, the International community–which one can argue means the Global North under its neoliberalism–did not have any mechanisms or willingness to hold the culprit accountable as means of resolving the conflict that left millions of people in the two countries poor. How would the international community hold such corrupt dictators accountable while the same Global North was the chief beneficiary of their theft? Moore (2001) notes that "underdeveloped states are too independent of their own citizens.... strong external financial and/or military support for state elites, even when they are in conflict with many of their own citizens; the heavy dependence of states on 'unearned income'" (p. 1). How would the former turn the tables against ones of their own? This shows how relationship between the Global North and the Global South is one of major causes of violent conflicts, poverty and underdevelopment in some countries in the Global South. Correspondingly, such unfair relationship has maintained corruption in the latter. The fact that many dictators in the latter still enjoy the backing of the former provided they vend their people and their resources mirrors how the macabre the situation is, as I will indicate later. To the contrary, while the relationship between the two has always authored conflict, poverty and underdevelopment, it has enabled the former to become richer and richer as opposed to its counterpart that has always become poorer and poorer.

Angola's long time conflict presents another example on how the former has undermined and underdeveloped the latter. Under the backing of the former, former terrorist group, the National Union for the Total Independence of Angola (UNITA) waged a protracted war simply because it openly enjoyed support from the former simply because such a conflict enabled the former to get cheap supply of resources from the latter. Therefore, there was no any international pressure the international community timely and equitably exerted on the UNITA to resolve to this conflict during the entire period of the Cold War. How would the international community pressurise the UNITA while the Global North was on the beneficiary of the resources looted from Angola chiefly being blood diamond it needed? Sogge (2007) argues that Angola's long-standing subjugation to a predatory world system is the cause of such a long war that left the country devastated with destruction. Furthermore, Sogge (*Ibid.*) in showing how the Global North exploits the Global North notes that in Angola that:

> Donor agencies have, with few exceptions, been largely irrelevant to citizen empowerment in the post-war period. Most Angolans have relied on their own resources. They are, moreover, captive to configurations of political power built on the basis not of donor power but of international flows of capital, whose deregulated status is protected by Western governments (p. 13).

The help, if any, which the former offered to the warring factions in Angola, was nothing but exorbitantly selling them weapons so that they could finish each while the former made away with cheap resources or just doing nothing. To the former, the blood and resources lost in this war meant nothing but business as usual. Human rights, principally the right to life did not matter then for the Angolan people. Moreover, this was not the first or the last time for the former to ignore and trample on human rights. Refer to genocides in the DRC under king Leopold, Namibia under German colonial rule and lately in Rwanda that have all hallmarks of the machinations by the former. Arguably, the former has always discriminated against the latter almost in everything. This is why it has been possible for it to commit such crimes against humanity without facing any accountability for its commission or omissions. Therefore, one of the solutions to the problems in the latter is to stop selling or supplying weapons to the former.

What happened in Angola is a typical replica of what happened in many countries in the Global South, chiefly those facing conflicts geared by the struggle for controlling resources. Resources have become another indicator for academics and practitioners as regards to predicting where the conflict is likely to occur. It is easy to tell where conflicts will erupt. Wherever there are resources that the former needs, conflicts will surely ensue there. Due to the international conspiracy and discrimination against them, the majority of Angolans are disgruntled. Such a situation is not good for any country. For, it helps opportunistic politicians to capitalise on it; and thereby start civil wars aimed at controlling resources they end up supplying the former. Ironically, the current international superstructure seems to reinforce and support an inequitable relationship between the Global North and the Global South. I would candidly argue that when Peace and Conflict academics do some predictions of conflict, one of the major components to examine should be the abundance of resources in certain countries; and the types of the governments such countries have in power. Looking at many countries that have already faced violent conflict such as Angola, the Central African Republic (CAR), the DRC, Ivory Coast, Liberia, Sierra Leone and Nigeria, I find that resources are the major causes of conflict simply because the former needs them; and it supplies weapons to greedy local elites to do its dirty laundry. However, there are countries without resources such as Burundi and Rwanda that also can experience conflict due to the scarcity of resources (Magnus Theisen 2008; Cilliers 2009; Evans 2011; and Selby and Hoffman 2014). In addition, such scarcity based on the population explosion can well act as a good predictor for future conflict. It is clear that who supplies what; and who get what regulates the relationship between the Global North and the Global South. This is why it has always remained to be clientèle and nobody tries to deconstruct and reconstruct it.

Consequently, too, countries without resources, supported by the former, can cause conflict in their neighbouring countries that happen to have resources. What transpired in the DRC in 1998 and 2000 when Burundi, Rwanda and Uganda invaded it provides an ideal example. Sutherland (2011) maintains that the U.S. Geological Survey records of tantalum imports reflect the extra-budgetary system implemented by the Rwandans and the Ugandans for exporting Congolese coltan. From 1998 to 2000, specifically listed tantalum imports to the US, originating from the Democratic

Republic of Congo. Yet, at that time, Rwanda and Uganda controlled the Congolese coltan mines, and the Congolese Ministry of Mines reported zero production of tantalum both in 1998 and 1999, and only 550 metric tons of tantalum in 2000 (p. 15). Ironically, Rwanda and Uganda do not have even single tantalum mine. I think; to avoid future conflicts, and tackle poverty and underdevelopment, the international community must put a stop on such double standard applied by the Global North. Without doing so, many conflicts will erupt and drag on provided that the wars emanating from such conflicts may take a long time and consume a lot of resources provided that such war are "self-financing" as Kagame cited in Sutherland *(Ibid.)* discloses. Such practices and conspiracies need to stop if the duo aims at deconstructing their relationship for the benefit of the world peace.

In spite of such the double standard, the Global North has always applied on the global South, many countries, mainly, African, still trust the former and its so-called International Organisations such as the United Nations (UN), the International Monetary Fund (IFM) and the World Bank (WB). The latter does so without underscoring the fact that such are tools created and used to safeguard its interests as opposed to the interests of the latter. Furthermore, Whitehead, Gerald and Kuklick *(Ibid.)* maintain that Africans' little knowledge about the UN as a creature of the US, not to mention its drab weakness when it tried to act without the say-so of the powerful. This rationale is in tandem with the aim of creating the North-South polarity of the colonising and colonised world (Pieterse 2015) whose legacies have gone on in the relationship between the former and the latter. Countries in the North do not respect the mandate of the international organisations unless only at the time they stand for their interests but not when they stand in their way. Due to ignoring such malpractices and power larceny, the Global North—under its neoliberalism policies, apart from showing double standard—shows great weakness and the lack of transparency in the process. Again, despite such flaws, still the Global North gets away with murder; why? Battersby and Siracusa (2009) maintain that actually, colonial regimes created incongruous colonial states designed to service the economic needs of the colonisers and not the communal or political interests of the colonised. Therefore, divisive politics and systems that the former introduced to the latter are still in place up until now. Those in the global South who subscribed to such manipulations were able to stay in power even if their people did not want them.

Thanks to such divisive tactics, many corrupt regimes in the Global South that opened their economies for the Global North's exploitation survived in power for a long time. This is why the so-called free market succeeded in the latter. The Global North made sure that corrupt rulers stay in power because they protect its interests. However, the Global North did all this at the expense of the citizens of the affected countries. What such rulers had to do is open their markets ready for the former's exploitation. For neoliberalism, opening the market that benefits Western economies surpasses democracy and human rights. Essentially, the notions, intentions and lulls of the neoliberalism based on market and personal liberty as solutions to world's problems is wrong. Mac Ginty and Williams (*Ibid.*) note that the thinking of the Global North is that "free markets made free men who would not be foolish to be involved in war" (p. 20). Does this rationale apply on the global South? Further, Mac Ginty and Williams maintain that free market prevents violent conflict that is an antithesis of market-induced inequality, causation, escalation and maintenance of violent conflict. This is because war is obviously the greatest world's industry in the ascendancy of neoliberalism. It is ironic to note that the former advocated free market without advocating free trade. Moreover, the Global North's predisposition of talking the talk without walking the walk, the move that ignores other mechanisms of dealing with conflicts is to blame. The major tactic the Global North uses is providing aid to the countries in the Global South. I think; the latter needs "trade not aid" (Lundsgaarde, Breunig & Prakash 2007); trade free of exploitation and *holier than thou* mentality that has existed for a long time since the inception of exploitative-neoliberal policies. When it comes to what should be done, Beyerlin (2006) observes that the industrialised states must take action towards reaching seven objectives namely opening their markets for the products of developing countries; acknowledging the developing countries' full and permanent sovereignty over natural resources; increasing the official development aid of industrialised states. Additionally, I would argue that the industrialised countries in the Global North must equivocally admit the wrongs they committed to the Global South. Admission will enable the countries in the former to take responsibility for the wrongs they committed to the latter; and thereby devise the mechanism of redressing the former instead of giving it discretionary handouts in the form of aid. This is the way forward given that aid has not solved a problem. Instead, aid has exacerbated the problem due to many reasons such as conditions attached to aid, corruption involving local elites in the latter and their counterparts in the former. The North lulls local elites in the South without any problem simply because it knows how their material hedonism as the legacies of colonialism, and results of criminalism, individualism and selfishness.

Briefly, it is important to conceive and entertain the idea of enacting international laws or instruments that deal with all wrongs the former committed and benefited from through exploiting the former. Why was it possible, for example, to enact international laws to redress the victims of the holocaust while it has become impossible to redress the latter? What do we call this? Is it not conspiracy and international discrimination against the latter? Essentially, the twosomes need to deconstruct the laws and regulations by enacting favourable and new laws and regulations governing their relationship in order to do justice for both sides shall they aspire to bring equity and parity in their relationship. This can act as a bulwark for the emancipation of the Global South while acts as tool for doing justice for the former. By enacting laws that force violators of others to clean up their deeds, the two halves will be inculcating global rule of law that binds both equally. There is no way the former can teach the latter rule of law without upholding it in their relationship. This is hypocritical and a double standard by all standards.

iii) Free Market as a Ruse to Penetrate and Exploit the Global South

Additionally, democracy, free markets and unjust economic relationship–that have always been neoliberalism's drives–cannot function well for the benefits of the citizenry in the Global South without involving accountability for both sides; which however have always benefited the former as it vexes the latter. Ironically, when neoliberalism maintains that democracy and free markets are the solution to conflicts resulting from poverty, it tends to; stereotypically apply double standards as it was in the case of Iraq where the US accused, former President Saddam Hussein, of, among others, being a dictator. Surprisingly, while the West was fighting to bring down Hussein, the same was protecting other dictatorial regimes in Kuwait and Saudi Arabia. Furthermore, by ignoring, and conspiring rulers such as Mobutu and Marcos–among others, to rob their countries–neoliberalism becomes causation of conflict. And indeed, Mobutu's mismanagement of the DRC resulted to the conflicts that are currently going on in the country which goes contrary to neoliberal assumption that econometrics would avert conflict. Sponsoring and installing Mobutu shows how neoliberal intervention in many countries experience conflict or coming out of conflict does not aim at benefiting countries in conflict but the Global North as Mac Ginty and Williams (2009) argue that "vast sums of money of dubious origin lubricate the international financial markets" (p. 35). This shows how the Global North aims at benefiting from corrupt and warring countries even at the expenses of the citizens of those countries.

It is an open secret that many Western capitals are good havens for money looted from poor countries. Ironically, the Global North has never underscored this to be a good causation of conflict because such tax havens motivate warlords to engage in war in order to print and mint money quickly. So, too, such greed-motivated governments or warlords disturb the distribution of resources which leaves the majority citizens out something that can inspire other political opportunists to embark on fighting in the name of liberating the citizens.

This is typically colonial superimposition by the Global North onto the Global South. Even if we consider the way the duo conducts the process, we find that the Global North has always dealt with, and used local elites thereby excluding the majority of citizens. Burrowes (1996) argues that the "structural nature of imperial relations between the North and the South facilitates the former's exploitation of the latter" (p. 142). The argument Burrowes makes is that the Global North uses governments and multinational organisations in conjunction with local elites–who form many governments–to exploit the Global South through structural arrangements aimed at securing the needs of the Global North on the expense of the needs of the generality of citizens of the Global South. In this exploitative relationship, capitalism uses markets as the master of the game in which the former gains while the latter loses. Besides, this has been so since colonial time up until now.

In sum, the relationship between the Global North and the Global South is inequitable and unfair. Therefore, it needs to be overhauled to see to it that this relationship between the Global North and the Global South equally and equitably serves the interests of both parties. Doing so will reduce conflicts resulting from unmet needs and struggle for control of resources in the Global South. The duo has a lot to do in addressing many shortfalls embedded in this unfair relationship. I would argue that such inequitable relationship that fosters exploitation of the Global South by the Global North is very fertile source for many violent conflicts. Hence, too, I would argue that neoliberal policies have completely failed to do justice for the Global South despite some gains. Importantly, one would argue that the relationship between the pair is more of an extended colonialism. Also, the international community and the international system with their empty vessels-like organisations need to be constructively reshaped and reorganised in order to do more justice than becoming the tools in the hands of the Global North.

Chapter Two

Nature of Exploitative Relationship

> *Early considerations of economic inequalities caused by unbalanced trade structures can be traced as far back as Adam Smith. He discussed the possibility of exploitation through trade, presenting the example of trade relations between towns and country-side characterized by different levels of wages and of profits* Raffer 1987 cited in Giljum and Eisenmenger (2004: 76).

As quoted above, the exploitation found in the relationship between the Global North and the Global South has all hallmarks of the exploitation between two different geographic and economic areas. For, the relationship between the Global North and the Global South, despite revolving around perpetual and systemic unfairness and injustices, has been going on for many years. However, this relationship is purely unequal, unfair and exploitative whereby the former exploits the latter. What should the duo do to rectify and better this relationship? You do not need to have high knowledge or a degree in quantum physics to feel and see the burden that the former has always placed on the latter, mainly economically and politically, among others. This chapter, *inter alia*, aims at digesting, exploring, analysing and contributing some solutions to the problem resulting from unfair relationship between the two halves. Arguably, the relationship between the two halves is built on arrogance, deceit, fear, gullibility, manipulations and *holier than thou* mentality in which one half is viewed as superior compared to large extent with its supposedly inferior counterpart. This said, there is a need of embarking on rectifying this collective clientelism (Ravenhill 2010) to see to it that the two halves are equally benefiting from their relationship. This chapter, as is the book in general, aims at generating some insights that can help us in seeing an improved relationship for the benefit of the duo as the means of correcting the evils and sufferings from this relationship. Correcting the evils and sufferings of this relationship that are primary facing the latter will not only presumably do justice but also will enhance productivity, development, peacefulness, and above wellbeing for the parties.

Arguably, everything is obvious. As argued above, that the former has always exploited the latter almost in every aspect of their dichotomous and hypocritical relationship. This being the situation, it raises the need of deconstructing the relationship in order to reconstruct it so that it can equally serve the duo. There is no way such an unequal relationship can be allowed to go on as it has been while one of the part in it is cascading to abject poverty while the other is becoming enormously rich. In addition, this unequal relationship has been going on ever since some countries in the global North introduced colonialism in the Global South. Therefore, we need to be clear here. When I say that the global North exploited the Global South I do not intend to condemn the entire Global North or all Western countries. For, some of them such as some of Scandinavian countries did not colonise the global South not to mention countries such as Northern Ireland that is still suffering from colonial and toxic relationship based on colonialism some countries in the Global North perpetrated. Implicating the global North causes confusion to many in the Global South, especially due to the victimhood position the people in the Global South have always suffered after the former colonised and exploited them. Chichilnisky (2006) maintains that the lack of property rights has a lot to do with the over extraction of resources in the South. Such an imbalanced relationship cannot go on without as it has been. It needs to total rectification to see to it that there is a balance in whatever transactions the duo enters. Equitable trade is one of such areas that need rectification. This will help to synchronise and tweak the balance of the trade and relationship between the two. Jaffee, Kloppenburg, and Monroy (2004) argue that "fair trade is typically understood as an alternative market system that aims to right the historically inequitable terms of trade between the geopolitical North and South" (p. 170).

Due to the archaic and anarchic nature of the global trade and relationship between the two halves, the latter does not only offer resources but it does also act as a major consumer of goods the former produces after processing the same materials from the latter.

We need to tip the balance all aimed at enabling the duo to equally benefit from their relationship which is vital for both. What makes this relationship more exploitative than constructive is the fact that the former sells its products to the latter at exorbitant prices compared to cheap ones it gets from the latter. People in the global North like and take such an anomaly as a normal thing; because they have always benefited from this exploitative and unfair relationship between the two. To the contrary, people in the latter see no benefit in the relationship except for a few elites in power that benefit from this toxic relationship.

So, too, what makes the relationship between the two even worse than ever is the fact that it has created another form of exploitation in which people in the Global South have perfected it as Matunhu (2011) maintains that "while Europe and America are busy exploiting Africa; the urban areas are also busy exploiting their rural areas" (p. 68). The gap between rural and urban areas almost everywhere in the latter, especially in Africa shows this form of adopted exploitation. Rural dwellers pay taxes to their governments that spend it on developing urban areas. Many cities in the latter have, at least, all amenities such as electricity, roads and water while the rural area has none of these amenities. Life in urban area is attractive compared to life in rural areas only. However, the situation is very different in the former where life in rural and urban areas is almost similar as far as the provision of services is concerned due to being rich. Here I am talking of urban-rural exploitative relationship. There is another offshoot in the exploitative and unfair relationship that the former has always maintained. Politicians exploit citizens in the Global South while, to the contrary, in the global North; politicians are the servants of the citizens; and whenever they fail to meet the expectations of the citizens, they are voted out of office. Ironically, in the Global South, local elites–whom the former uses to exploit the majority of poor citizens in various countries–are at home with ineptness and nihilism. In many corrupt countries in the Global South, rulers are not afraid of what the voters can do to ouster them. They rig elections; and sometimes, the former provides support to such rulers as an opportunity they and their masters use in plundering the latter. Corrupt rulers the former supports see to it that they vend whatever resources under their control to it. Additionally, citizens in the former have the constitutional rights to enjoy the resources and wealth of their nations while the situation is completely different in the latter. Ironically, despite this anomaly being visibly unattended, the former still preach human rights based on freedoms to some rights but not cultural, economic or other rights that citizens enjoy in the former. Due to this double standard, many corrupt and inept governments and their officials make a lot of personal wealth resulting from this unfair business relationship maintained by corruption and rent-seeking practices that both parties pretend not to see; and when they address them, they, for those who try to, just offer lip services. Arguably, the interests of the former surpass the rights of the citizens in the latter; that is, itself, neocolonialism and exploitation based on this exploitative relationship between the twosomes. Many corrupt and undemocratic rulers in the South spend much more money obtained in this unfair business to buy critics and maintain their armies and instruments of power to remain in power even unconstitutionally. Aleksynska and Havrylchyk (2013) note that:

> Most of the explanations found in the literature relate to the rents that are generated due to exploitation of natural resources and that are easily appropriated. A "rentier effect" occurs because revenues from the export of fuels and minerals allow governments to mollify dissent (buy off critics through lavish infrastructure projects or outright graft) and avoid accountability pressures (because taxes are low) (p. 41).

The quote above shows how the former preaches democracy to the latter; then goes against it and colludes with corrupt rulers in the latter. Concerning preaching true democracy to the latter, the former does exactly the opposite from what it does at home. Moreover, this is not new, especially in Africa where the Global North protected many corrupt tin-pot dictators who were able rule for many years in some countries such as Congo, Gabon and Uganda, among others, for over three decades thanks to this protection. Currently, Equatorial Guinea is an ideal example. Its dictator has been in power for over thirty years simply because he agreed to offer oil to the former. Who would hate to be in bed with the ruler of the country that has a couple of billion barrels of oil that Equatorial Guinea is? Who would hate the ruler of a tiny-but-rich country whose GDP is bigger than those of France, Japan and the UK are? Who does not want to do business with Mr. Moneybag like this one who is above the law? The Global North has been reluctant in taking some dictatorship on simply because one of theirs, the US, is always in bed with Equatorial Guinea's long-time president Theodoro Obiang Nguema whose country despite beating many countries in the Global North is still poor.

Diamond and Mosbacher (2013) disclose that the majority of 700,000 people in Equatorial Guinea—whose population is relatively small compared to country's endowment of resources—live on fewer than 2 dollars a day. This is the real situation in many African countries, principally those endowed with resources. The former applies double standards in dealing with the latter in order to benefit both ways. The question we can ask here is where does money garnered from such immense resources go? Silverstein (2011) answers disclosing that in 2004, the son of Nguema, Theodorin controlled $700 million in state funds deposited in Riggs Bank in Washington, D.C. (p. 58). Arguably, this is but the tip of the iceberg *vis-à-vis* how much Nguema's family controls; also see Solo-Trillo (2013); and Ngambi (2011). Here I am talking of one family that has usurped power and thrived while the majority of the citizens are suffering unnecessarily. The countries in the Global North would like to protect such a tyrant to see to it that it goes on enjoying the loots from the Global South. Again, this is a very typical replica of what has for, a long time, been going on in many countries in the Global South. What of other famous corrupt first families in Africa such as the Abachas (Nigeria), Mobutus (DRC), Eyademas (Togo), Bongos (Gabon), Mois (Kenya), Zumas (South Africa), and many more who wantonly robbed Africa in conjunction with the Global North where they stash the loots? By cooperating or supporting what Wood (2004) calls criminal government or states, the former faces criminal liability; however, the current international law regimes does not deal with such criminality that criminal enterprises or state commit. English sage has it: show me your friends; I will tell you who you are. Again, we can see the inequality and unfairness of the relationship between North and South by looting at the latter. The former uses gullible and myopic rulers to rob their countries. Once, such rulers are kicked out or became obsoletely unwanted and useless, the former abandon them to carry their own crosses as it happened when former rulers were booted out in the DRC, the CAR and elsewhere in the latter. Even regarding criminal liability, the courts of law in both halves do not prosecute thieves from the former along with those they conspired with in the latter to face the music. Besides, no workable mechanism that forces thieves to return the loots stashed in the former to the poor countries in the latter it from which they originated.

The *African Union* (2002 cited in the OECD 2014) estimates that 25% of the GDP of African states amounting to US$148 billion, is lost to corruption every year (p. 3). Despite knowing such stinking and damning reality, the duo has always doing business as usual by ignoring it. Instead of reining in, the former, in many instances, has helped corrupt dictators to rob Africa as they deem fit provided they share the loot with it.

Now that China and India have joined the looting splurge of Africa's resources, the continent should brace itself for yet more exploitation because those supposed to arrest this criminality are the same people in power and in bed with the former. Alexander (2009) observes that the "Europeans, who have traditionally viewed Africa as their domain, both India and China are investing heavily in many countries, with an eye toward the vast mineral resources that can be found there" (p. 5). In a united or organised, such competition of powers would help it to secure a good deal due to the fact they both need the same resources Africa has in abundance. This said, it is upon academics, especially from the latter that have the duty to alleviate the situation. When it comes to the coming of China and India, Mhango (2015) admonishes Africa to clutch and latch on this opportunity; and secure a good deal provided that Africa must be reunited: and thereby act as one country instead of acting severally as it currently is. North's indifference forces me to put their seriousness in to question as far as justice and human rights are concerned. Mhango reprimands African countries and the ways they do business severally. Instead, he stresses that they must reunite Africa so that they can present a unified front that, apart from making them stronger, will also have positive impacts on international affairs. There is something the latter needs to learn from the former that, for many years, has presented a united front in dealing with the latter almost in all matters in their relationship. There is no way, in particular for Africa; the Global South in general can succeed in deconstructing and reconstructing this toxic relationship without learning the art of acting unitedly.

One thing that makes the Global North an accomplice to robbing Africa specifically is the fact that the Global North has always turned a blind eye on African rulers who loot and misuse their countries' abundant resources. Ironically, while the Global North preaches good governance, rule of law and human rights to the Global South, it does not take such corrupt gangs in power on because it benefits from their criminality. So, one can evidentially argue that, among other things, corruption in the Global South has been maintained by the Global North because, in such deals, the latter gets cheap resources it sells at extortionate price to the former. Moreover, if anything, this is among the reasons why the former has always languished in utter paucity while the former stuck it rich thanks to exploiting the latter.

Again, for the victims of this paradoxical and toxic relationship, the mentioning of the former brings to mind anger and resentments resulting from a long-time exploitation that ended up fuelling and financing wars all aimed at maintaining the struggle of controlling and extracting resources. This is a crystallised reality that is clearly known to both partners in this wanting relationship. For rulers whose regimes the Global North maintain through handouts it provides in the names of aid, loans, military and technical assistance, the relationship between the duo is healthy. However, the same relationship–for the victims who pick the tab after their compromised and corrupt rulers squander monies obtained through thievish and dupery loans and unfair business deals–is the source of many economic miseries they have ever known. Citizens in the

Global South have always withstood the worst of footing the bills resulting from extravagant lives of their rulers. They hate and want their rulers out of power. However, they cannot kick them out of power; because they are big nations behind them enhancing their perpetual exploitation to go on and on. Many corrupt rulers in the Global South live large while those they call their people wallow in squalor all manmade; if I may say so. Again, the same North that has always portrayed itself as the guardian of human rights does not say anything; simply because the said rulers are doing whatever they do for the advantage of the North. Whether what the Global North does as far as corruption and exploitation in the Global South are concerned is an issue the former is supposed to take on and thwarts all depending on which side of the equation on is to make sense of it. For example, von Weizsäcker, Lovins and Lovins (1995 cited in Giljum and Eisenmenger 2004) argue that 20%of the world population found in the former is appropriating 80% of the world's natural resources (p. 75). How do you call this? Is not this moral corruption next to a sacrilege? You can go further and call over-consumerism a type of systemic corruption former has always exported to the latter under the pretext of business as espoused by neoliberal exploitative policies.

i) The Economies of Dominance and Exploitation

Economically, the Global North means all affluent Western and two American countries namely Canada, the United States of America (USA) and Western European countries in general. You can go ahead adding rich countries such as some Scandinavian countries whose history does not have the baggage of colonialism. Apart from unfair relationship between North and South, there are evolving countries that form its own club whose name is not yet socially constructed. These are South Korea, Singapore, Taiwan, Hong Kong, China, and India among others. We see the formation of the economies of exploitation on how the two halves treat each other. You need to be rich or a rising power such as China and India that is when the former can listen to and respect you. Therefore, sometimes, you shall not wonder to find that rising powers are behaving like the Global North or are in good terms with it simply because they have economic and financial muscles.

Consequently, too, when I talk of the Global South, emerging countries whose economies are doing better than the rest, it is important to exclude them due to the fact they, too, are now exploiting other poor countries in the Global South. Maybe, we can call these emerging powers the *North* of the Global South if not the *West* of the same. They can differ by definition and history from the Global North; however, what they are doing now is almost the same. As it is in the case of exploitation between the centre and the periphery and rural and urban, emerging powers have created another type of problem. For example, currently, the Global North is currently accusing China and India of depleting some resources in Africa thanks to their hunger for resources; which is a fact. Cheru and Obi (2010) disclose that Chinese "networks for the import and distribution of Chinese prints are also associated with illegality (including smuggling and tax evasion)" (p. 139) not to mention substandard and fake products that have resulted in killing traditional products such as Kente cloth in Ghana (Boateng 2011). Alike, China and India do not only export their substandard products massively to Africa, but they also exploit African massively through exporting their armies of jobless people who have already caused stirs in countries such as Angola, Ghana and Zambia the *BBC* (August 5, 2012). The situation is tense, particularly among the common citizens of some countries. On Angola and China business, relationship, Coroado and Brock (2015) quote 35-year-old cook Marisa as saying that "the agreements with China are a benefit for them and the president and not for us." This shows how rent-seeking practices are sanctions in the upper echelons of power in both countries.

Ding (2008) maintains that Beijing has never bothered itself dealing with corrupt, even brutal dictators in the former simply because it benefits from their corrupt practices. Here you can see that when it comes to exploitation, even emerging economies are as worse as the Global North has always been.

Politically, the meaning shifts and reduces the number of players. For instance, Japan does not have any input in Western model of democracy as an imposition. Scandinavian countries or occupied countries such as Northern Ireland or Switzerland have no inputs at all. Hence, when one considers the Global North must be carefully in making such distinction. Apart from espousing deconstruction, this book aims at trying to show how deconstructing and overhauling the said relationship is imminent for the world to enjoy everlasting peace apart from development and prosperity. No doubt; violent conflicts resulting from unfair relationship between the two global halves have many more negative effects to the world, especially to the Global South that lack peace and prosperity. For example, while the Global North sells weapons to the Global South, it does not bear the brunt of refugees–however; recently it has faced some–at the same magnitude as the latter does after economic immigrants flooded Europe seeking greener pastures. So, the major argument I am making here is: Invest in peace; and save many lives and economies by so doing and live at peace without being bugged by economic immigrants. Selling weapons to the Global South in order to create conducive environment for obtaining cheap resources by selling hiked weapons will not sustain or bring peace to the world. Instead, such practices will exacerbate the problem by increasing insecurity all over the world. Consequently, insecurity will curtail production in order to negatively affect production; and thereby development. Therefore, deconstructing unfair relationship between the two is not the matter of choice but, instead, it is the matter of necessity for both parties.

Many–especially victims of the crime resulting from unfair relationship between the duo–wonder how the former sells arms freely under the international market as espouse by neoliberalism without considering collective effects it will cause to peace in the world at large. One would argue; given that the world is now more globalised than ever before is likely to be equally affected. The take here would be to consider the world as one unit instead of everybody to act solo which embeds arms race that has some racist characteristics if we consider how superpowers prevent other countries to acquire dangerous weapons such as nuclear as the world evidenced recently when Iran tried to acquire ones. Powerful states fear that if weaker countries acquire nukes, they would turn them against them; and thus become easy prey as Africa and other weak states have always been. In addition, the countries in the Global North would not stomach watching weak states use the nukes to tip the balance of the world *status quo*. Their fear is that when such weapons land in the hands of the so-called rogue states (Danilovic 2007; and Lebovic 2007), such a move will put the former at the risk so as to force superpowers in the Global North to renegotiate their relationship with such countries. If this happens, these countries will lose their economic dominance that has enabled them to exploit weak states in the Global South. So, too, they feel threatened the way they threaten others. Actually, to stop arms race, there must be a danger aimed at the West.

Ironically, when arms race danger is against the Global South, arms business goes on as usual. When I argue that the relationship between the former and the latter is dichotomous, hypocritical and paradoxical, I mean exactly that. Keller and Nolan (1997) argue that on "rare occasions, some countries deny advanced weapons to unstable regions or to so-called pariah states" (p. 113). Keller and Nolan make a good point showing how double standard, self-serving, self-saving and self-preservation of the Global North are the rules of the game of deceit and discrimination; while burden bearing is the only thing the Global South has ever known. They go on arguing that arms proliferation is but an impediment to world security, and peace. Ironically, world peace and security only matter when the former faces a threat as evidenced in 2001 when the United States (US) declared that former Iraq dictator Saddam Hussein–whom the US had cloned–had the *Weapons of Mass Destruction* (WMDs). Later it became clear that the so-called weapons of mass destruction was a hoax-cum-pretext of pulling the dictator down after compromised the interests of the big brother (Lewis and Reading-Smith 2008). When making such allegations, those making them failed to tell the world who cloned or supplied the said WMDs. This was not an issue at the time. The issue was to get rid of the dictator by all means, legal and illegal, altogether. Thus, in this context though, I can argue that, one of the best things to do to normalise and harmonise the relationship between the two, is addressing the issue of arms-free trade. For, it has become a good backer and enabler of conflicts in the Global South where resources motivate all players to take up arms and cause apocalypse that kills and displaces millions of innocent people such as children, elderly, girls and women raped not to forget long-time economic hardships. No doubt, the former has created a combat economy in order to swiftly and perpetually exploit the latter. Ballentine and Nitzschke (2005) argue that:

> The combat economy is based on economic interactions that directly sustain actual combat. It is dominated by a variety of actors, including the security apparatus of the state (military, paramilitary groups, police) and rebel groups, as well as domestic and foreign "conflict entrepreneurs" who supply the necessary weapons and military material (p. 7).

In the relationship between the Global North and the Global South, two things are obvious that the former supply weapons and get cheap resources; and the latter receives weapons and loses its resources. So, too, the latter lacks the propitious environment for production on top of selling whatever unprocessed products at cheap prices. Furthermore, the latter has no free access to the market in the former while it is vice versa to the former. Under combat economy, the extraction of resources on the expenses of the citizens in the latter is rife simply because the economies in the former need the resources. This is why international complicity has always been higher against the latter. The Global South has witnessed one crisis after another; all resulting from elites' struggles to get in power so that they could control resources to sell to the former. Due to the exploitative nature between the two, the conflict in the latter has always revolved around controlling resources that, likewise, involves controlling humans, especially during the war in which they suffer a lot individually and collectively.

Another face of the feature of the relationship between the two is the complicity and duplicity of the international community. Arguably, the extraction of resources–that the Western economies need–hampers the international community from intervening decisively. This ties *realpolitik* of the world to the situation. Currently, international media has totally ignored the predicaments of the latter. Instead, the news of terrorist attacking the interests of the former has taken over. For example, the conflict in Syria, in which the former is fighting to safeguard its hegemony, has taken a long time to be resolved due to the fact that it involves two powers namely the US and Russia which makes the news important not because of the Syrian people but because of the interests of the former.

Further, take, for example, the consequences of violent conflict resulting from struggle to control resources in the DRC. According to Peterman, Palermo and Bredenkamp (2011), approximately 1.69 to 1.80 million women are reported as having been raped in their lifetime (with 407397–433785 women reporting having been raped in the preceding 12 months), and approximately 3.07 to 3.37 million women reported experiencing intimate partner sexual violence (p. 1060). The figures noted above are high. However, it is not easy to know the percentage of rape victims in the DRC compared to the general population. Peterman, Palermo and Bredenkamp (*Ibid.*) note that the most recent DRC's recent census is the one it did in 1984. Therefore, current population estimates are imprecise and suffer from several limitations. The lack of census also shows how failing the country has become. For, without knowing the population of the citizens, the country is unable to plan. Such a weakness negatively affects the provision of health services for rape victims in the DRC.

Try to imagine. What would have been the reaction of the world if those victims were from the Global North? The answer comes from Kosovo 1999. Schabas (2000) argues that in 1999 the Serb militias drove Kosovar Albanians from their homes within Kosovo using terrible violence in order to accomplish their objective. Such an operation was intended to culminate into "the ethnic cleansing of the territory and the forced displacement of the Albanians to neighbouring states, principally Albania and the former Yugoslav Republic of Macedonia" (p. 293). After the news of the tragedy broke, the North Atlantic Treaty Organisation (NATO) started bombing the areas in order to dislodge Serb militias even without waiting to obtain the leave from the UN Security Council as the international law stipulates (Reisman 2007). The NATO was in hurry to save its people while at the same time, five years before, a tiny country of Rwanda experienced genocide that Rwandan radical militants perpetrated for 100 days unabated, and no power wasted time to stop it. After ignoring Rwanda, then what did the international community do? Uvin (2001) answers the question noting that "it is interesting to see all the young PhD candidates from good American and European universities running around eagerly in this remote and traumatised country to advance their academic carriers" (p. 76). The quote is self-explanatory that the academics from the Global North are exploiting Rwanda using it for self-preservation. In other words, Rwanda is like a guinea pig or a museum where they have been going to learn for their professional benefits but not of the victims. Moreover, this has always been the tendency of the Global North to use the Global South as an experimental object or guinea pig almost in everything. The former is pregnant with almost all information about the latter while the latter does not have any gist of the same from the former. This is why the former has almost every type of *experts* on the latter while the latter seems to be satisfied with as regards to defining and study the former. It astounds to find that, after over five decades of independence in the latter; many countries still look at the former for the solutions to their problems. Although the world tends to ignore such academic theft, it has its long time consequences for the latter. Many years to come, people will go to the former to learn about Rwandan genocide due to the fact that the Global South has no academic and systemic structures of preserving and protecting its knowledge and the sources of knowledge.

I am trying to ponder on one important issue. Had what happened in Rwanda occurred in the former, would students from poor countries have such free access to knowledge while the fear has always been that they would end up stowing away due to poor conditions in their countries that result from this unjust and unfair relationship? Will the former allow academics from the latter to use it to advance and treasure knowledge about it for the future dominatingly use? In trying to vent her anger and frustrations about how the international community maltreats; and treats the Global South with indifference and double standards, Chouchou Namegabe cited in Victoor (2011), addressing the US senate, observes that when one woman is pushed down or raped the whole community follow. She wonders why the so-called developed world has always been silent about such predicaments people face in the DRC while the same are concern about the killings of gorillas. She says that militants raped more than 500,000; and still, the silence went on while at the same time resources for conserving and saving gorillas were available. She ends saying "Never Again" (p. 55).

Essentially, Namegabe shows how vulnerable and invaluable humans are in the Global South despite the Universal Declaration of Human Rights (UNDHR) in 1948. She finds that endangered gorillas attract more attention than victims of rape receive; that is ironic to the international community. Indeed, this has been ongoing unquestionably. Currently, there are many *animanthropists* or *betenthropists* from the West advocating for the rights of endangered animals such as rhinoceros and elephants to mention but a few. Furthermore, Mhango (2015) makes a good point asking why almost all *experts* on Africa–for example–are from the Global North while there are no experts on the same from the latter. He goes on adducing evidence to prove that the so-called human rights accrue only to the people in the former since it took over twenty years for colonised people to enjoy the human rights after proclamation of the UNDHR. His major argument is that colonialism was a crime, and was characterised by gross violations of human rights in the Global South but yet the colonial masters were not brought to book or forced to redress the victims of their crimes that were perpetrated for many generations so as to leave behind many traumatic and systematic ills.

In analysing or dealing with any conflict–be it big or small, interpersonal, intergroup or international, violent or otherwise, there are important elements academics and practitioners consider. Such considerations become yardsticks by, and with which to resolve, manage, contain, or transform the said conflict. Again, this depends on how creative the persons trying to resolve the conflict becomes or acts based on and aimed at leading to specific outcomes that revolve around non-zero-sum rationale (Ploetner and Ehret 2006). So, the conflict at hand begs for creativity of both parties to see to it that they embark on inclusivity when it comes to resolving it. In dealing with the conflictual relationship between the Global North and the Global South, creativity must dictate the process in that the desired outcomes should be a non-zero-sum in that both parties must win under win-win formula.

What are the inputs of the parties as far as the duo is concerned? Is there power balance or power over in this equation? Essentially, the relationship between the former and the latter lacks inclusivity and parity. To do away with such an anomaly, the duo needs to, equally, decide the modality of their relationship based on equality and equity. Right answers to such questions help in unearthing hidden and underlying strata of the conflict. They unveil the bigger part of the *iceberg* that is always under water. Thus, conflict experts aim at dealing with relationship in order to enable the parties to move on. For, the two globes in point to move on, they need to consider such elements. The analysis does not end up here. Other things such as interests, points of view, history, and envisaged commonality, interdependent and interconnected future are also important.

How entrenched and unequal features of the relationship in point are, it is not easy to enumerate. Schein (1985) cited in Tikkamäki (2013) notes that, like an iceberg analogue, we just see a small part of the iceberg above water. For most of the iceberg is naturally invisible under the water. What we see or what the parties tell about the conflict is not enough. We need to creatively delve into the "water" and see the size and nature of the *iceberg* we want to deal with. What you see is but the surface of the conflict. There are many hidden layers, any person or organisation dealing with a particular conflict needs to appreciate; and thereby deal with decisively and painstakingly to reach the resolution of the conflict. In trying to unearth hidden layers of the *iceberg*, we need to brace ourselves for an unforgiving task of facing the truth as it is even if it is bitter and provocative as it is in the relationship in point. Professor Sean Byrne used to tell me that dealing with conflict is as painful and demanding as peeling the onions. We all know how onion juices attacks our senses, particularly eyes and nose. If anything, the parties to this conflict must prepare themselves to face the *onion* and *peel* it by looking for, and finding hidden layers in their conflict, relationship and process altogether. For example, there is no way one can normalise the relationship between the two rondures without appreciating the history, and, of course, the obnoxiously detrimental role colonialism played in pauperising the Global South. This is a fact backed by findings. Rodney (2010) in his epic book *How Europe Underdeveloped Africa* poses a crucial question: "What did colonial governments do in the interests of Africans?" (p. 440) at the period, they colonised Africa for longer time than time since Africa became independent from them. The answer to this question is obviously zilch. If there is anything that colonialism did to the colonies is nothing but robbing them and destroying their civilisations and their ways of life. However, Rodney admits that colonial governments built hospitals, railroads and schools. He goes on maintaining that the "these services were amazingly small," (*Ibid*) compared to what they destroyed or robbed. Considering how much colonial masters gained and how much Africa lost, if there is anything colonial governments did was nothing but shamelessly brutalising and virtually exploiting Africans. Had brutality and exploitation ended up here, maybe, Africa would be different from what it is now.

When I talk of reconciling two globes or repairing their relationship such things need to be considered and solutions given to problems rising thereof. There is no way two unequal partners may keep such relationship based on honorific intentions. The whole idea of independence is practically a hoax because the majority of Africans are still suffering from prolonged manmade miseries under neoliberal policies. Essentially, colonialism has been going on unabated despite fake aura by local elites who benefit from clientele system cheating themselves and their people that former colonies are independent politically; but not economically and culturally one may argue. Again, when the Global North faces blames, its spin-doctors say that those doing so are blaming the *chimpanzees* by ignoring the *monkeys*. In blaming *monkeys*, some blame Africa for having poor priorities such as the lack of rule of law, corruption and irresponsibility without considering who finance and support such malpractices. Mhango (2015) espouses the formation or cartels or cartelisation of African products the same way Middle East countries and petroleum producing countries did with their major commodity, oil. After noting the power oil wielded, some oil-producing countries came together and former what we now know as the Organisation of Petroleum Countries (OPEC). After all, the idea of cartelisation of Africa's produces is not new. Ghanaian first president, the late Dr Kwame Nkrumah, championed the cartelisation of cocoa, the then chief produce of Ghana as a preliminary approach towards spreading the whole idea to cover the entire continent. His efforts to set pace and tone for the entire Africa did not come to fruition. The Global North toppled him; and that was the end of the cartel dream for Africa (Mhango 2016).

There are those who argue that Nkrumah had to go simply because his ideas did not appeal to imperialists who aimed at exploiting Africa forever as they have always done. What makes the idea of creating cartels for African products new is the fact that, ever since Nkrumah championed it, those he targeted have never put it to action. Ironically, Africa has many cartels of criminals such as tax evaders, drug barons, corrupt government officials and the whole host of netherworlds as far as criminality and corruption are concerned. It is even sad to note that African countries have always seen how oil benefited Gulf States; yet they have never envisaged such an emancipatory approach of cartelising their products. Again, how can African countries form strong cartels while they are divided along colonial lines not to mention some having *petit* interests? One of the tools that may enable poor countries in the Global South, mainly Sub-Sahara Africa (SSA) is the cartelisation of their produces. Africa still can cartelise its products even without necessarily embarking on its unification. At this moment and time, African countries can ape the Gulf States model and get good returns of their produces. Sometimes, it makes more sense to argue that Africa's economic backwardness is caused by poor priorities resulting from bad policies, for the most part, based on receiving misleading templates for their economic plans from the West as espoused by the IFIs.

Historical narrative brings us to another important element of conflict between the former and the latter. This is nothing other than power. Conflict is about power. Who has more or less power between the parties? Does power relationship revolve around power over or power between? After knowing the nature of power dynamics in a conflict, anybody dealing with it tries as much as one can to balance it in order to go on the process knowingly that doing so would make the process just. Essentially, it is possible to attain power balance just through by giving voice to the party that does not have it or reducing the ability for one party to influence another by levelling their power. When it comes to the Global North, as indicated above, has more power than the Global South. This relationship is more of power over than equal or balanced power or power with. Tough it is seemingly impossible to recalibrate, shall the latter come together and come up with a sound argument of doing so, nothing is impossible under the Sun.

Academics have one major role to play in the North-South conflict, among others, to see to it that this situation is effectively addressed so that the duo can move forward together as equal partners but not as donors and recipients as it currently is. Since Rodney (1972) wrote his aforementioned book, no books on the same came forth ever since. Therefore, the role of academics has always been to diagnose the problem, and thereby prescribe the mechanisms of managing, resolving or transforming the conflict in point. Some call this diagnostic-cum-prognostic approach since the academics do diagnostic and prognostic works. Again, working on the problem or using the advice academics offer is one thing and using their advice is another thing. Everything solely hinges and latches upon the policy makers to decide. I therefore, respect and apply this tradition of diagnosing and prescribing what is important to do. Whether those we target take or ignore our advice, is none of our business so to speak.

ii)   It Takes Two to Tango: Two-Part Liability

How can the Third World catch up with the West? The starting conditions for growth are irretrievably different. The West was behind the Chinese and

> *Islamic civilizations, at the time its growth took off. There is also nothing to suggest that the west deliberately created a merchant, entrepreneurial, capitalist class. It developed out of internal dynamics. But this gap was not as large* Rosenberg, Birdzell and Mitchel (1986).

The quote above sheds some little bit light on what the Global South is supposed to do in order to move forward. Apart from that, the quote shows how those viewed as inferior and underdeveloped can develop if they take up the challenge seriously, as it was for the former. What is important *vis-à-vis* the above quote is the courage and preparedness one has to have in order to beat the odds. However, there is no need of accommodating such a statement by ignoring other factors that propelled the former to prosperity such as slavery, colonialism and now neocolonialism. What we need to learn here is the courage, preparedness and readiness to take our challenges on. After all, it is not the first time for Africa to face challenges of development as Amin (1991) argues that theories of Being, Arithmetic etc. are not new to Africa noting that:

> Universal knowledge runs from the Nile Valley towards the rest of the world in particular to Greece which serves as the intermediary. As a result, no thought, no ideology is foreign to Africa which was the land of their birth. Consequently, Africans must draw from the Theoretical Perspectives common intellectual heritage of humanity, guided by notions of what is useful and effective (pp. 53-54).

Amin makes a good point saying that the predicament of any person or society is not a sealed one. Anything good can crop up from whatever situation one is facing. The most famous house on earth, the White House or the first mega-highway project in the world that black slaves built in the US; although they have never been appreciated provide an ideal example. Who would think that such despised and exploited people would put an indelible mark on the history of such great nation? Amin (*Ibid.*) observes that "once a set of basic and shared human predicaments have become reasonably well understood both locally, and in a broader historical and cultural context, what remains to be 'put into practice' is predicament-motivated action" (p. 5). Actually, this is true that human nature is dynamic but not static *vis-à-vis* change and facing and taking up challenges.

Sometimes, we blame everything on the Global North for exploiting the Global South without considering what enhances this growing exploitation. The former does depend on some of the behaviours, weakness and sometimes, unpreparedness of the latter to take the challenge up. This said, sometimes, the latter needs to act and blame responsibly by reflecting on itself and others. This is the right thing to do; however, the latter, too, has its fair share of culpabilities. The latter can primarily never pull out of the impasse it is in if it will not look at all sides of the coins by accepting some policy and systemic failures on its side. There are some failures and issues the latter needs to seriously and timely address in order to move forward. For example, keeping on trusting the former even when it is clear that transparency does not exist is the failure of the latter. You can go as far back as to colonial era wherein the agents of colonialism duped and misled the latter. This must act as a wake-up call for the latter to start doing things and thinking differently. It needs a mind-set reawakening, exclusively when it comes to policymaking and business in general. For example, many companies, from the former go to the latter to invest which is good. On its side, you find that the latter enter in such agreements unpreparedly or by using unqualified on untrustworthy personnel. The results of such unpreparedness are obvious that the prepared side will gain while the unprepared one will lose. This speaks to the need to seriously, fight corruption in the latter. This is obvious. There is no way anybody can treat you properly if you treat yourself improperly.

Currently, corruption has been legalised through the back door in many countries in the latter, especially in Africa because it mainly involves the high and the mighty. Arguably, the latter is duty bound to embark on amending and improving most of its pieces of laws in order to suit in the current way of doing things. Such a move is crucial in order to bring its corrupt and irresponsible officials to books. In simple terms, while the latter cries for justice, it too, must do justice to itself and its people by doing things competently and transparently. By so doing, the latter will have all reasons and right to pat itself in the back.

One way of moving forward for the latter is to, unitedly agitate to change the current biased international system that favours the former as it victimises the latter. This is where historical realities help both parties to appreciate the successes and failures of each other. For example, the Global North formed the many so-called international instruments at the time many countries in the latter were still under colonialism. This means that the latter did not participate in the formation of such organisations. Therefore, this move did not accommodate aspirations, expectations and interests of the latter. The warning however in whatever is undertaken; the latter must make sure that it does not do things like a headless chicken as it has always done.

As the sage has it, it takes two to tango. Some factors namely, the laxity of the latter to systemically, put its house in order to competently, conform to, instead of confronting, the former to address the problem have enabled the exploitation of the latter. Essentially, the policymakers and politicians have the blames squarely on their shoulders for taking advantage of their people. This is evident in many dealings the policymakers and politicians in the latter enter with the former. It is no secret. Local elites and foreign elites from both camps are in the same bed doing the same business at the detriment of their citizens in the Global South and vice versa for the Global North.

As I will show later, the ongoing exploitation between the two has been going on for a long time. Arguably, the nature of the international system with roots back to colonialism has exacerbated the exploitation of the latter. Since the system was put in place, it has never been overhauled in order to serve the interests of all humanity as it is duty-bound supposed to do. What do you expect from the system that the one side of the divide enacted and controlled? The answer is obvious that who pays the piper calls the tune. In relational matter such as this, two parts need to have their strategies. For, this relationship is like any game in which everybody seeks a trophy, sometimes, by all means, or otherwise as it has been in this relationship.

Circumstantially, the former has always acted as a united force–the lesson it got from the world war–the latter seems not to get any lesson from slavery and colonialism. If there is anything the latter needs to learn from the former is nothing but unity. I will address these lacking elements in the foregoing chapters independently in order to put the emphasis about the necessity and essence for the latter to act collectively. Ayoob and Zierler (2005) note that the urge for the industrialised countries to act unitedly was reinforced by the end of the cold war at which the tug of war and competition among superpowers was removed based on the reality of a North-South division. Instead of languishing in the politics of division, industrialised states embarked on civilisational, economic, military, political and cultural drive to survive. This is lacking in the latter. You can see this on how colonial masters divided, for example, Africa to remain divided up until now. Why and who is to blame? Swahili sage has it that if you wake up a slept person, you will fall asleep yourself. Arguably, there is no way the latter can develop without learning from its past. The latter has many strings to its bow to exploit based on its past mistakes if it uses them as a class in order to move forward, chiefly if we consider the fact that almost all countries, however at different magnitudes, face the same problems resulting from a shared history of colonialism and partly slavery.

Another asset the countries in the latter share is powerlessness, vulnerability and hard and unpredictable future. Here I think; the countries in the latter need to learn from ants. Weak as they naturally are, ants use their weakness as strength by pulling together in everything they do. They know that if they act solo, they will all perish and vanish. If small creatures with small brains can underscore this, why humans do humans in the latter fail to do and underscore the same? If the powerful are embarking on unions in dealing with the powerless, what is the logic for the powerless to remain divided in dealing with the powerful while they know the consequences of their commission and omission in this matter? Look at the unities of the powerful such as the European Union (EU) or the NATO. Despite its challenges and squabbling, the EU has stood to see to it that the members sail through or sink together. Modern challenges in the modern world need unity as the only weapons–like the ants–available for the powerless. Instead of maintaining hostile and divisive behaviours, petty politics and mistrusts, the latter needs to embark on unifying strategies in order to competently and successfully deal with the former. Immanuel Wallerstein cited in Silver and Arrighi (2005) admonishes the citizens in the latter to 'accommodate the combined demands for everybody' (p. 56). Silver and Arrighi address workers' challenges in both halves arguing that the inter-imperialist conflicts created an opportune moment for the explosion of labour unrest in wealthier countries; and also, the spread of communism in poor countries; also see Narman (2014). If workers in the latter keep quite as they know they are not deservedly paid, they become the part of the problem instead of becoming a solution to their eminent problems that will double due to exploitative relationship between the two. Although the international community does not follow human rights to the letter, we can, arguably say that, at least, there is a framework that the workers, in the latter, can use to agitate for their rights. Active workers who demand their rights can force their governments to change the way they have been doing things. The workers and citizens in general need to put their force together. We have seen this in South Africa during the struggle to bring Apartheid down. Labour organisations played a crucial role that, in the end, brought down Apartheid. Political parties, too, can team up with trade unions in various countries in the latter to bring their governments to accountability. Like the ants, if workers put their weakness together, there can be born strength out of it. There are some theoretical and practical proofs in some countries in the former. There is development in unity and underdevelopment in disunity. Simon (2014) observes that "developmentalists often still ignore or fail adequately to address the reasons for widespread 'development failure', especially in poor countries and; among large subordinate unpowerful groups" (p. 24). This is obvious that elephants cannot in anyway be concerned with the problems of the ants. Workers have a great role to play in stopping exploitation between North and South. They are the ones who oil the cog and run the engine of any country almost in everything. Like ants in their termite hills, in whatever they do, all ants play their parts. While many countries in the latter, mainly in Africa, are strengthening their individuality, the countries in the former, specifically in the UE are embarking on collectivistic moves. Keating, Hooghe and Tatham (2006) note that the EU has challenged the national state while it ironically has itself acted the same manner in policymaking for the member states. Do countries in the latter have any collective-policymaking body or systems in place particularly in dealing with such a united and powerful entity such as the EU? Do you think Africa can gain from any agreement or business resulting from such dichotomous policy-and-structural arrangements? If anything, time for creating one nation out of the many existing states for Africa is around now. What is amiss the will and understanding of its rewards thanks to selfishness, myopia and colonial legacies. Without arming themselves without the spirit and strategy of unity, countries in the latter are wasting time. What is obvious is that the countries in the latter are likely to suffer even more in their division while, to the contrary, countries in the former will gain more thanks to their oneness, togetherness and unity of the purpose.

The other part that shares the blame for the predicaments of the latter is the citizens in both halves. The blame falls on the citizens in both halves for not taking their governments and organisations on to see to it that justice is done. Citizens in both side accepted the role of onlookers as if the business of their countries is not theirs. Citizens, particularly in the latter, have left everything in the hands of their policymakers and rulers something that gives corrupt and greedy rulers an upper hand to do as pleased but not as required and expected. For example, many citizens in the latter have accepted corruption and rent seeking to become normal things and practices. This does not need any uncle from the former to deal with. Given that the relationship between the two is purely commercial, the latter needs to change the way it has being doing things by taking their rulers on to make sure that people are getting what they expect of their governments. They need to amend their constitutions in order to bring accountability for their rulers; failure to which, nothing will change itself.

On their part, the citizens in the former must challenge their governments to do clean business with the latter. By so doing, such citizens will reduce the magnitude of violent conflicts that are chronic in the latter as they revolve around the struggle for controlling resources the latter supplies to the former. Although this may seem as a farfetched suggestion, currently, conflict resulting from poverty that makes some countries in the latter supply terror groups good recruiting grounds, it is the innocent citizens from the former who suffer when they happen to fall in the hands of terrorist groups that are now mushrooming in the latter thanks to exploitative and hegemonic relationship. For the members of families that terrorist activities such as kidnapping and killing have already affected, know too well what equitable and harmonious relationship between the two mean. I do not want to defend terrorism. However, when I look at its true causes and sources, I find that the relationship between the two plus the way they treat each other have a lot to do with the phenomenon.

iii) The Role of Technology in the North-South Relationship

Modern advancement in technology has contributed hugely to the interdependence even dependence of all humans in the globe. While the Global North produces massively, for example, cell phones have bigger market is in the latter; which also plays a role of supplying raw materials for the production of these gadgets. This, if anything, is one of many examples wherein technology; and its unfair uses, always, shapes the unfair relationship between the two. Such a nexus based on business and service, connects the duo however inequitably and unequally it is something that needs to be deconstructed. With the coming of the new information technology, the world has become smaller and smaller and the market bigger and bigger. Tranos and Nijkamp (2014) call this interconnection "the death of distance" noting that there is distance decay thanks to the introduction of internet (p. 3). Distance is no longer a barrier as it used before the introduction of internet. Those who lived in the Global South before the invention of internet remember how letters and postal services played a very significant role in their communication and lives. After the introduction of the internet, letter writing is dying naturally.

Additionally, there is the death of time in that what used to take a long time to move from one place to another as far as communication is concerned. Communication is no longer a big barrier it used to be. One person can massively communicate with anybody on earth in just a second by writing an email that the sender can replicate in many by just writing as many address of the receiver wherever they are on earth. However, when it comes to the use and enjoyment of what internet has to offer, the former still supplies the latter almost everything *vis-à-vis* programs and what is to consume. Such a relationship has led to cultural exploitation-cum-imperialism in which the latter is losing its ways of life and culture by prodigiously consuming whatever comes from the former. In such a relationship, the former passes on some cultural garbage to the latter from the former. For example, Farley (2006) discloses that the normalisation of prostitution in the US as "a glamourous and wealth producing job" (p. 112) has negative impacts on the latter whereby currently, sexual slave, human trafficking and other vices are on the rise. Culturally, the normalisation of prostitution results from Western materialistic nature based on individualism as opposed to collectivism. How do you buy a person connected to you without exploiting her? If anything, this is a systemic degradation and exploitation of a woman. I can argue that this is neoliberal gender based violence (GBV) that has been legalised in the name of making wealth. Ironically, despite such a role it has played in gender-based crimes, the former still preaches women rights to the latter without underscoring the fact that some of its practices are the pillars of this crime against humanity.

Culturally, especially for many African countries, prostitution is unacceptable; it is a sacrilege and abuse of human dignity. It becomes even harsher when one calls it a job that can produce wealth. While prostitution is a glamourous and wealth-creating job in the former, in Africa, the situation is to the contrary. Farley (*Ibid.*) admits that actually "prostitution is a lucrative form of oppression." For example, in Mauritania, Arabs enslaved 90,000 Africans for exploiting them sexually. Again, prostitution is as old as the society in the former while the situation is different in the latter. Sometimes, when one argues that foreign countries and cultures exported and superimposed prostitution and many cultural rots purposely to Africa, some critics say this is but the romanticising Africa as a society of angels. Let us see where the problem commences. Gausset (2001) discloses that:

> During the Victorian period, and that colonization was legitimized by "the white man's burden"–the European's moral obligation to bring their "higher civilization" to others. Africans were presented as the exact opposite of idealized Europeans, also in their sexuality, in order to give an ideological legitimization to the colonization (p. 510).

Who allowed such *armchair researchers*–whom Gausset (*Ibid.*) refers to as *armchair anthropologists*–who even to date still conduct researches; and under what conditions or guidelines? What would one expect from such biased and corrupt researches that paved the way for colonialism in the Global South? Webb (2012) maintains that actually "white racist supremacy continues to seek the desecration of Black bodies, especially through the debasement of Black sexuality. Violence against one Black body does violence to all" (p. 204). Up until now, the former has become a self-appointed prophet of almost everything in the latter. The former has an upper hand almost in everything *vis-à-vis* research, knowledge and what have you compared to the latter. I do not think that the former can allow academics from the latter to inundate the former to conduct research on their prostitutes or other abused and exploited people in the former. When I talk of the lack of reciprocity, I mean exactly such a relationship.

Up until now, African sexuality depends on concoctions that missionaries created in order to show that their fake religions brought the light to Africa, while, in fact, they brought the opposite. To legitimise prostitution in Africa, neoliberal stress that prostitution is one of touristic attractions. Once again, this tells us why colonial government introduced prostitution to Africa. There are views that prostitution does not only financially benefit women in the Global South but also *benefits* various sectors including tourist agencies, hotels, tour operators, pimps, police and government officials, as well as the airlines and foreign travel agencies not to mention increasing women powers (Graburn (1983: Kibicho 2016) which may sound ridiculous for countries sitting on plenty of resources. In the eyes of the pro-North thinkers, such benefits are the economy of prostitution (Persak and Vermeulen 2014). Interestingly, there is a United Nations Convention 1949 against Trafficking in Persons and the exploitation of prostitution of others through sexual exploitation. This instrument seeks to make the so-called free prostitution industry (Jeffreys 2008) which, in a sense, is contradictory to morality and many African cultures and religions that denounce and illegalise prostitution. I think, if the Global South had a say in such a decision, it would not have consented to it. This is because prostitution is unacceptable per societal norms (Galdamez 2016). Again, if you examine the history of colonialism, when such an instrument came into force, many countries in the latter were still colonies. Therefore, such so-called international instrument is the creature of the former. I think; this is why prostitution, either geared by poverty or conflicts, has never been human right issue is supposed to practically cover. Notably, the whole charade of human rights is contradictory in that it agitates for the right to dignified life of a person without necessarily defining the dignified life not to mention how the same allows people to treat their bodies the way they like even if it is to vend them which is immoral by all standards. Again, I am not trying to castigate prostitution where it is a human right resulting from the freedom of an individual. Importantly, we must draw the line between the values of the former and those of the latter in order to see how acceptable or unacceptable prostitution is shall we examine the consensus of the duo.

When it comes to the exploitation of prostitutes in Africa, it is true that many prostitutes in African cities target tourists who are mostly from the latter. Once again, the former exploits the latter in such a business it legalised. This means that the former does not only benefit from the resources in the latter but also the souls and bodies of the occupants of the latter. Thanks to being the recipient of almost everything, the governments in the latter that heavily depend on such dirty tourism that degrades and robs women of their dignity cannot fight against this unfair relationship provided it does not touch on the powers of the heads of these governments. Even when it comes to local exploitation of prostitutes, it is the rich who do so most of who are the elites that control power in poor countries in the latter. The situation is now surreal because prostitution now involves children (Curtis, Terry, Dank, Dombrowski and Khan 2008) chiefly in countries facing violent conflict such as in the DRC.

Although there is a schism between the acceptability and unacceptability of prostitution, Farley (*op.cit.*) notes that "in prostitution, a woman does not stay whole; she loses her name, her identity, and her feelings" (p. 115) which, ironically, has never become the concern for the international community, especially when the victims are from the so-called third world like the DRC. Again, thanks to cultural imperialism, as the former has always entrenched in the latter, such reality is always under the rug simply because the dominant culture legalises prostitution in order to turn it into an international industry. Does it mean that the world has become so bankrupt morally and mentally to the extent that it has failed to find another alternative means of production that can replace prostitution? For the Global South to avert the dangers of witnessing the objectification of its people, it needs to agitate for equal cooperation in which it can have a say about everything involved in the relationship with the Global North. Essentially, decolonising every aspect of relationship is the only way forward.

Here, I am talking about prostitution as the cultural exploitation based on this traditionally exploitative relationship between the twosomes. How much do the latter suffer from crimes such as drug trafficking that involves people in high places of power in the latter? What about money laundering, capital flight, bogus investment contracts, land grabbing and unfair trade among others. The list is long.

You can go further and interrogate the rationale behind the former to define the latter almost in everything. Many lies and fabrications were unleashed about Africa for example. Thanks to the former's technological advancement, it can inundate the latter with whatever garbage in the name of modernity through internet. My experience, for example, shows that many African countries used to hear about serial killers in the former because culturally there was none of them. Again, due to internalised inferiority, some youths are now aping their counterparts in the former to the extent of indulging themselves in such criminality. Currently, another crop of technological colonisation is terrorism that has attracted many youths from the latter due to the spread of internet, ignorance and poverty among others. The looming danger is that the former still dominates and monopolises internet that uses it to flood the latter with denting, manipulative and pornographic materials.

Nowadays, one does not need to be in a certain locality or location to buy, sell something or work online. E-commerce is becoming a norm almost everywhere; and thus, "e-citizens and e-services" (Heeks 2002: 1) in which the duo will never be at par due to the dominance of the former. One can work online without necessarily moving from home. One can attend a meeting hundreds of kilometres away from home. Arguably, Information Technology (IT) has smashed the barriers humans used to encounter all over the world. This is a good thing. However, such improvement has come with a heavy price the latter is now paying dearly. For, when you examine the whole exercise, you find that the former is making more gains than the latter that is losing tremendously due to depending on the former. For, the former controls all internet services that it discretionary provides to the latter without any censorship or agreement on what to offer and what not to. Such a trend enforces even more dependency on the part of the latter. This is how information technology has deconstructed and reconstituted the world to the favourable and advantageous behest of the former.

Hence, I can argue that technology has enhanced our awareness in the sense that it has expanded our worldviews to the extent that the world has never evidenced in the history of humankind. However, when I look at how the world currently views the world, the worldview of the former seems to have altered the worldview of the latter due to giving it the lenses by which to use to view the world. This is why prostitution and other Western cultural and political carryovers, for example, are slowly becoming relevant in the latter. Currently, no part of the world is immune of the virus of technology, especially information technology and its carryover all aimed at conditioning the latter to accept former's values and lifestyle so that it can make a killing. In other words, the South is offering fresh products including its culture while it is in return receiving leftovers and toxic materials. Krugman (1979) argues that the advantage of the former does not lie on nonhuman endowment but its superiority in exploiting technology. Moreover, this is true because such a rationale is internalised among the twosomes. It is easy to sum up this type of business-cum-relationship as crazy one shall the latter keep on believing that it cannot get out of the vicious circle of exploitation is in. For, the former does not bother to use technology whenever it surfaces for the equal benefit of the twosomes. In this unfairly unequal relationship, the former benefits twofold while, to the contrary, the latter suffers the same way. You can see this on how it is using countries such as Japan, China, India and others to boost their technological dominance even by exploiting the countries in the Global South for their advantage. Exploitation and unfair relationship does not end up here. Matsuyama (2000) argues that whenever the Global North acquires a new technology, it exports the old to the latter because the law of trade in this relationship is against the latter. I think the duo needs to agree to invest on modern technology on areas such as renewable, sustainable and acquirable for both sides.

If the volume of technology the former exports to the latter would match the volume of resources it imports from the latter, the duo would be able to seal gap between them; and thereby end up at par. However, thanks to benefiting many folds from such unfair relationship between the two, the former would like the situation to remain as it currently is while the former does not pull all the stops to bring such relationship to parity. This is why the duo has been living in two different worlds (Cardoso 2009) without necessarily seeking to, deliberately deconstruct such an anomaly in which the latter is the loser and the former is the gainer. Arguably, due to individuality and consumerism nature of the latter, the former does all this as way of self-preservation on the expenses of others. It is not a secret that the Global North is now phasing out polluting industries to the Global South without underscoring that the dangers of pollution is affecting the entire globe. The former fails to underscore the fact that earth is like a boat in which all creatures are sailing. You can see this naked conspiracy on vehicular products that the former exports to the latter as the way of fazing them out on top of making money to finance and afford new technologies.

Among all technological domains, the cell phones lead whereby others follow. First, it is cheaper to buy, use and maintain. With the genesis of the cell phones, the whole globe has become like a small technological village or a block so to speak. Anybody can be in contact with anybody anywhere in the world at a fraction of the second. Again, information technology is the product of the Global North. However, such technology cannot exist without materials from the Global South. The truth is; without coltan, computers and other gadget cannot function. Larji (2007) notes that:

> Columbite-tantalum is the formal name for coltan, a metal base, which is little known outside Silicon Valley and high-technology institutions. Its strength, high density, and chemical properties make it a valuable metal used in the manufacture of capacitors in high-tech and medical devices, including mobile phones and laptop computers [Sic] (p. 35).

If the Global South, just as it was the OPEC, underscores the important role such a mineral plays in the economy of the world, it would decide to use it, *inter alia*, as a bargaining chip for deconstructing this detrimental and manipulative relationship. One may ask why the Global South does not apply this rationale to emancipate it from the craws and fangs of the former. The answer is simple that ruling elites in the Global South are in bed with the Global North to see to it that the *status quo* prevails for their personal and myopic interests. Had many countries in the Global South had the minds like that of Gulf States that used their only one resource, oil to set themselves free, such a volume would become illogical. With oil, there is even an exception in that there are other resources that can produce energy while for the coltan there is no alternative currently. Due to such importance of the Global South, the Global North has made sure that the latter remains divided and conflicting in order to not sit down and do the right thing, deconstructing exploitative and unfair relationship between the two. There is no way the latter can keep on waiting for academics and policymakers in the former to do this emancipatory and noble work. The latter needs accept to carry its own cross for its true emancipation. Over fifty years of independence must have given the latter enough experience it can use in seeing; and thereby addressing the problem resulting from this damningly unfair relationship.

Although the Global South benefits from this advanced technology, compared to the Global North, the latter lags behind, and the major role it plays is that of the supplier of the raw materials and the consumer of processed ones. Given that the two parties in this conflict contribute in technological advancement by contributing knowledge for the former and materials for the latter, there are reasons for the duo to sit down and renegotiate the terms of their relationship in order to minimise poverty, miseries, conflicts and imbalances in their relationship.

iv) Is It Democracy or Demicracy?

> *Alexis de Tocqueville and John Stuart Mill were apprehensive about full-fledged democracy, and they were not alone in this. Their fear of "false democracy" (Mill)* Rueschemeyer, Stephens and Stephens (1992: 243).

I have chosen this quote to show how democracy can be controversial and imperfect, especially when some countries use it as cudgel to bully and exploit others. Therefore, I must state it from the outset that my understanding of democracy is that it empowers those who preach it to others to force them to believe or embrace it as it is. This is why the former has always attached conditions of democratisation to the aid they offer the latter. Indeed, it is undemocratic (Derham 2002) or undemocratic liberalism (Norton 2012) by all standards. Being a creature of human creation, democracy is as imperfect as anything else that needs dialogues among its stakeholders. It becomes even worse when such a creature who created democracy is the former coloniser. The concept of democracy fits well in this discourse since the Global North has always taught it to the Global South without equality, reciprocity and a level ground. Always, the former has used democracy to seek linkage and leverage (Levitsky and Way 2006) in the former; even when it means to do so undemocratically provided its interests are achieved, protected and safeguarded even at the detriment of the latter as it has been for a long time.

Etymologically, the word democracy draws its roots from Greek words *demos* "the people" and *kratein* (rule) (Atelhe 2014: 495). Therefore, we can construe the term democracy to mean the rule of the people. Again, which people and how, this needs its own volume. Furthermore, Hollyer and Rosendorff (2011) define democracy as "the contestability of elections" (p. 1193) based on Western ways of administration even if it is not accepted globally however universalised as it has been superimposed on others. The former introduced modern democracy in the latter after the fall of the Berlin Wall in 1991. Before this historical event, democracy did not matter to both parties in this relationship. Thanks to the nature of Western democracy, it seems to work only when it serves the interests of the Global North. However, this is nothing but a superimposition the Global South has always copied. If it were a good thing that serves the interests of all, the former would not have always pushed its model of democracy down the throats of poor countries in the latter. Essentially, what the both halves refer to as democracy is nothing but a ruse the former use to secure its interests in the latter. Levitsky and Way (2002, 2010 cited in Lazarus 2010) describe this type of democracy as 'competitive authoritarianism' (page not provided). Indeed, democracy from the former has created a competition among local elites who seek to control the reins of power; and thereby easily remain in bed with the former. Such a competition has produced oligarchy that is now terrorising many countries in the latter for the benefit of the former. Nails (2006) argue that in Athens, the birthplace of democracy, there came time, chiefly in the fifth century, when democracy and oligarch were ubiquitous in which democrats and oligarchs changed side. Such characteristics are evident today where politicians change side to defend their interests under what they ironically refer to as democratic rights. No doubt; the former has legalised and universalised its *diktats* even where the so universalised issue is not universal. The former always believes that it is better than other is; and thus, whatever it created, so, too, is better than others are. Tony Blair cited Harvey (2007) in justifies this view saying that "ours are not western values; they are the universal values of the human spirit" (p. 3). Suppose everybody takes such a stand on her or his values and culture. I think, if all human beings are equal, as well, their values are supposed to be equal. Therefore, any universalisation of one culture by sidelining others as the Global North has always done, is but colonialism and racism.

Again, the latter tolerates such carbuncular tendencies in the latter while in the former nobody can easily change sides in order to protect personal interests. This is the area where I trace inequality in relationship. It is a normal thing to find that corrupt and anti-democratic figures and forces becoming *politically born again* over the night and be accepted as democrats in the latter. Furthermore, here is where the two breed and braid corruption and rent-seeking practices. If democracy were essentially well intended, why did the latter not exist during the Cold War in which two dominant colonial powers the Union of Soviet Socialist Republics (USSR) on the one hand, and the United States (US) on the other hand were able to secure and safeguard their interest in the absence of the said democracy. This shows and tells us as to why democracy, the former applies and forces others to embrace, is completely different from the one it exports to the latter. Due to its controversies and underperformances, it is not exaggeration to call this democracy defective and feeble simply because it aims at safeguarding the interests of the former simultaneously endangers the latter through perpetual and systemic exploitation that has been going on for many years. Why should democracy matter now and not then? Nevertheless, neither the former nor the latter is ready to ask and answer such looming questions about the sincerity of introducing democracy in the latter by the former. As academics, we need to ask these questions; and make sure there receive right answers as a way of deconstructing almost everything with regard to the relationship between the two strange bedfellows in question.

However controversial and deficient as it has always been, Western democracy is one of the elements that unite the Global North and the Global South. However, the said democracy is spread undemocratically through a one-way traffic in which the former dictates what the latter should do as far as democracy is concerned. Therefore, when I talk about democracy in this volume, I mean Western democracy whose values are more suitable for individualistic people in the former than collectivistic ones in the latter. This is because this brand of democracy mostly defends more of individual rights than the rights of the group. You can see this by gauging how two halves fair democratically, especially *vis-à-vis* human rights. When I posit that the democracy the former spreads is undemocratic, I mean the whole superimposition and discrimination in applying it. To know how undemocratic this democracy is, refer to what happened to dictators the former created and fell out with them so as to destroy them while protecting other like that are still in bed with it.

Ironically, Western or the so-called modern democracy advocates human rights that do not exist in the latter when the duo deals with issues such as economy and finance. Mawere and Marongwe (2016) define democracy as an amorphous thing that can mean different things for different people. I concur with this definition on one factor that democracy misses one important aspect of treating the duo equally. However too general and too simplistic, it enables us to know why many dictators are in bed with the *democrats* from the Global North. Such a take can explain nicely what has been ongoing in some countries in in Africa and the Middle East. However, as per Western conceptualisation of democracy, it must enable the majority to win over the minority without trampling over their rights. Further, democracy must bring accountability despite the fact that this sort of accountability is prejudiced in that the latter is forced to accountable while the former is free not to. Even within the countries in the latter, not all leaders are accountable to their people. Are there any democratic and international systems that hold all corrupt African rulers for their dirty actions? How many dictators are in power in the Global South not to mention the past ones? Are the people in the latter empowered enough to take on their venal rulers? Is it not the fact that the former in protecting such unscrupulous rulers who also reciprocate by protecting its right when the citizenry try to take them on is a double standard and colonial mentality? I think what befits Africa is that some leaders in some few countries are held accountable while in the majority of countries, in the above mentioned localities, it depends on how leaders or rulers offer to their masters in the former. Again, despite its flaws, some call such brand of democracy a representative democracy that is not, primarily in Africa due to the fact that many so-called representatives–thanks to corruption and Western double standards–end up representing their stomachs after conning their voters.

The question the duo needs to ask and answer is necessarily; do the so-called representatives in the latter represent those they say they represent? If the answer is affirmative, then how has it been possible for the latter to languish in poverty while it sits on immense resources compared to the former? In case this is seen as a far-fetched reason-cum-question, ask yourself; if there has been representative democracy in Africa, as it has been in the Global North, why then Africa lags behind in terms of economic development? Stein (2001) underscores the abnormality of the current neoliberal democracy in that it entails 'a space free of public power for individual and group action (civil society), and a free market sector" (p. 493). What is free market is for, if at all, the latter has never enjoyed it? Again, is there any agreement the two have ever reached in defining democracy? Has the latter really enjoyed this free market? Why are economic rights not enshrined in the human rights regime? Due to its archaic and anarchic nature, Peck and Tickell (2002) compare the victims in the latter with religious converts who strictly follow the *diktat* of the church as it was in Latinate Church in medieval Europe dealt brutally and savagely whoever opposed it. We all know how brutal and conservative the Latinate church was; and how it destroyed the lives of many people in Europe. Again, despite the fact that Western democracy has all hallmarks of dictatorship and one-sidedness, the former still forces the latter to accept it as a way of bringing justice where it does not exist! To me, democracy allows dialogue, disagreements and agreements all reached through a free and fair means mainly elections that in the latter ended up being charades reached at after election rigging and manipulations. Nevertheless, when it comes to the relationship between the two, such ingredients–that would perfect democracy–are missing; and nobody is agitating that they be included in the process based on fifty-fifty power dynamics. One would call what is referred to as neoliberalism as old-conservatism if not authoritarianism.

Another undisputable fact that helped the former to lord it over the latter is the truth that almost all policies operating in the latter are made in Washington, New York, Paris and London among others. Even democracy I am talking about follows the same patterns. What is good for the former is automatically good for the latter and the world in general; which is strange and purely hegemonic.

I wonder about the logic of Western democracy that empowers Western countries to bully the world on the one hand, while on the other hand, encourages citizens in the countries that export, exploit and misuse it to hold their leaders accountable for their actions. How African citizens can hold their leaders accountable for their actions while the Global South cannot question the Global North for its actions? With such twisted or contrived democracy (Nhemachena in Mawere and Mwanaka 2015) that gives justice to one side and denies others the same, the world cannot enjoy true peace. If true democracy means the representation of the people, one would think the leaders of the Global South would have that power of holding leaders of the Global North in international matters the same way the former do thanks to having bigger population than the former. There are issues such exploitation, arms race, arms trade and production that escaped the rationale of democracy internationally; not to mention ecological threats global warming resulting from carbon emission the Global North has always caused; and posed for the detriment of the whole globe. If democracy were truly about the majority, the latter is more populous than the former. I still wonder how the Global North with a small population compared to the Global South to have more power in the United Nations (UN) without using the same rationale of the Latin maxim *vox populi vox dei* or majoritan rule. Why the majority is a determinant at national level but not at international level as far as power of decision-making is concerned.

However, imposed as it has always been, arguably, ideology–which revolves around the values and norms of the former–is now another unifying factor for the latter. Democracy, as the Global North invented it, is now taking a centre stage in the Global South. There is no way conditional democracy can bring about any positive changes anywhere. Strait-jacket-like democracy is harmful; for those who enacted it did so for their interests as opposed to the interests of others. Had democracy been uniform for all, it would make sense despite its shortfalls. I do not get it to see–for example–on the one hand, the United States of America (USA) has always protected monarchs and Emirs in the Middle East while, on the other hand, the same is baying for the blood of those it perceives to be dictators and undemocratic rulers. This is a double standard. Moreover, it speaks to the hidden factor that democracy, those behind Western democracy, use as a ploy of safeguarding the interest of the superpowers. Why should democracy be a *sine qua non* to say Tanzania but not for Saudi Arabia? The Global North forces many countries to gulp its brand of democracy without questioning it in order to get aid. With its prescribed democracy, the former does not bother to think about the customs and norms of the latter. Sweeping democracy, with strings attached to it, is now amidst almost everything the Global North offers to the Global South, especially when it comes to aid. Countries, in the latter, are encouraged to borrow big sums of money to finance elections that, in turn, produces corrupt rulers. I think that there cannot be democracy without justice. Arguably, what is referred to as aid to the latter is–like resource curse (Van der Ploeg 2011: Mehlum, Moene, and Torvik 2006; Robinson, Torvik, and Verdier 2006) that the latter has suffered for long–more of "the curse of aid" (Djankov, Montalvo, and Reynal-Querol 2008). Unfortunately, aid the latter has wrongly viewed as something benevolent while, in actuality, is but malevolent ruse the former uses to get leverage from the latter besides subjecting the it to many conditions it attaches to every aid. The truth is clear that aid has not helped the latter. Instead, the former has used aid dubiously as a ruse to keep the latter at bay for easy and perpetual exploitation. Under the Rational Political Business Cycle Model (RPBC), which predicts that opportunistic behaviour pays off (Aidt, Veiga and Veiga 2011), especially through "the opportunistic politician framework" (Block 2002: 4), many countries in the latter are in debts. This is simply because they irresponsibly borrowed; and unwisely spent a lot of aid monies in funding their sham elections that brought just the same cabal of corrupt politicians. Ironically, despite outright rigging, such elections still receive funds as democratic! Block (*Ibid.*) goes on noting that:

> The interaction of opportunistic governments and naive voters leads to the prediction that governments will systematically intervene to create regular multi-year cycles in growth and unemployment in which growth is above normal and unemployment below normal prior to elections, followed by corrective contractions after elections (p. 5).

Paradoxically though, when some countries are able to get loans or aid for elections, their donors are not ready to provide the same to crucial sectors such as education and health in the same countries. Even by considering political correctness and responsibility, the duty of making the government and its institutions in any country is solely on the shoulders of the citizens of that country. Again, when someone finances your elections, by implications and logic, is that leaders such elections produce are likely to be under the influence of the donor or donors.

Who pays the piper calls the tune. This shows how many African democratic leaders elected by the support of donors' money are the creatures of those donors. Therefore, they will pay back for the kindness of the donors who enabled them to come to power. I think this is why most of African rulers are above the laws in their countries as opposed to the leaders of their donor countries. While accountability in the Global North is *sine qua non*, the same is an option in the Global South. Arguably, donors like it that way so that they can use leaders obtained by their donations to rule indirectly for them or protect their interests in those countries. The other day former Zimbabwe strongman, Robert Mugabe, happily supported the suggestion by African countries to send election observers to the US that scalded and scoffed Mugabe for such an idea. Pricketl (2000) quotes quotes Mugabe as saying that "perhaps now we have reached a time when they can learn a lot from us. Maybe Africans and others should send observers to help Americans deal with their democracy." Although the former ignored such an idea, plundered countries were trying to show the shortfalls and the double standard of liberal democracy. The AFP goes on quoting Congo's independent *La Reference Plus* as saying that "if this happens in the United States, how you want everything to be clean and transparent in the poor African continent." Again, the police of the world sealed its ears and went on with its controversial elections that saw George W. Bush trounce Al Gore despite such anomalies and controversy. Had this happened in any country in the Global South, the same police of the world would issue threats and condemnations accusing such a country of trampling on democracy! This is a type of relationship between the two spanning decades as it revolves around superiority and inferiority complexes so to speak.

Despite all, rich countries in the Global North think it is their God-given right and duty to man poor countries in the Global South by sending their election observers. They give legality, credibility and integrity to the elections by deciding which elections are free and fair or not based on their *fairness* scale. Essentially, poor countries in the latter are checked like a baby to see if there is any untidiness or not. What do you do with the baby? You keep on checking her or his diapers to see if there is any mess so that you can clean her or him. Such relationship is not equitable and equal. It degrades, and above all, lacks respectability and reciprocity. The same applies to the presidential terms that are now two terms in many African countries. However, some countries went around this prerequisite of African democracy by repealing their constitutions to enable their strongmen to serve more than two terms. Uganda leads in this murky sort of perquisite of democracy of deceit. Ugandan president Yoweri Museveni has been in power for 30 years. Given that he has assured his masters in the former he can protect their dubious interests in Uganda and in the region, he still gets money and a nod from them despite ruling Uganda as his private estate. This shows that if the guardians of democracy in the Global North are satisfied with the protection and security of their interests, a person can misrule the country for as much time as he deems fit. This reminds us what the former Libya strongman, the late Col. Muamar Gaddafi, questioned. When Western countries required him to relinquish power because he had served for a long time, he asked them why did they not tell the Queen Elizabeth II of the United Kingdom (UK), Canada, Australia, and New Zealand who—at that the time—had cloaked longer time longer than Gaddafi. Poor Gaddafi, after snubbing his argument, the answer was to topple him.

Looking at what has been going on in Africa since 1992, sometimes, it become harder to see the importance of democracy that makes people free politically while the same people remains dependent economically. Democracy would make more sense if it could accommodate economic freedom from dependence for the Global South. It is clear that many countries in the latter may view themselves as free. Again, can there be any meaningful freedom amidst of dependence? Another element that makes the said democracy to be paradoxical-cum-hypocritical is the fact that the same differs in the two globes in point. While democracy in the Global North is there to serve the population, the situation is different in the Global South where democracy seems to serve local elites more than the *hoi polloi*. Without turning around this stance, arguably, democracy becomes meaningless or less important in the Global South; because it has always been inconsistent and controversial in its double-standard applications, which, in a sense, is but espousing undemocratic settings or rules. Again, looking at the Middle East and its lack of democracy, for example, one thinks otherwise. Despite lacking democracy, the Middle East has used its norms and cultures to renegotiate its relationship with the West;

and thereby benefit from its resources more meaningful than many African countries. Can people eat democracy really? Can there be democracy amongst injustices, poverty and unfair relationships? Why is democracy important between the rulers and citizens in the countries in the Global South but immaterial in the relationship between the two global halves? I like and concur with the capability approach that puts justice amidst everything as far as democracy is concerned. Srinivasan (2007) argues that "the capabilities approach has much to say on the subject of what freedom should be really about, in all societies, and offers more nuanced understanding of justice and the importance of democracy" (p. 458). To me, there cannot be true and real democracy without justice for all but not for some as it currently is in the duo and between them. Likewise, the said true democracy must exist between the Global North and the Global South. Is this democracy or demicracy?

Chapter Three

When Dependency Hampers Interdependency

There is no way one can address the anomalies of the relationship between the Global North and the Global South without touching on dependency. If you look at relative deprivation, modernisation and dependency and development theories, you find that what is known as dependency in the Global South is nothing but imperialism that needs to be treated based on the history of the Global South, chiefly *vis-à-vis* the concepts of colonialism and underdevelopment resulting from historical realities. First, the duo is interdependent on each other however at different magnitudes. The former needs resources from the latter that needs aid from the former. Such needs need a systemic overhaul mainly in the latter where almost all systems, apart from being archaic and wanting, depend on the former as it created them. When it comes to theories, aim at maintaining international *status quo* championed by the Global North under the neoliberalism and capitalism not to mention imperialism (Gilpin 2016), such a rationale is practically and theoretical right, especially in that the former uses its capitalistic, imperialistic and liberalistic systems under either globalisation or internationalism to exploit the latter. You can see this on how the latter conducts its business. Currently, many poor countries in the latter are striving to attract investments from the former while they discourage the same among themselves. Therefore, the Global South needs to attract intra-investments as the means of lessening its dependency on the former (Mhango 2015). Statistically, not many African countries are investing within their boundaries. African countries need to change this mentality-cum-trend by, for example, either allowing their sister states and companies to invest collectively or every country to attract invests from each other. According to Ngugi (2016), it is only Kenya and South African that, currently have invested in other African countries. Further, Ngugi notes that "South Africa however beat Kenya in terms of the worth of the projects as it had Sh200 billion compared to Kenya's Sh100 billion." These figures are still small compared to say Chinese or investments from the former.

Importantly, Gilpin (*Ibid.*) goes on to brazenly call the dependency theory a thunderclap which it actually is, exclusively for those robbing the Global South who are known for paying no attention to unfairness and injustices they have always applied and committed to the latter. Amin (1976 cited in Gilpin *(op. cit.)* simply puts that the latter is poor simply because of the exploitation of the core or the former whose development is the underdevelopment of the latter (Mhango 2018). Arguably, as indicated hereinabove, the underdevelopment of the latter has all hallmarks of the former's colonialism and contemporary imperialism we know of today. How do you call the half that produces almost all raw materials the economy of the former depends on dependent by excluding the former that, so, too, depends on such materials? I think what the former refers to as dependency to denote the backwardness of the latter needs to receive its true meaning namely interdependence as the way of bringing equality and justice in the relationship between duo.

McGowan (1976) argues of that "dependent countries, because of their subordinate role in the world's capitalist system, are unable to make autonomous decisions concerning the pace and direction of growth of their national economies" (pp. 25-26). If anything, McGowan points at the crux of the matter as far as unequal relationship between the duo is concerned. How do you say that the customer is dependent of a shopkeeper while the both depend on each other? This is a cardinal rule of any business that is simple to comprehend. This is a natural phenomenon that even dogs know when trading bones. Again, is it out of malice and ignorance that the former does not appreciate and comprehend such a simply matter? Adam Smith is among scholars from the Global North who contributed immensely as far as modern trade is concerned. He wrote in his famous book *The Wealth of Nations* that trade is about profit but not humanity. Based on this different rationale from the way the same many countries in the Global South understood this concept, the latter is nothing but an engine of the relationship between the duo. The former has always served its interests on the expenses of the interests of the latter. This is obvious that the duo uses different ethical and moral principles. For example, the SSA has its famous Ubuntu philosophy, which means I am because you are or there cannot be you without me and vice versa. Everybody depends on everybody; and this is the cardinal rule that regulates almost everything *vis-à-vis* relationships. Some perspectives and empirical studies have proved to have some impacts on the understanding of the concept of Ubuntu, specifically the role that it can play in business ethics (West 2014). This is a stark difference between the two as far as business meaning and ethics are concerned. While Smith (*Ibid.*) postulates that, essentially the aim of business is purely to make profits, Ubuntu everything revolved around ethics and morality.

Despite ethical flaws in its approaches and systems, ironically, the former has always portrayed itself as a saviour of the latter while it actually is the tick on the back of the latter. The latter knows everything save that its indifferent *ignorance* is the tool that enables the former to rip the latter off easily. However, many Western thinkers have always pushed some historical and scientific realities under the carpet such as heavy dependence of the former to the latter in supplying natural materials. If the world faces it, it needs to treat the Global North the same way it treats the Global South when it comes to the former's historical independency. It needs to embark on the demythologisation of North's superiority hidden in fabrications and colonialism. Arguably, there are no miracles that enabled the former to become more prosperous than the latter other than the leg up it got from colonialism, slavery, and, currently neo-imperialism. These crimes, *inter alia*, are the issues this tome seeks to address in a conciliatory manner revolving around renegotiating new terms of relationship in order to enable the duo move forward as a civilised society of a people guided by equality, equity and justice all entrenched on pragmatic appreciation of equal human rights and destiny. Nyerere (1977) strongly argues that poor countries unfairly locked the latter together in poverty; thus, there is a need of changing the whole system regulating this relationship. Being one of African leaders who championed social justice,

Nyerere knew the situation first hand as a leader and as a victim; and the former did not like his noises based on equality and equity.

If we put greed and lust aside, it is obvious that both parties are well aware of the injustices one part has been doing to another. What is lacking, however, is political will geared by new awakening that such unfair relationship needs to address in order to avoid unnecessary conflicts in the Global South. So, too, the Global South needs to worry when such *kindness* revolving around aid from the former comes to an end. This issue has always boggled my mind. What will happen shall the former stop offering its handouts to the latter? When will the latter return the *gentility* it has enjoyed for many years for its peril?

I purposely chose Nyerere's argument above to substantiate the fact that the problems resulting from Global South's long-time dependency on the Global North needs an overhaul save that there have never been any efforts or will to address this anomaly. Ironically, some countries in the Global South seem to be satisfied with their dependence despite claiming to have political independence. Without deconstructing and debunking hegemonic relationship that has been going on because of historical realities; thereby making the latter being satisfied with underdevelopment and economic backwardness, is as good as offering yourself to the lion to devour you. Nevertheless, the former makes the latter believe that it cannot live without receiving handouts from the Global North or cannot pull itself out of this modern slavery. Some have gone further to suggest that the Global South is responsible for its failure though not all (Sheppard and Nagar 2004; and Amin 2011). Many countries in the Global South, despite knowing that policies from the former hurt their economies, still do not want to think out of the box by rebelling against; and thereby, initiate policies suitable for their interests and economies. They wantonly believe that the Global North will always be there to solve their problems while in reality it will always be there to exacerbate them.

However, Kipling's book *Whiteman's Burden* attracted much criticism in order to be termed as racist; it has some nuggets for the countries in the Global South. Time for deconstructing and faulting wrong beliefs that the Global North has a messianic role over the latter altogether is now. It is sad that Kipling's metaphor of Whiteman's encumbrance is ambiguous in that some think that the white man has the burden of civilising others while pragmatic meaning based on the history of colonial misdeeds, the burden is a white man himself and what the Whiteman caused to those he colonised. For this book, the white man's burden is colonialism of all forms news and old. In other words, the white man does not have any burden. The burden is on the oppressed. This is why I diagnostically call North-South relationship a horse-jokey one. For, whenever the jokey and the horse do business, the former strives to make the latter believe that their business is productive; and everybody is playing his part. Despite such deceit and silence, the burden is always on the horse but not on the jokey. It is even sad that the jokey had perpetually made the poor horse to accept a lie that the burden is not on its back but on the head of the jokey. Thus, the jokey wants such ridiculous relationship to remain as it has always been by making the horse believe that the jokey is there to carry its burden while the burden actually is the jokey himself. It becomes so sad when the horse knows the whole reality yet keeps on ignoring it, or does not work on it. Humans do not deserve such animalisation.

North-South relationship is perfectly the same as jokey-horse one. And the duo know too well that their relationship is not normal; and without normalising it by deconstructing, peace and prosperity in the world will become a very scarce item. It strikes to see how the international community burns billions and billions of dollars in dealing with the outcomes of the conflict without investing in the sojourn to address the root cause. I know this may sound strange for neoliberalists who think that the Global South has to copy their trajectory without allowing conducive environment that enabled the Global North to reach where it is now, the apex of development in the world. For countries that colonised other countries and acquired the capital that enabled them to become rich it is sheer double standard and hypocrisy to propose such a solution. As McGowan (*Ibid.*) argues, the question: How will the Global South make headways without decision-making freedom supported by the duo; remains begging for accurate and practical answers. For, some thinkers espouse that the Global North should give money to the latter and development will happen. Hulme, Hanlon and Barrientos (2012) argue that "in industrialized countries, there was a major change in thinking in the 20th century, and cash transfers are now considered an effective and normal means of addressing poverty" (p. 3). Wrong. How do you offer or transfer monies to countries without legal frameworks that protect the rights of their people or to countries without decisionmaking clout in the world market? How do you funnel money to countries governed by corrupt and inept governments; and logically expect anything? Money cannot be a solution for the Global South. Why the latter, with such immense resources, depend on money instead of giving it a fair deal in trade? How can such money make a difference if, at all, the Global North scoops and takes back the same money offered as aid? How can such money make any sensible change in the countries wherein the heads of the governments are above the law? Why does the Global North not want to learn from living examples such as those corrupt regimes they supported in the DRC, the Philippines and elsewhere? As I will prove later, the Global North siphons much of the money the Global South receives in the form of aid. It is like giving with the left and taking it with the right on the same table if we consider the role the IFIs do on behalf of the former.

The evidence is clear that multinational corporations, backed by neoliberal institutions such as the World Bank (WB) and the International Monetary Fund (IMF), *inter alia*, are wantonly plundering the Global South. Ironically, they call such trade. In effect, giving money to a corrupt regime is as good as giving a sword to a killer. He will spend the money on self-protection and self-preservation after wronged the population that, in the main, he hijacked. Experience shows that such money maintains kleptocratic regimes. Omar Bongo (Gabon) and Mobutu Seseseko (DRC) are a good example of how money from the Global North entrenched dictatorship and corruption in the Global South. Again, it does not mean that the Global North or neoliberalists do not know this. They know it too well. However, they offer such monies to make more money. For, the debts such money cause make the Global

South more dependent and compliant when the former wants its interests protected and promoted on the expense of the majority of suffering citizenry. A Chinese proverb avers that: Teach somebody to fish; he will become independent instead of giving him a fish. The Global South needs to know how to fish but not a fish. It has fish and water even skill shall it be treated fairly and equitably. It is pure colonialism to keep on helping the people in the Global South that can help themselves if the use their resources freely and fairly under international systems. Hence, what the duo needs here are true cooperation, meaningful and reciprocal interdependency and partnership.

i) **Inevitable Interdependency Partnering and Partnership**

Fair trade is a commercial partnership, based on dialogue, transparency, and respect, the aim of which is to create greater equity in world trade. It contributes to sustainable development by ensuring better trading conditions and guaranteeing the rights of producers and marginalized workers, particularly in the global south FINE (an informal umbrella of fair-trade organisations) cited in Pirotte, Pleyers, and Poncelet 2006: 442).

Legally speaking, partnership is the agreement of association of more than one person that the partners co-own according to the agreement on how to run such a partnership. I can say that partnership has three major elements namely partners, and agreement on terms of ownership. Again, when such a legal definition of partnership is entertained–which in this case is the relationship between the Global North and the Global South–all elements seem to miss. Therefore, due to the lack of the current relationship that I view as partnership however, lacking legally it may be, methinks the duo should sign a new contract based on collaboration and partnership than just mere relationship. So doing, will help the duo to treat each other with dignity and equally and equitably. When it comes to collaborating, Bygballe, Jahre, and Swärd (2010) define it as a long time commitment between two or more parties with a shared understanding of the partnership. Looking at these two definitions, this volume looks at them as the same concepts despite with different magnitudes. Therefore, to make a point clear, I have decided to use both terms in order to give a reader a choice in understanding the relationship between the duo; and the way it is supposed to look like in order to equally serve all parties in it.

In dealing with the North-South relationship, I prefer interdependence to dependence, especially when the independence seemingly becomes a hoax as it has been for many countries in the latter whose independence has never freed it from dependency on the former. Sin (2010: 984-985) cited in Noxolo, Raghuram, and Madge (2012) notes that "'the notion of 'responsibility'...is often shaped and constructed around the view that the privileged 'developed world'" (page not provided) which is true. However, humiliating it is, such a view, sometimes, can be wrong and misleading, especially when one treats it as a rule for underdeveloped countries to get satisfied with such economic political and social dependency. Apart from lacking independence, I, also, see the lack of justice and equality between the two. However, Waltz (2010) argues that arguably "everything is related to everything else, and one domain cannot be separated from others" (p. 8). Although the former views the latter as dependent, likewise, it depends on it; however, indirectly or covertly. Try to image what would happen to the economies of the countries in the former if the countries in the latter stop supplying them with raw materials not to mention stopping consuming their processed goods from the raw material the latter supplies the former. The world has changed tremendously as far as obvious interdependence and interconnectedness are concerned. Everybody almost knows everybody due to various factors. There are some factors making this knowing-each-other awareness quite obvious and strong. Our awareness about the existence of each other is becoming more obvious because a person in remote villages in Papua New Guinea knows the existence of the others in mega cities such as New York, London and many more. As well, the persons in mega cities mentioned are aware of the existence of others in remote areas of Vanuatu.

History has a vital role to play in this interdependency. The former, particularly countries that colonised others, cannot deny the fact that they accumulated their capital by ways of colonising and enslaving other countries. This is why they have always owned powerful financial institutions that operate based on their goals and interests. Financial systems in the former have become another type of government within governments. They have immense and discretionary powers to do as pleased. So, too, such financial systems are new to the Global South, especially Africa and partly the Middle East where, for example, which do not need to have interests or usury attached on their financial services or transactions.

When I look at the world across the board, I sometimes, wonder; what the world has become. I wonder even more to find that banks all over the world operate based on just mere trust. More often than not, banks do not have money in their vaults; yet they can do business despite having no money. Essentially, the banks use their registration to solicit trust among themselves and customers simply because they are registered and insured. When it comes to Africa's immense resources, are they not sufficient to act as an insurance that may enable countries endowed with them to trade with whomever they want? Insurance and registrations are mere papers that do not carry as much weight as resources some African countries are endowed. This means, we need to change our laws and policies to reflect on such concrete realities *vis-à-vis* African resources. Why is it possible to trust a person or an institution based on papers but not based on resources? Why is it possible for an individual to use her or his house to secure a loan but not a country to use its resources to get the same? Really, the value of anything is what we ascribe to it; otherwise, the so-called value is nothing but the product of agreement. This said, the latter has always lost a great deal due to not having any inputs in the formulation of the valuable mediums of exchange such as the US dollar. This is why the money we use has value even though what makes it are but mere papers some can print and produce massively as it is in the case of hard currencies the former uses to exploit the latter. Suppose the latter uses its immense resources such as gold and others as its media of trade through stifling the former, can the former perform as it has always done.

It is time now to declare Africa's untapped resources as wealth that need to guarantee Africa trust in international business and instruments. This said, it is time that Africa uses its abundant and huge resources as a guarantee in doing business with those who do not have such resources. Here is where the importance of cooperation and partnership comes into the big picture. There is no question. Western rich countries made many gains by ignoring and underrating Africa's potentials based on its resources, humans and materials.

To pull Africa out of this manmade debacle-cum-impasse, the international community needs to incorporate resources in its legal framework. If a person can secure a loan from the bank by using his parcel of land or a house, why can Africa not do the same based on its resources? Under neoliberal exploitative policies made by the West, even the definition of property concurs with the logic that Africa is supposed to own its resources against other persons or the world. When it comes to the validity of property Smith (2012) makes a good conclusion arguing that "is a right to a thing good against the world—it is an in rem right" (p. 1706). Legally and logically speaking, the value of anything or property depends on the relationship between things and persons and the world. In this case, Africa needs to advocate and agitate for the incorporation of its property even in the definition and evaluation of wealth, generally, the wealth of the world. It, sometimes, boggles my mind when I come across UNESCO heritage sites all over Africa. This is not supposed to be with some precious resources that Africa is supposed to enjoy and use without necessarily kowtowing before UNESCO's law. Take an example Aïr and Ténéré National Nature Reserve in Niger that is a UNESCO site. Supposed Niger discovers oil or any precious resources underneath this site; can it exploit them without necessarily breaking UNESCO's rules? I am not quite sure if African governments have any inputs, when it comes to deciding which part of Africa is a UNESCO heritage site or not. Instead, they rather blindly subscribing to neoliberal policies without knowing their future ramifications. I do not know if they know whose interests such heritage serves. Why the former likes to declare some area World heritage without considering the resources of the latter in calculating countries wealth? Why is American dollar–the paper that the US can print at will–recognised as wealth but not Africa's minerals, forests, Lakes and whatnots that can be used to secure some loans internationally? I would argue that fair and genuine partnership is the only way forward. Sometimes, I wonder to find that our resources even animals are more valued that our people. Again, you may argue that animals and things are not obstacles to exploitation. Although the majority of Africans have no role to play in the affairs of their countries, they still are obstacles through reproduction.

ii)   Essentialised and Internalised Colonialism

In his book, *Africa Reunite or Perish* Mhango (2015) poses a very provoking question asking if colonialism is a type of positive or meaningful civilisation. Further, Mhango argues that colonialism–just like genocide and other crimes against humanity–and he urges the international community to, legally declare them crimes against humanity intentionally and internationally in order to force all countries that profited from such evils to redress the countries they colonised and robbed. Nonetheless, being the beneficiaries of such crimes, the international community seems to have consented to the internalisation and essentialisation of colonialism. It is a normal thing, under current international laws, for the Global North to bully and exploit the Global South without being legally liable for such crimes committed to many countries in the Global South for many years in order to generate the capital the Global North is now enjoying and using to bully the latter. Many instances prove how the existence of international legal law is a conspiracy against poor countries in the latter. For example, plundered countries in the Global South have always complained about unjust and bully trade relationship between the two halves and no international laws have ever addressed this problem. Ya'u (2004) cited in Ezema (2010) argues notes that:

In order to understand globalisation, as a tool for cultural imperialism, there must a review on the economic root and the underlining cultural implications *vis-à-vis* the IFIs. For, example, armed with international treaties, the World Trade Organisation (WTO) propagated the gospel of liberalisation and privatisation–the twin-working tools of globalisation. Liberalisation and privatisation created opportunities for multi-national companies with their vast political and economic resources to install themselves as key players in the critical sectors of the economy. With privatisation, these companies took over investments in social services such as health care, education, power supply, telecommunication among others. The control of access to education means that such services became costly beyond the reach of so many Africans children–thereby laying the foundation of cultural imperialism.

Remember; this is the WTO which Peet (2009) ties to other two notorious IFIs namely the IMF and the WB; and calls them unholy trinity.

Just like in any sphere of life, what is playing here is power dynamics based on unequal formulation and equilibria in which the former has much discretionary power over the latter. What makes this power game advantageous to the former and detrimental to the latter is the fact that the latter has internalised this inequality to the extent that it sounds as a normal and natural thing. For example, a doctor, professor, politician or beggar from the former feels he or she is superior to the counterpart in the latter. Likewise, the appreciation of services between the two is very different. Elites in the latter go to the former for services such as education, health and leisure. The former knows everything; and make do with this anomaly knowing that it makes big profits from such elites it has always been in bed with. Such elites destroy and sabotage social services in the latter knowing that they have alternative in the former. If you look at the history of Africa, for example, you find that many African leaders died in hospitals in the latter but not at home where health services are poor and in many countries non-existent. Power is about relationship (Dahl 1957: 201 cited in Meehan and Wright 2012) that denotes the dint by which anybody can use to achieve what he or she wants to achieve. Despite propounding this definition, power is among many concepts whose real definitions have always been difficult to, unanimously find. Kroes (1997) cited in White (2005) argues that power depends on "causal relations which are neither observable nor deducible;" for, they are induced from observable event (p. 678). Therefore, when dealing with power, we must ask ourselves if it is power with whom or what in relation with who or what. We can go ahead asking if this is power over or power with in this equation. When it comes to the relationship between the two in question, the power dynamics is extemporaneously power over. The former—as indicated above—has the power to dictate the latter in whatever matter the duo enters or shares such as business, politics even social affairs such as what is good for the people in the latter. You can see this in some unacceptable cultures to the latter that are an issue without considering the ethics, feelings, mores, norms and practices of the latter. This is that cultural imperialism is all about. Indeed, power is about relationship based on the event and the way we observe it. For example, Kroes (2001) cited in Kim (2017) argues that American imperial drive has "translated its symbols and myths into an international iconographic language, visual lingua franca" (p. 42). This is obvious, especially when any one looks at the impacts and effects of such iconographic language. By turning America's symbols and myths into an international iconographic language, the former created an opportunity to define the latter without allowing it to define itself or question whatever definition it expounded on the latter. Mhango (2017) argues that it is crucial to interrogate the definitions we use, who defines what, why and how such a thing or concept is defined so. In other words, we need to define and redefine definitions instead of picking them up blindly without interrogating their validity and logic not to mention the rationale and reason of reaching at them. This is obvious in that the latter does not question or doubt the definitions or tags the former pointlessly puts on it.

Currently, the world views American consumerism and greed as the signs of modernity. Who questions or resists American rot that it forcefully and propagandistically spread all over the world intended to keep on exploiting it? For example, the latter is now facing the dangers from tobacco overconsumption thanks to the advertisement of Marlboro culture. The former, *inter alia*, has for many decades, inundated the latter with Coca-Cola, MacDonald and all other cultural garbage. Again, what makes this relationship between the twosomes itchy is the fact that it lacks reciprocity and impartiality. There is no way a two-role culture of a belligerent donor and a silent recipient can regulate a true relationship. The other day, I was looking at how the latter consumes cultural items such as Hollywood films. It is only through the ruse of international film festivals the films–for example, from Africa, that I will concentrate on much more than other countries in the latter–make headways to the former for just the shortest time of their broadcasting to end up quickly disappearing thereafter. Ask yourself what is in the Hollywood films apart from violence, machoism and over consumption. All this is the role and trickeries of power, principally when its uses are unfairly as it is in the relationship between the former and the latter. To add more salt to injury, even some countries in the latter such as India are now exploiting African countries culturally by littering it with its Bollywood films without consuming any from Africa. Again, how many people see this cultural imperialism based on power dynamics this way?

The major question everybody needs to ask is does the Global South have any tangible contribution in operating a globalised economy. At policy level, the latter has nothing despite supplying almost all raw materials the economies in the former depend on. Furthermore, if there is the role the latter plays, is nothing but receiving orders from the former; that uses its IFIs to bully and confuse the latter. With the exception of China, India and Asian Tigers, who else has the upper hand in trade and business policymaking in the world market? During the cold war, the former blamed socialist countries for protecting their economies. After the world exited a cold war quagmire, we evidenced the same protectionism the West used to demonise being legalised. Refer to how the US government offered stimuli money to private companies during the 2007–08's Credit Crunch. Had such a measure taken during the cold war, the country doing so would be reprimanded by the WB and the IMF which in, practices, are not world or international organisations but Western agents of new colonialism. Again, when it comes to the world, by implications and praxis, the Global North becomes the world as if other countries in the Global South are not the world.

Theoretically, colonialism ended in the 60s and the 70s when the last countries in Africa acquired their independence. Again, when I maintain that colonialism ended in the abovementioned period, I mean external colonialism. For, practically, colonialism has existed since its creation. For, without changing the *status quo*, chances that more epidemic colonialism will go on existing as it claims the lives of many people due to fuelling and maintaining many conflicts in poor countries in the Global South. However, what seem to have changed are the styles of colonisation. Instead of using direct rule–that became more expensive after colonial masters accumulated the capital from colonies–they embarked on indirect rule through appointing and sponsoring local elites to rule for them. Such elites that the Global North appointed to rule for it vicariously–like their masters–invented another type of colonialism, internal colonialism perpetrated by homegrown colonialists. Sometimes, homegrown colonialists are more ferocious and more destructive than external ones. For, they have what it takes to stop external colonialism but they do not want. Even when you evaluate the damage they cause to their countries, you find that its effects and impacts to the future generations are huge. Arguably, the enemy that operates *ab intra* is more lethal than does so *ab extra*. It becomes even worse when the internal enemies conspire with external ones as it has always been in Africa where internal colonialists have clung unto power for a long time due to the backing and support they enjoy from the Global North. There are so many examples of such internal colonialists who ruined their countries. I have touched on them hereinabove in the DRC, Equatorial Guinea, Gabon, Nigeria and Uganda among others.

Further, the Global North created beneficial environment for unseen exploitation under the pretext of freedom. For, a common villager in rural Africa, there is no difference between colonial times and post-colonial ones. His or her life is still meaningless; and the exploitation has changed from the head tax to serving foreign debts superimposed on his or her country under neoliberal capitalistic exploitation. Since then, the situation seems to remain unchanged, and if it did, it is for the worst. Is the Global North ready to take up the challenge that seeks to do away with exploitation, double standard and hypocrisy? Arguably, the answer is yes. Drawing from the current exodus of economic immigrants from the Global South, recently the European Union (EU) summoned African leaders to address the issue. The first proposal was to offer some financial assistance to Africa so that African governments can create favourable environment that will make life liveable in Africa. However, African leaders refused flatly saying that what they need is not money but instead, justice in doing business with the Global North. If anything, this is a good beginning that is likely to deconstruct hegemonic and exploitative relationship between the two shall African countries press on for such radical change. Pop and Legorano (2015) note:

> Faced with an unprecedented influx of migrants and refugees mainly from the Middle East, the European Union is seeking to give incentives to African countries to take back some of the Africans who have arrived in Europe for economic reasons in return for more financial aid, scholarships and training programs (page not provided).

Due to the hegemonic and *holier than thou* nature of the relationship in point, one may pose one crucial question: Why should Europe return back African immigrants while the same welcomes Syrian refugees? Is this not racism and unaccountability because much of poverty in Africa results from colonialism and neocolonialism? Are Syrian refugees better than African ones just because two world powers Russia and the US are fighting proxy war in Syria thus, they are concerned with the victims of its war?

Ironically, during the EU-Africa meeting, the former offered Euros two billion to address the problem that is laughable and ridiculous if we consider the fact that a single country of Germany spent ten times as much to accommodate a few refugees it allowed into its borders. Staff (2015) notes that, according to the

Association of German Cities, Germany's federal states and municipalities could face costs of up to 16 billion euros (11.47 billion pound) in 2016 to deal with the refugee crisis. On their side, if willingly and ably apply it, African leaders have the arsenal or a bargaining chip that will change everything shall they cling unto it and use it wisely to their advantage. Thanks to the huge and many types of resources they have under their control; African leaders may tip the balance by using their much-needed resources.

Why it is logical for one country to spend such humongous amount of money just in a year and yet sees it reasonable to offer one tenth of the same to over 50 African countries? One may argue that the EU is indifferent in dealing with the crisis colonialism and neocolonialism created due to unfair and unjust relationship between the Global North and the Global South. Another argument I espouse is that the Global North has always been racist in dealing with whomever it deems to be black. Why Syrian refugees are more important than Haitian who suffered from natural calamities and the international community did nothing to offer them asylum.

In sum, I can posit that colonialism in this essentialised relationship is for the benefits of the former. This is one of important things academics and stakeholders need to deconstruct to see to it that they decolonise the latter so that it can do away with the essentialisation of colonialism.

iii) Global Warming as a Unifying Force

Although all countries in both halves played a role in causing global warming, significantly the former and East Asian countries have done more harm than to earth the latter due to being industrialised (Gore 2006) or overpopulated. Concerning who should redress whom, the former has a moral obligation to redress the latter; because it created a lot of wealth in the period and process of creating global warming. As an industrialised half, the former's industries have a lot to do with global warming and other environmental hazards resulting from emission, e-wastes and radioactive materials.

Looking at how imminent global warming is, some academics decided to point at the problem; and proposed some solutions to the problem. Timmons Roberts and Parks (2007) concur with this assertion by making a bold proposition for the duo in addressing global warming. By linking global warming to inequality *vis-à-vis* who will suffer the most and who is responsible and willing to address the problem. They accuse the Global North of adversarial negotiations on environment.

Denying responsibility or dialoguing adversely will never solve the problem. Once again, this shows how hypocritical the international community is. What is obvious however is the truth that this phenomenon affects all even if at different times and magnitude. Instead of wasting time and living in the state of denial, those responsible for global warming should stand up and take responsibility. What makes global warming interesting is the fact that it does not chose whom to affect even though the Global South face more consequences due to its imposed poverty. In addressing global warming, the Paris 2015 Agreement on Environment proposes that the world must makes a "shift away from investment in coal, oil and gas as primary energy sources of the world" (Davenport 2015: 5). Ironically, the same did not encourage rich countries to not only invest in renewable energy but also made sure that they distribute such technologies where they do not exist in order to avoid solving the problem on one side as it grows on the other. If equity and equality, in investing in and using technology, remains amiss, chances are that the former will exploit the latter even more by phasing out and export its old technology to the latter. The international community needs to enact laws that will practically deal with polluters who export old technology to the latter. As Timmons Roberts and Parks (*Ibid.*) put it, uneven investment in technology will fuel injustice through globalisation revolving around ecologically unequal exchange and climate change whereby the latter will suffer even more.

Importantly, those thinking they can keep on playing politics and politicising global warming must remember one thing; if farmers in the latter are left out, they will keep on causing global warming due to being poor. Additionally, given that corrupt, greedy, myopic and self-seeking rulers still misrule many countries in the latter, there is a possibility of turning their countries into dumpsters for old technologies so much that all efforts of curbing global warming become fruitless. For example, Nnoroma and Osibanjo (2008) note that, after environment laws became stringent in the former, dumpers or waste brokers have turned to Africa in doing their deadly and toxic trade. Nnorom and Osibanjo give Nigeria as an ideal example where many countries from the former dump their perilous materials; also see Milmo (2009). What would happen has the trend been vice versa? Why the international community is silent on such criminality the former has always committed to the latter? Further, Sepúlveda, Schluep, Renaud, Streicher, Kuehr, Hagelüken and Gerecke (2010) cited in Bisschop 2012) name African countries that receive a lot of e-waste from Europe to include Nigeria, Ghana, Cameroon, Togo and Senegal, partially due to Antwerp's trade connections with this region. Further, they note that Ghana, Benin, Ivory Coast, Liberia and Nigeria import about 250,000 tonnes of e-waster per annum illegally (p. 10). For how long will this go on; when did it start; and how much vulnerability has it already caused nobody knows up until now. Some countries in the former, such as France, have already entered agreements with some countries in the former to dump their radioactive materials without bothering about the danger such materials will cause to the people in the latter. Kimani (2009) discloses that in 1988, the government of Benin negotiated a bilateral deal with the French government to import radioactive and industrial waste in return for $1.6 million down payment and 30 years of economic assistance (p. 50). Is this really assistance or exploitation? Can you call such an agreement anything rather than criminality? Here the issue is not if or when Africa will become a dumpster for e-waste or radioactive materials despite producing the smallest amount of 0.04 kg/capital-year compared to Switzerland with 2.7 kg/capital-year as a replica of the volume of waste materials in the former (Müller, Schluep, Widmer, Gottschalk and Böni 2009). Ironically, when the Berlin Wall fell, the former acted quickly to make sure that nuclear materials did not fall in wrong hands to the extent of endangering its security. I think such a spirit and style must prevail in addressing global warming; and now toxic trade as evidenced in Benin. For, experience shows that industrialised countries have always imposed their will on the Global South that fears the limits of their economic growth and care for basic human needs (Timmons Parks and Roberts, *op.cit*).

Logically, as any human could do, why is it important and possible for the former to defend and safeguard its citizens' human needs while it is impossible for the latter? Common sense dictates that the latter will never sit and watch while its people are perishing. For such a people, livelihood and survival are more important than environment. Therefore, it is upon the former to; understandably accept that its stasis and double standard will never solve the problem. Instead, they will exacerbate the problem; and cause more harm for both sides. Concerning pending contribution to environment degradation by the latter, the rise and coming of China provides an ideal example. Currently, China is exploiting resources in the latter without any regard to environment security. Despite China being in the Global South, its relationship with Africa seem to benefit the international market (Vicente 2011 cited in Juma 2015); thus bringing it in the possibility of cooperating with the Global North to keep on exploiting Africa. This is very possible just like the bohemians and bourgeois (bobos) resulted into cooperation after long time opposition (Brooks 2010). Rising powers are like fish. There is no time the shark will favour other smaller fish despite facing the same danger from the whale. The former is a whale as opposed to China and India that are sharks braced to devour small countries from the same pond they have share for generations. This fish-eat-fish theory dictates that unity and shrewdness must prevail for the world to survive.

Due to capitalistic lust for wealth, some unscrupulous people, using their shady companies, will want to make big bucks out of everything including toxic waste or exporting old technology to the latter even if they know the danger such activities pose to the humankind. Here is where environmental degradation geared by greed and bad policies equally becomes a challenge to the duo. Hence, the international community needs to wake up from slumber and put a stop to this deadly trade by enacting binding laws to punish deadly traders. Thanks to individualistic drive, greed and unfair neoliberal policies, shall the former keep on doing its stasis, business as usual and *holier than thou*, all will end up in vain with regards to stopping whatever type of exploitation from North to South. Annan (2005) proposes partnership between poor and rich countries in combating this phenomenon. Again, is partnership alone enough if it lacks equal footing and doing justice for all partners without discriminating against or exploiting one another as it has always been in the relationship between North and South?

Essentially, as argued above, partnership and collaboration are vital almost in everything. This is because, in reality, North and South are like yin and yang on their livelihood and survival. However, I do not know which is yin and which is yang. I just see a yin-and-yang sort of thing in this equation; if viewed with a naked eye as it is.

Chapter Four

What Worked and What Did Not in the North-South Rapport

Although, North-South relationship in dealing with conflict and development has worked in some places, it is still hugely inequitable; and enables the Global North to exploit and dominate the Global South; thus causes conflict based on struggle for resource control as a means of meeting unmet needs. This struggle has always attracted political opportunists and warlords in many countries fighting for power as the means of exploiting resources for selling to either the former or make money or get weapons that guarantee them the grip on power. The relationship in point is exploitative, hegemonic, unfair, unjust and paternalistic by nature. In this chapter, I apply some theories to shed light on ontological relationship between the two globes as extension of colonialism embedded in how the two deal with conflict and development. The major aim of this tome is to earmark the problem; and thereby suggest the solution. So, too, this tome applies prognostic method in suggesting the solutions to the problems found in this relationship in point. Furthermore, the tome earmarks the area in which the former superimposes its will on the latter through intrusion, exploitation and exclusion.

By using a prognostic analysis, it is easy to note that the Global North has been more of the causation of conflicts in the Global South than a solution. Due to its hegemonic nature in this relationship, the Global North uses its market-oriented neoliberal intervention in conflict and development it regards to be as a cure-all mechanism while it is not. After either suffocating and ignoring or sidelining the Global South, the Global North created a paternalistic and clientele system wherein the latter is at the receiving end that puts the former in a position of dictating everything pertaining with the relationship between the duo. Jiang (2009) maintains that over the past three decades, China embarked on modernisation of its economy based on traditional economic model that allows low labour and environmental damage that are concurrently occurring in Africa and China without any efforts to stop them. Who will stop China while those supposed to do so have their blames and baggage in this anomaly? While China is carelessly and massively depleting and devouring resources in Africa, Zartman (1976) cited in Taylor (2010) notes that the North still depends on the South despite shifting its presence in Africa. However, Zartman adds that through eliminating its presence through the military occupation and sovereign control over African territories, Europe has maintained political influence, economic preponderance, and cultural conditioning that gave birth to the dominance by corrupt local elites that China is now buying easily. Further, Zartman posits that there is an irreconcilable gap between developing countries in the South and developed countries in the North.

Apart from environmental degradation, there is another aspect that causes more harm to the latter. This is nothing but economy and politics in the latter as controlled by the former. What aggravates the situation in the latter is the fact that the formation of international organisations responsible for finance, politics and economy have never worked on, or accommodated any mechanism that can rectify such anomaly and exploitation that this volume views as an extension of colonialism or neocolonialism under neoliberalism. There is no contribution from the latter when it comes to the formation of these organisations. For example, Wapenhans 1994: 37) cited in Toye, Harrigan and Mosley (2015) notes that the intention of the WB in introducing structural adjustment was to demolish those structures of policy which it blamed; and thereby connected to the increasing incidence of failure of its projects. Ironically, the duo treats such anomaly as a normal way of relating to each other in this zero-sum-game. QUiLiConi (2006) poses a question: this a path to the future or a dead-end street?"; also see Zartman (2013). In this respect, the formation of the OPEC provides the *modus* by which the duo can address the problem. Arguably, the realisation of the OPEC helped member countries to increase oil prices as a political weapon. I wonder what can happen if the Global South can use its abundant resources as its bargaining chip to see to it that the current relationship undergoes some deconstruction and overhaul to suit the needs and interests of both parties. This is the only alternative available for the Global South to do away with the current exploitative *status quo* that benefits the Global North more than it does to the Global South. If taken, such a stance can avert the Global South the danger of purchasing weapons as a guarantee of its security. Weapons cannot maintain peace in the countries wherein basic human needs are unmet. The money spent on weaponry can bring about change in the lives of people in the Global South. The fact that the Global North depends on economic exploitation of the Global South more than it does on its weapons that it sells to the Global South to fuel and maintain conflicts at the detriment of the latter provides an ideal example.

In addition, the conflicts of interests and unfair relationship between the Global North and the Global South have given rise to many other ethnic, ethnonationalistic and international conflicts among others. For, the conflict in point, to be precise, gravitates towards the unregulated international market as neoliberal policies of exploitation espouse it. It is noteworthy to aver from the outset that the relationship between the Global North and the Global South is more of conflictual than peaceful. This is because, under the basic needs theory, there are many unmet need in the Global South due to the exploitative nature of the relationship between the two. This Staub (2003) argues that "human beings have fundamental, shared needs" (p. 2). Consequently, once such needs are ignored or unmet, chances of becoming a good source of conflict are high. However, Staub points at a "them" versus "us" acrimony that revolves around devaluing to the extent of causing violence as opposed to positive view of the same that creates conducive environment of helping the duo. Such a rationale applies precisely on the North-South relationship wherein the Global North seems to "other" the Global South in the between-us-and-them axis. Again, despite basic human needs theory Western scholars propound and prescribe, never has the Global North practically and equitably applied its rationale when it comes to dealing the Global South. The neglect of basic human needs in the

Global South has led to many conflicts resulting from uneven and unfair distribution of resources of which the Global North buys and consumes. The conflict resulting from North-South relationship, regulated by capitalistic market, seems to have escaped scrutiny either purposely or ignorantly as a good cause of conflict in the Global South.

Arguably, such an unfair relationship has fuelled violent conflicts that have always preoccupied the international community. In a word, the conflicts, in case and point, seem to have been internalised so much that the duo views it as a reality under the international system. Such understanding has caused blindness resulting to the failure on how to, adequately and truly, address it. The international community in its intervention to resolve the conflicts uses immense resources in trying to resolve violent conflicts by ignoring the North-South unequal relationship that, in essence, is a major cause of conflict in many countries in the Global South. There are some flaws in Global North's intervention in violent conflicts resulting from its exploitative relationship under its neoliberal strategies in post-war countries. The approach that the international community has taken under the *diktat* of the Global North massages the conflict that makes the parties to overlook it as a major causation of many conflicts. The Global North has been using intervention as a pretext or a scapegoat from its original intentions motivated by its self-interests under neoliberal peace initiatives. Under international relations theory, the state has the task of protecting its interests even if it means to go to war with another state or suppress its people. Hauss (2010) argues that the "stakes of a conflict can be magnified by security dilemma in which the actions of one state to protect its own security actually serve to weaken its opponents" (p. 30). Hauss makes a good point, especially when we consider what happened to "rogue" states such as Iraq and Libya whereby the West conspired and cooperated in toppling the governments in these two countries in order to safeguard their interests but not the interests of the citizens of those countries. Hence, we can vividly see that anarchic nature of the international system as the Global North created it after World Wars I and II still serves its interests even at the expenses of other countries in the Global South in particular. In other words, I can contend that the Global North has always depended on its fashion of the anarchic international system to commit structural violence based on its norms, *diktats* and intervention. This becomes eminent because, under current anarchic international system, the Global North conspires with a few elites from the Global South to safeguard interests of the two conspirators. In addition, this becomes a very good causation of conflict in the Global South. What is currently going on in Syria speaks volume whereby two superpowers, Russia and the US, are waging proxy war on the expenses of Syrians.

Under Structural theory, the relationship between the two is nothing but a type of neocolonialism that essentially operates and revolves around core-periphery relationship. Boshoff (2009) notes that due to structural inequalities and historical patterns of dominance partnership, the two have the potential risk of not being a true partnership but the control by the foreign partner in a semi-colonial fashion. The fact that this toxic relationship between the two has now created an internalised superstructure makes it a major obstacle for the latter. If anything, this is where the root cause of many violent conflicts emanating from superimposed structures in the Global South emanates. For, in many developing countries, where conflicts emanating from struggle over resource control, some areas with abundant resources lack the service they deserve; and this creates resentment and drives for control from the people living around those resources. Such people feel disconnected from the governing structures. Mac Ginty and Williams (2009) cite a good example from Ogoni, Delta in Nigeria where people surrounding this rich area in resources live in abject poverty while their resources enrich a cabal of corrupt politicians in Lagos. There has been the tendency whereby the Global North dictates the Global South about what to do in dealing with conflict and development. Such tendency would not be a problem if the Global North would not use its intrusion aimed at reshaping existing structures through imposing its ideals, norms and structure based on free market, democracy and human rights all aimed at connecting the economies of the countries in the Global South to the world market as envisaged by neoliberalism. If we question the whole concept of the free market, we find that, naturally the market is a free place for exchange of goods and service. Smith (2005) cited in Bonefeld (2013) argues that market has to regulate itself depending on demand and supply as the sign of invisible hand. Looking at the neoliberal concept of free market, I find that the so-called free market is free for some and unfree for others. This is why the former has always enjoyed free access to the market in the latter while the latter without any form equality or reciprocity. In the relationship in question, the former has an upper hand almost in everything *vis-à-vis* the said free market. It controls the rules by deciding about what it should supply to the latter and who should do so. Haphazardly and dubiously, the free market the neoliberalism proposes benefits the former as it sabotages and robs the latter. This is why the latter–despite sitting on huge quantity of resources has never benefited from them thanks to this unfairness in treatment and relating. Further, this reality does not need one to have a degree in economics or commerce. It is obvious that exploitation is the rule of the game between the two.

Practically, when the hyenas set the rule of the game between them and antelopes, chances are obviously that equity, fairness and justice suffer some miscarriages. If the market is naturally free, where does this free market come from? We need to know whom, how and by whom the free market intends to serve. How free is the free market and for whom? Practically, we can blame such intrusion on weakening, ignoring or destroying the existing structure, ideals, ideas and norms that seem to be incompatible with the interests of the Global North. Once anybody encroaches on, ignores, intrudes or wipes out existing structures, chances of creating conflicts are high. Under dependency theory, what is going on is detrimental to the Global South. Kay (2010) notes that the core imports primary goods from the periphery at cheap price while the periphery imports processed goods at a much-hiked price. I can maintain that North-South way of dealing with conflict and development is totally antithesis to dependency theory that, too, is an antithesis of modernisation theory that has always a neoliberal drive to exploiting the Global South. Modernisation theory is nothing but westernisation hidden behind the theory. Who is modernising what and how; and for what reasons? Who defines the term[s] and its conditions? Nkrumah (1966) answers the questions noting that "so long as neo-colonialism can prevent political and economic conditions for optimum development, the developing countries, whether they are under neo-colonialist control or not, will be unable to create a large enough market to support industrialization" (p. 3). This speaks to the fact that the relationship between the duo has prevented the creation of a reliable and viable market for the latter. Since the former annihilated the latter from creating its economic policies and the market, the latter started to cascade into dependency and poverty wantonly.

Apart from controlling and manipulating the market, ever since the Global North envisaged exploiting countries in the Global South—through colonialism, and thereafter, through neo-colonialism. As noted above, through installing its stooges to run some countries for its own benefits as opposed to the interests of the citizens of these countries, the former has always benefited from this unfair relationship.

Additionally, one may argue that democracy, free markets and economics—that have always been neoliberalism's drives—cannot function well for the benefits of the citizenry in the Global South without involving equal accountability of the duo. Ironically, when neoliberalism maintains that democracy and free markets are the solution to conflicts resulting from poverty, it tends to; stereotypically apply double standards as it was in the case of Iraq, as hereinabove noted, where former President, Saddam Hussein, whom the West toppled for—among other reasons—being a dictator. Surprisingly, while the West was fighting to bring down Hussein, the same was protecting other dictatorial regimes in Kuwait and Saudi Arabia. Furthermore, by ignoring, and conspiring with corrupt rulers such as Mobutu and Marcos—among others, to rob their countries—neoliberalism becomes causation of conflict. And indeed, Mobutu's mismanagement of the DRC resulted to the conflicts that are currently going on in the country which goes contrary to neoliberal assumption that econometrics would avert conflict. By sponsoring and installing corrupt dictators, such a tendency shows how neoliberal intervention in many countries experiencing or coming out of conflict does not aim at benefiting them but the Global North. Mac Ginty and Williams (2009) argue that vast sums of money stolen from the latter maintain the international financial markets. Once again, this shows how the Global North aims at benefiting from corrupt and warring countries even at the expenses of the citizens of those countries.

It is an open secret that many Western capitals are good havens for money looted from the Global South. In spite of knowing everything, the Global North has never underscored this theft as a root causation of conflict. It is a fact that such tax havens motivate warlords to engage in war in order to print and mint money quickly even if doing so at the expense of innocent citizens as it has always been the case in the Global South. So, too, such corrupt governments or greedy warlords disturb the distribution of resources so as to leave the majority citizens out something that can inspire other political opportunists to embark on fighting in the name of liberating the citizens; thus creating a circle of violence.

Evidentially, the Global South loses a lot of money through capital flight, tax evasion and other corrupt means. Boyce and Ndikumana (2012) disclose that:

> The group of 33 SSA countries covered by this report has lost a total of $814 billion dollars (constant 2010 US$) from 1970 to 2010. This exceeds the amount of official development aid ($659 billion) and foreign direct investment ($306 billion) received by these countries. Oil-rich countries account for 72 percent of the total capital flight from the sub-region ($591 billion) (p. 1).

Had the latter sealed all loopholes for capital flight, it would have been debt free with the balance of many US$ billions. Again, where did all this money go? The answer is obvious that it went to the former. Once again, this shows how the former has tremendously benefitted from the latter. Essentially, exploitation is one of the major causes of poverty in the latter. Shaxson (2012) argues that illicit flows from developing to developed countries amounted to GFI's $1.3 trillion in 2008. If you compare this humungous amount to what the latter received in terms of aid and technical assistance, you can understand how the relationship between the Global North and the Global South is toxic and obnoxious. Shaxson (2007) asks a good question: "Why should the corruption debate not expand to include this crucial global aspect of the problem?" (p. 1130) such as declaring economic and social services rights as mandatory human rights.

It seems that economic rights have never been the concern of the Global South. For example, since the inception of the African Charter on Human and People's Rights (ACHPR) to deal with the rights of the people, it concentrates more on liminal rights of women instead of the rights of all people specifically economic ones. Throughout the whole charter, economics rights for all people are amiss. Is it because the charter came into being at the time women rights were an in-thing or just because women's rights appeal to donors more than anything does? Where are the economic rights of the people in the Global South against exploitation by the Global North? I argue that corruption, capital flights and bad governance–the Global North condones–are the major causes of conflicts in the Global South due to exploitation by the Global North. Moreover, exploitation by the former is the sole cause of poverty in the latter to which other causes latch.

As I will indicate repeatedly, the money stolen from the Global South end up in the capitals of the Global North that has never done anything to arrest the crime. While citizens of the countries in the Global South stand to fend for themselves, the situation is very different to the citizens of the Global North. Bakker (2007) notes that "many citizens of capitalist democracies accept that commodities are not inconsistent with human rights (such as food, shelter), but that some sort of public, collective "safety net" must exist if these rights are to be met for all citizens" (p. 439). Why is it logical for citizens in the Global North to enjoy human rights such as food and house, *inter alia*, while the state does not mandatorily provide such things to its citizens in the Global South? I know many may argue that it needs economic and financial affluence for the government to offer such services to its citizens. Well, is the Global South very poor with all such abundance resources that have helped the Global North to become richer and richer while the latter become poorer and poorer? If anything, the need the latter needs to, adequately address here is none other than commuting resources abundantly found in the Global South into wealth. To do so, there is a need of deconstructing the current neoliberal policies the Global North has always superimposed on the Global South.

Arguably, not all money Africa loses to corruption and capital flight is accounted for; because the *modus operandi* and schemes those involved use to evade justice are not addressed. It becomes even harder when such corruption involves the heads of the states as it was in the case of Mobutu cited above. Here, I am talking of venal heads of state. How much money did corrupt local and foreign businesspeople and companies rob the former; and stash mostly in the former?

Additionally, there is another aspect of loss the former cause the latter. For example, Africa alone loses almost US$ 17.5 billion annually through brain drain compared to only US$ 4 billion Africa receives as technical assistance from all sources from the former (p. Ndulu (2004: 66). It is an open secret that many African countries spend billions of dollars in educating their people to end up conspiring with the former to steal them. If you look at the number of professionals, experts and skilled personnel Africa has lost to the former, you wonder how Africa will develop while the former sucks its *crème de crème*. I suggest that the aid that the former extends to the latter should be directed either in educating many more experts from the latter or be directed to motivating them to return to their countries so that they can develop them. I call this brain regain shall it be accepted and applied. Another important element in helping the latter to catch up with the former is through encouraging or conditioning countries in the latter to accept their skilled people instead of fearing and discouraging them from returning from the former. During the dark era of dictatorships, many professionals were either killed or forced to go to exile to the former. This is no longer the fact today; however, they are still some brain-phobic governments that do not utilise their skilled people, especially when they do not subscribe to malpractices such governments commit.

Again, we need to underscore the fact that due to the protection and support that corrupt and inert regimes get from the former, academics and professionals are not entertained to use their expertise and skills in Africa where it is needed the most. Corrupt and dictatorial regimes in Africa perceive academics as a threat to their illegal businesses in the upper echelons of power. Despite complaining about brain drain, there is a good face of it in that some of the professionals working in the former remit huge sums of money to their countries. Russel (1998 cited in Ndulu *Ibid.*) notes that global remittances was approximately US$ 71 billion of which US$ 31 billion went to developing countries in the latter which is equivalent to nearly three quarters of Overseas Development Assistance (ODA) (p. 71). Based on the amount remitted to the latter, one can think that this money is huge which it is. Again, how much, those remitting this money, make in the former that did enable them to have a surplus to remit to their countries? This is a very important question given that the amount of money the Africans in diaspora remit is smaller than what they produce. However, there are two opposing views of this brain drain phenomenon. Tadoro and Smith (2006 cited in Beine, Docquier, and Rapoport 2008) argue that brain drain represents a loss of valuable human resources that could prove to be a serious impediment to the development in the latter. To the contrary, Beine, Docquier and Rapopor cited in Beine, Docquier and Schiff (2008) argue that actually "brain gain is equal to about half the brain drain in small developing states" (p. 20). Whether brain drain or brain gain is productive or otherwise to the latter depends on how one looks at it. One would argue, however, that if brain drain has positive impacts on development and wellbeing, why is this phenomenon a one-way one but not reciprocal by nature? Some would argue that the money so remitted to the latter could fuel development. How will this money make change while the systems in the latter are corrupted, especially because nobody holds rulers accountable for their deeds? I would strongly argue that remittances help to maintain decadent regimes in the latter. For, they lessen the magnitude of suffering citizens; and thus, thereby make them fail or see no forces or reasons to take their corrupt regimes on. I do not think that the money remitted to the DRC under Mobutu had any positive impacts on the lives of Congolese other than helping the regime to survive because it lessened the suffering of the citizens.

The findings about the brain drain as opposed to the brain gain generally show how the latter loses as opposed to dealing with a few elites benefits them and their Western conspirators. Interestingly, much of the money stolen from poor countries ends up in many Western capitals where the headquarters of many IFIs are. Essentially, Mobutu represents thousands of corrupt African officials who robbed their countries and stashed the loot in Western banks; and the governments in these countries have never said or done anything. However, things are changing slowly. There are some calls for Western countries to stop their double standards and hypocrisy. Switzerland has already mirrored the willingness to overhaul its banking system. In one incident, the Swiss Authorities reported to Tanzanian authorities its willingness to cooperate to trace Tanzanian government officials with account in Swiss Banks. Ironically, the Tanzanian government did not like the idea. Thus, it frustrated Swiss efforts to retrieve the stolen monies Swiss authorities were ready to release. Analo and Olingo (2015) note that East Africa's elite have stashed away more than $700 million in offshore accounts with the multinational HSBC banking group, a leaked cache of documents reveals. Such humongous money involves just a single bank. How many billions corrupt rulers from the South stole are lying idle in Western banks? Further, Analo and Olingo quote the International Consortium of Investigative Journalists (ICIJ) that notes that a total of $102 billion lied idle in secret accounts on behalf of more than 100,000 people and entities from 203 countries that I am sure many are from the latter. In 2013, the Swiss ambassador to Tanzania, Olivier Chave, disclosed that Tanzanian authorities were frustrating his country's efforts to return the monies after then Tanzania Attorney General, Fredrick Werema, threatened him with legal measures for interfering in country's internal affairs. The Swahili Daily, *Mwananchi* (January, 19th 2013) quotes Werema as reprimanding the ambassador despite having diplomatic immunity. Werema went on saying that the ambassador had no right to reprimand a foreign country; and doing so was disrespect of such a country. How big is the problem? Ndikumana and Boyce (2008) note that:

> Real capital flight over the 35-year period amounted to about $420 billion (in 2004 dollars) for the 40 countries as a whole. Including imputed interest earnings, the accumulated stock of capital flight was about $607 billion as of end-004. Together, this group of SSA countries is a "net creditor" to the rest of the world in the sense that their private assets held abroad, as measured by capital flight including interest earnings, exceed their total liabilities as measured by the stock of external debt (p. 6).

Looking at the enormity of the money stolen compared to the sheer magnitude of poverty in the Global South, it is obvious; such an amount would have changed the economies and the lives of the people. Again, who benefited from such humungous amount apart from the Global North? Again, neoliberal policies still make us believe that the Global South will advance slowly amidst such robbery. Why is it becoming harder to trace the culprits and retrieve the stolen and stashed money? Ironically, those supposed to hunt down the criminals stashing looted money abroad are the same culprits. Swahili sage has it that all monkeys are guilty of stealing maize or all mudfish have moustaches. Therefore, it dcannotoes not make sense to ask a monkey to preside over baboon's case. If this occurs, the justice will never avail itself to all.

Even if we consider the styles and types of investments the Global North has in the Global South, they end up developing urban areas as they negate rural areas. Ironically, neoliberal prophets like to commend them although it is purely dichotomous base of core-periphery setting between rural and urban in the Global South. Such investments and the way recipient countries spend their returns can deceive many thinking that development in urban areas the former funds by depriving the rural areas would, in the end, trickle down. Why is it that in the Global North development plans and policies does not discriminate between rural and urban areas? Whatever is available in urban areas in the Global North is almost available in rural areas. Is this not itself economic total deprivation that, in many countries, is a good source of conflicts? Due to this core-periphery setting enhanced by internal colonisation, the Global South has currently evidenced the exodus of mass immigration from rural to urban areas that leaves the question: Who will produce in agricultural sector? Underscoring the danger of such mass movements, the Global North is producing foodstuffs in billions of metric tons ready to sell to the Global South that used to feed itself before colonisation. Lerner and Eakin (2011) argue that such a setting poses conceptual understanding of the situation; thus, failing to understand the way of addressing the problem. Due to the nature of problematic, exploitative, morbid and unfair relationship between the duo, the latter has always been a loser as McMichael (2005) puts it that:

> The losing battle within the global North nevertheless conditions the construction of 'world agriculture.' The combined dumping of subsidized food surpluses and growing agribusiness access to land, labor, and markets in the global South clears the way for corporate-driven food supply chains binding together a (selective) global consumer class [Sic] (p. 274).

Knowing that the Global South will have population explosion while its agricultural prowess is dwindling, the Global North purposely invented Genetically Modified Food (GM) that are now forced onto the Global South after destroying its economy and ecology altogether. As argued above, the Global South used to feed itself up until the Global North colonised it and felled all of its systems, skills, plans and whatnot to give way to neoliberal and capitalistic exploitation to take place. Agriculturalists, politicians and scientists from the former are now preaching the gospel of GM production to the latter without underscoring how this move is going to destroy already dwindling traditional foods in the latter.

I must say it unmistakably that the society that cannot feed itself is insecure and vulnerable. Mhango (2015) equates such a society to the society of the hens that produce what they do not eat and eat what they do not produce. Such a society will never meet the basic human needs of its people. The failure to meet the BHN will automatically lead to conflict; because the elites and rich people in the latter will be able to bring food on the table while the majority citizens will never do so. I can predict that, due to the explosion of population, especially in the Global South, the major causes of conflicts will be none other than food scarcity coupled with resource depletion after economic powers from the former and the emerging ones, greedily and massively deplete them in order to quench their thirsty for such resources. As well, the rise of China and India will put more pressure on resources and food of course to the extent that making a prediction about conflicts resulting from food scarcity to become easy to predict and occur. Without deconstructing and overhauling the current regime of production, it is obvious that the world will face many avoidable conflicts shall the current relationship between the Global North and the Global South not be deconstructed, overhauled and reconstructed as well.

i) Liberal Peace: A Quick Fix

When it comes to economic ailments, the former has appointed itself to nurse and cure them in the latter. Many experiments carried on the latter as an experimental object have since undertaken with bold and sweet names such as structural adjustment and economic restructuring. However, when you look at what such projects attained in the latter, the situation is always grim. For, if you consider why the International Financial Institutions (IFIs) came into being; and the roles they played thereafter, you concur with me that they have nothing to do with what they are doing in the latter. Vreeland (2003) notes for example that the International Monetary Fund (IMF), the former has always used to *fix* the economies of poor countries in the latter, is the creature of just 44 countries that aims at maintaining exchange rate for international free trade but not to rescuing or fixing the economies of poor countries. Vreeland goes on saying that "despite constant references to a failure of political will, however, the IMF is notoriously bad at defining exactly what the term means" (p. 5). As I will show later, whenever anybody defines any concepts, he or she does so without escaping the trap of biases or interests. This is obvious *vis-à-vis* the formation and activities of the IFIs in the latter that does not have its own IFIs. Let us interrogate this claim. If the IMF is "notoriously bad at defining exactly what the term means, first of all why, secondly, how can its program succeed in the countries where terms are ambiguous and flaw? Ironically, the latter has always fulfilled the requirements of whatever programs and projects the former gives it with its entirety without anything changed *mutatis mutandis*.

Again, when IMF's programs failed in the latter, the IMF impugned countries involved; and thereby their efforts and reputation took a hit! The same has been the case in conflict resolution whereby the emphasis is to secure a deal or win hearts and minds. Prescriptive as Western mechanism for conflict resolution have been, seems to have failed in the latter; because it excludes local conflict resolution mechanism by applying prescriptive solutions. Lederach (1995) observes that, sometimes, prescriptive model of conflict resolution exaggerates some aspects and leaves others out in order to highlight the extreme case. Why is it fair to exaggerate; and why leaving other aspects out? How extreme case is extreme; and in whose eyes the same is? Such are the questions that indicate how impractical superimposed models or programs can be, especially when they are not cognisant of local methods of dealing with problem[s]. Essentially, this prescriptivism has always been the policy of the IMF and other so-called IFIs whose targets have been to benefit the former under neoliberalism as superimposed on others. Santomé (2007) posits that in the 1990s and the years of the new millennium and the rise of neoliberalism have benefited from the success attained by this reductionism in terms of social analysis, and has been able to impose the economy as the benchmark against which all its (mercantile) analysis is measured. This is telling as to why the latter needs to reassess its cooperation with the former.

As it is in prescriptive model of conflict resolution, the IMF, too, uses the same model by exaggerating some aspects that are important to the former as it leaves out others that are not important to the former but are important to the latter. Due to vague terms and *holier than thou* mentality, the latter ends up receiving toxic expertise that results in failure the former always blames it for.

While the aim of the IFIs is to, quickly fix the economies in the latter, in dealing with conflict, the former seeks a deal and win hearts and minds of conflicants ready to prepare the countries in conflict for the free market to exploit. Schmitz, Matyók, Sloan and James (2012) underscore another importance of elicitive approach saying that in developing a mind-set and process for change, community members who, in this sense, are the countries in the latter, gain the skills and knowledge necessary to participate in the ongoing process of civic (economic) engagement. Here the rationale is clear; the stakeholders need to participate in; and own the process in order to contribute their inputs based on their needs. Thanks to our academic specialisation and biases, I am using conflict resolution jargon even in economic matters. For example, if the IFIs only use prescriptive approach, do we expect countries they tutor to succeed while they do not know the meaning and definitions of the terms of the projects or programs the IFIs introduce to them? I think the latter needs to emphasise that in this relationship, both approaches, namely elicitive and prescriptive, must apply based on the needs and interests of the recipients and donors. I think if the IFIs would ask the stakeholders in the latter to generate ideas and views on what they need in order to address their problems such as poverty and underdevelopment; chances are that programs would succeed. For, apart from generating their views, they will feel like owning the projects, programs, and above all, the process. As Schmitz, Matyók, Sloan and James *(Ibid.)* put it, whatever recipe introduced to the latter should seek to address the interests and objectives of stakeholders or participants based on equality and equity for the benefits of both sides. This makes sense even in the political dispensation in the latter today wherein conflicts resulting from terrorism are rife. The former has always superimposed its militaristic models of dealing with the scourge without underscoring that there are other mechanisms those involved in such a crime understand better.

When it comes to resolving conflict or dealing with developmental issues, those involved should not obsessed themselves with wining hearts and minds or getting peace deals signed, even if there is an imposition on conflicants. The same occurred recently in South Sudan where the Intergovernmental Authority for Development (IGAD) forced the parties to conflict to enter an agreement first without addressing other pressing issues such as meeting basic human needs, the inclusivity of victims and citizens in general. Here is where liberal interventionist strategies become more a problem than a solution; because the strategies put in place do not abide by ideas of neutrality and impartiality in order to do justice for all participants in the process. This is the model the IGAD copied from the IFIs that intervene for its interests. For, what concerned the former most is to created opportune environment for a free market with the aim of exploiting the latter. Thus, whenever the IFIs fund peace talks or other developmental projects, they aimed at resolving or managing the conflict in order to get an opportunity for exploitation of the latter. In so doing, they purposely ignore or overlook important issues such as stakeholders' inputs, historical realities and *geopolitics* of the time. The ongoing conflict in South Sudan presents an ideal example in which ignorance of the realities of the conflict has exacerbated the conflict (De Waal, 2014); also see Gorsevski, Kasischke, Dempewolf, Loboda and Grossmann (2012). Once lip and glib services hurriedly apply as they aim at *dousing the fire*, the conflict drags on or causes more economic harm. Once this happens, the former arrogantly blames the latter for not doing things rightly. Arguably, this is a type of systemic and international corruption, geared by greed and self-seeking as evidenced in the latter, the world has known. Thanks to this type of corruption, many conflicts remained unsolved; and the economies of the affected countries ended up becoming obsolete or collapsing as it currently is in South Sudan.

Iheukwumere and Iheukwumere (2003) note that:

> Corruption among African leaders and officials in turn is then, unfortunately and regrettably, aided and abetted by the banking and economic policies of the same colonial powers which initially heaped misery and savagery upon the continent, and helped ensure the

despotism of some of the worst pretenders who branded themselves leaders (p. 5).

Unfortunately, this trend is still going despite the introduction of deceptive and chimeric democracy the former uses as a yardstick to evaluate the unquestioning Global South. When it comes to rulers that can use and abuse their countries as pleased, I think it is the latter that has most of them compared to the former wherein leaders thanks to its leaders being responsible and accountable for everything they do as opposed to the latter. This is where the double, standard the former uses, is evident due to using democracy as a yardstick of almost everything economic, political and social in the latter.

ii) Is aid a Panacea or a Mere Panegyric?

Among ruses the Global North has employed to keep the Global South at bay, is nothing but aid. With strings attached on it, aid has become another type of colonisation for the latter. Much money the former grant to the latter is uncounted for, particularly when the recipients are in good books of the former. The DRC under Mobutu Seseseko's kleptocratic regime provides an ideal example. Byrne (2010) argues that economic aid can reinforce ethnic divisions by disrupting balances of power. Corrupt rulers backed by the former, apart from robbing their countries and performing poorly, they become immune to accountability and democracy given that they enable the former to exploit resources found in these countries. Further, apart reinforcing ethnic divisions, Ryan (2007) cited in Byrne (*Ibid.*) argues that economic aid can reinforce group egotism; and therefore, exacerbates and fuels conflict resulting to poverty, insecurity and underdevelopment. This has been the case in some cases in the Global South, principally where corrupt and dictatorial regimes, the former installed, backed and supported corrupt as mentioned above in the case of the DRC. Apart from the DRC, the situation was exactly the same in South Africa during Apartheid when some Western powers, especially the US and the UK, openly supported the regime knowingly that doing so was enabling it to suppress and humiliate the majority South African indigenous people.

Truly, aid has always been the conduit through which the Global North has been robbing the Global South. After conspiring with local elites and greedy politicians that form governments in the Global South in some countries, the Global North extends aid and loans to the Global South, in one hand; and takes it back by the other hand. The money so given as aid does not end up being "creamed off" by Western consultants only but corrupt rulers and their cronies as well steal it; and stash it in offshore accounts in the former. For example, Nigerian former dictator, Sani Abacha, robbed Nigeria over $3billion—more than a million dollars for every day in office, including weekends–in this state robbery (Agbiboa 2012). Again, nobody knows exactly how much Abacha stole from public coffers. For, the monies African elites stash in many unknown banks in the former, up until now, nobody knows exactly how much the latter lost. Similarly, this is the same trend in many Africa countries. How much does Africa lose to this state robbery? It is not easy to know.

Another conduit of robbing; and thereby burdening the Global South (which is done by China and India too) is forcing any country receiving aid, specifically technical aid, to make sure that the said country uses the companies, experts and sometimes, materials from the donor countries. Recently, China has been aping this Western style of robbing the Global South by forcing countries receiving grants and loans from it to use its workforce as the jobless people in the receiving countries go on suffering from joblessness. Whenever citizens are employed, they are employed in low-paying jobs Sun (2014) notes that "China's "tied aid" for infrastructure usually favours Chinese companies (especially state-owned enterprises), while its loans are in many cases backed by African natural resources" (p. 75). One can say that most of aid extended to the Global South is nothing but a ploy for future exploitation and colonisation by those extending such aid and technical assistance. For, many poor citizens in the Global South are becoming poorer and poorer for paying and servicing debts from the money elites dubiously borrowed to end up being given their cuts and stash in

Western banks. The rise of China was mistaken as a reprieve for the Global South without underscoring the fact that China will never play a fair game. It is currently doing what the former has always done. Looking at the manner in which China does business with developing countries in the Global South, nothing has changed but the player. The rules of the game are the same; and the consequences, too, are the same.

Other types of aid involve arms that aim to enable one pro-Western country to attack and destabilise another country that seems not to be up to standard. Such have been the case and practices with Israel in the Middle East whereby military aid extended to Israel has helped it to suppress, kill, torture, displace and subjugate Palestinians in their country. In addition, Israel's military power has become another threat to any country in the region that threatens the interests of the former. Sharp (2015) notes that:

> U.S. military aid has helped transform Israel's armed forces into one of the most technologically sophisticated militaries in the world. U.S. military aid for Israel has been designed to maintain Israel's "qualitative military edge" (QME) over neighbouring militaries, since Israel must rely on better equipment and training to compensate for a manpower deficit in any potential regional conflict. U.S. military aid, a portion of which may be spent on procurement from Israeli defense companies, also has helped Israel build a domestic defense industry, which ranks as one of the top 10 suppliers of arms worldwide (p. 1).

Ironically, while the US offers such humongous and advanced military capabilities to Israel, it is well aware of what such aid does to the Palestinians who niggardly fend for themselves not to mention other countries in the region. Israel has become a bully in the region. Moreover, it does so unabated so to speak. Since its creation in 1948, Israel has always been an untouchable-cum-irreproachable country on earth that can commit atrocities as pleased. It can displace and humiliate Palestinians as it deems fit and the international organisation responsible such as the UN are just standing by and watching! When I strongly maintain that relationship between the Global North and the Global South deserves to change through systematic overhaul in order to reduce conflict, I mean exactly this. Why should countries pride themselves to be the champions of human rights do such things knowingly that their aid ends up causing many conflicts and hardships to innocent people in the Global South as it is in the example above?

US aid to Israel, at least, has security connotation. When it comes to other despotic regimes such as that of Mobutu in the DRC, the UNITA, former terrorist group in Angola, and Apartheid South Africa, the aid the Global North offered created more conflicts that ended up destabilising the countries for plunder by the West. One would argue that–excluding Israel and a few lucky countries–this was during the cold war. Now that the cold war is over, what is making the Global North hesitant to deconstruct the current relationship in order to serve the two parties equally and justly? Again, looking at neoliberalism and its market drive, it becomes harder for the Global North to let go the easy business it has always enjoyed by exploiting the Global South. Will this situation be changed or deconstructed in the near future? The answer is maybe, yes, maybe, no. All depends on how the rising superpower, China will play the cards however, even with the coming of China, exploitative and uneven relationship is still the same save that there is the new kid on the bloc. Given that China has aped what the Global North has perfected for many decades, developing countries will still suffer even more than they have always been.

However, China has tried to apply exchange between goods and technology, the type of technology and the modicum so applied are not equitable, just and reciprocal. We can see the exodus of many Chinese in African Countries. Some known poachers and smugglers to the authorities make their present counterproductive to their host countries; and their hosts do nothing provided some of government officials share the loots. This phenomenon becomes even worse in poor countries manned by corrupt governments. The state tour by Chinese president Xi Jinping to Tanzania on 24th March 2013 provides an ideal example. The media disclosed that his presidential jet carried illegal ivory when he left Tanzania. Suleiman

Mochiwa cited in Smith-Spark (2014) says that, at the time the Chinese government and business delegation arrived, ivory prices in the local market doubled to $700 (£438) per kilo. News was rife in the streets of Dar es Salaam; and this was but an open secret. Despite all such tainting revelations, neither the governments of China nor Tanzania came out forcefully to prove how such allegations were mere lies and concoctions. Arguably, I see no difference between the presidents who authorise military aid to the country he or she knows will use the same weapons and skills to destroy others and the one who allows his officials to purchase the products of endangered species such as elephants and rhinoceros. They all contribute to the instability of some countries in the Global South; because their aid does not aim at human development. It is sad to note that the Global South has never gotten the opportunity to choose the types of aid it needs. Many countries–under neoliberal economic policies–found themselves in a catch-22 trap of borrowing in order to carry on neoliberal policies such as structural adjustment that has not work. The tug of war under cold war enabled some dictators to thrive as Fleck and Kilby (2010) put it that:

> Anti–communist dictators such as Suharto in Indonesia, Marcos in the Philippines, and Mobutu in Zaire could count on US substantial funding despite widespread corruption, human rights abuse, and often counterproductive domestic policies. In contrast, support for the poor, for emerging democracies, for developmental regimes, and governments with good human rights records was inconsistent (p. 1).

Sometimes back during the cold war, things were better for some countries, especially those aligned to the East. However, all two evils, namely the East and West were hegemonic, to some countries; there was less interference in their internal affairs. Tanzania, for example, under the cold war, was able to provide free social services to its citizens (Mamdani and Bangser 2004); also see Songstad, Rekdal, Massay, and Blystad (2011). This ambitious move benefitted millions of Tanzania and became one of the countries with high level of literacy in Africa at the time. While the IFIs denied Tanzania to provide social services such as education and health, some countries in the former such as Germany (Busch 2010) still provide the same to their citizens. Inferentially, free health services countries such Canada and some Scandinavian countries still offer to their people shows the double standard. For, the IFIs, that introduced such stern policies aimed at making the latter produce many sick and illiterate people, have never reproached them. As for Tanzania, I do not know if literacy rates are still high now. Inversely though, in the 90s when the Berlin Wall fell, neoliberal policies kicked in; and forced Tanzania to abandon its socialistic policies. Two competing power were competing to win followers. Therefore, they offered aid with less conditional than it currently is whereby the Global North has no direct competitor except China that seems to do the same as I have indicated hereinabove. The cold war is long gone. What the Global South needs to do is to put its acts together and agitate for the deconstruction of the current unfair and exploitative relationship. The Global South still has the chance to influence things shall it underscore the fact that its abundant resources are the wealth that needs to be recognised by both parties as the engine of the economy of the world.

Knowing the reliance of the Global North on the Global South's resources, as it was in the case of the OPEC, chances of backing off from the current stance are very high. The Global South needs to make its resources viable bargaining chips in this catch-22 situation. With the exception of Israel, many countries in the Global South fend for themselves as they are now wrestle with aid with fulsome of strings attached to it. No more danger as it was during the cold war whereby every camp was afraid that its enemies would influence; and thereby take its allies something that would endanger its position and interests. As noted above, one country that benefited from aid under the cold war era was Tanzania that was an ally of the Eastern camp. This poor and young country was able to provide free social services without failing due to enjoying grants and aid from China and the then Union of Soviet Socialist Republics (USSR). Since the fall of the Berlin War, such glorious time is long gone. Tanzanians are now paying almost for everything they used to get free. Currently, Tanzania is in bed with China. However, the relationship is still unfair and exploitative just like it is in the Global South generally.

We can conclude this section arguing that aid is not a panacea however *sine qua non* it may be if it addresses and serves the interests of both parties to this relationship. Likewise, the former is not the latter's *sine quibus non sum*. For, it has always exploited it because instead of bringing parity and development, it has perpetuated undesirable dependency for the latter while it has acted like a spoon for the former used to scoop wealth from the latter. To do away with this anomaly, the duo must invest in; and treat each other equally based on justice. For, they both have what each other needs from each other. As suggested in foregoing chapter, the former should invest in educating skilled people from the latter for purposely developing it after exploiting it for many decades. This is why I strongly suggest that the duo must invest in brain regain in order to do away with the brain drain.

iii) New Economic Model and New Superstructure

One of the efforts-cum-solutions to the ongoing exploitation between the Global North and the Global South is to remodel it based on a new model [s] upon which the duo will agree. I logically think there must be one supermodel to replace one exploitative supermodel that has been in place for a long time. I would like to call this model, the Global North and the Global South are supposed to use, *yin yang* or *coin model* in that the two face of the coin depend on each other equally while yin and yang also do the same. All this aims at having developed, prosperous and violent conflict-free world built on interdependence and interconnection whereby no one is better than another is or is above another or others. Under the human needs and the 'cobweb' model, all humans have so complex interdependence (Richmond 2008). Although the former views the latter as *tabula rasa* in that it has always received almost everything from the former, it still has a lot to offer as far as stumping out systemic inequality and exploitation. When it comes to economic models, the latter, just like the former, has its own traditional models. For example, in business and financial models, the latter has various traceable models that it needs to, purposely, bring to the table in order to agree upon how to incorporate or top them up to the Western models. Chinese have their business models whereby business depends on connectivity among those doing trade under the system famously known as quanxi (Luo 2007), while the Middle East has its Islamic hawala system (David and Faith 2011) (in which money or business is conducted through a series of connected people or organisations) and Africa has its model which is basically built on trust. All these business models are different from the Western model built on Ponzi-scheme-like system. I know; many people do not know that Africa has its own traditional business models in various places. For example, there is Ubuntu system that used to govern almost everything in Bantu speaking people. Kalsten and Illa (2005) concur with this claim. They note that truly "Ubuntu refers to the collective solidarity in Africa but it can become convertible in other modern forms of entrepreneurship, leadership, business organisations and management" (p. 613). Although colonialism wiped out and ignored African models of business after its introduction, their remnants helped Africans to make do with colonial, neocolonial, and neoliberal exploitations. You can see this in rural areas where poor farmers are able to support each other to educate their children. So, too, you can see these systems in the social-capital oriented practices in many places in Africa and the way cooperation helps to solve many problems. Posner (1980) cited in Collier (2002) notes that social capital is about a complete traditional social interaction which members of a village or kin-based group use to overcome almost every problem; also see Acquaah 2012). As for the Middle East, Ali (1992) observes that business was based on friendship devoid of underhand activities of competition; all aimed at maintaining cohesion and peace in the society. Such a model aimed at meeting human needs of the society; is different from Western model that careless about human needs. Instead, the Western model cares about profits only. This is why it is easy one person to exploit another not to mention using illegal means to make profits even at the expenses of others as it has been in the relationship between the Global North and the Global South.

If anything, despite inexplicable exploitation, only social capital has enabled Africans to soldier on. Although, when faced with assertion that Africa had its own models of almost everything, cynics wrongly think that those making such an assertion aim at romanticising Africa, the truth is everywhere in Africa. There is nothing like romanticism but the plain truth. Go to many African countries. You will practically see, feel and experience this age-long system. What else do the two partners need to harmonise their systems if at all they are all serious? Therefore, the latter should not accept the role of being recipient while it has a lot to offer.

As indicated hereinabove, this volume uses both diagnostic and prognostic approaches to address the anomalies and problems resulting from the relationship between the two halves of the world. The intentions, *inter alia*, are to show possible elements that can make the relationship between the duo healthy and productive for both. Likewise, I must emphasise that deconstructing the current unfair relationship begs the deconstruction of the whole system the former has created and enshrined in this relationship. Thus, one needs to look into the functioning and setting of the international structure which I call superstructure in highlighting what should be done to make the relationship between the Global North and the Global South equitable and just for the benefit of both parties. Whatever inputs are available may contribute in helping the parties to conflict to become partners; and thereby constructively address the anomalies, conflicts, flaws and grievances by embarking on some changes such as appreciating the existence of inalienable rights of enjoying the resources and technologies the partners have. Actually, it is vital to exchange models from both; and thereby create a new one in which everybody will offer what he or she has.

Fundamentally, I am offering views on how the Global North to treat the Global South in order to stop the superimposition of its will on the Global South through intrusion, exploitation of resources and exclusion from decisionmaking. Instead, the two must embark on a peaceful and constructive journey of mending their relationship based on interdependence, interconnectivity, and above all, coexistence; all aimed at creating and welcoming a harmonious world.

Using prognostic analysis as introduced above, it is easy to note that the Global North has more causation of anomalies and problems in the Global South than the solutions. So, too, when it comes to causation of stumbling blocks, it seems: in this relationship, it is a one-way traffic in which the former causes problems to the latter without evidentially the latter reciprocating. Show me any problem that the latter has either accidentally or maliciously, caused to the former. You can go to the history of the world from slavery, colonialism to neocolonialism. No recorded history showing the latter has ever wronged the former. Underscoring such innocence, I think, the former needs to have morally opened up for the reconciliation with the latter.

Concerning exploitation, the major tool the Global North uses to exploit the Global South is nothing but its neoliberal economic and political policies that–for a long-time–have suffocated the Global South. Further, the same has caused the latter to end up servicing the economies of the former as Battersby and Siracusa (2009) note that the former created servicing states it has always used even after granting them political but not economic independence. One can argue that many countries in the Global South–especially many in Africa–have never been free at all. Their independence is fake and fickle so to speak. Arguably, the right thing to do, in this circumstance, is to, truly decolonise developing countries economically so that they can enjoy fair trade based on equality, equity and justice altogether. Current relationship between the former and the latter is purely hegemonic and colonial. Thus, it needs to be completely overhauled to enable it serve the two parties equally as means of reducing or stopping conflicts and exploitation in the world.

Another vital area is to strengthen (Landsberg 2006), deconstruct and reconstruct the paternalistic and clientele nature of the system that enables the Global North to, perpetually, exploit the Global South. Arguably, there is no need for the latter to depend on the former while it is sitting on immense resources that run the economies of the countries in the former. Instead, the international community should introduce a just and fair trade that will enable the latter to benefit from its resources; and thus, thereby reduce all causes of conflict such as struggle for controlling resources, poverty, unmet needs for the citizens. Above all, accountability for both sides is *sine qua non* in resolving the conflict; and thereby normalising their relationship. The duo, however artificially and socially constructed, need to depend on each other instead one depending on another. The good term to use here is reciprocity. Healthy relationship of whatever kind is a two-way traffic but not a one-way traffic as this relationship has always been.

Philosophically, the Global North has essentialised its exploitative and unfair relationship with the Global South by wrongly implying that it helps the latter under the belief that latter depends on the former while it is vice versa. To, nicely, resolve the conflict, this I propose the following:

1.) The former must truly open its market for the latter without any conditions or double standard,

2.) The former must redress the latter for the loss it has incurred on it for a long time,

3.) The superstructure and the system governing the relationship and the world in general must be deconstructed through consultations and agreements whereby both parties will agree on the structure to be used in their relationship, business and whatnot,

4.) The two should clearly and legally state that their relationship should be based on exchange of goods and knowledge and partnership instead of clientelism and donor-donee axes,

5.) Moreover, all in all, and above all, the envisaged relationship should, equally and equitably look like yin and yang.

iv) **Meaningful and Practical Policy Change**

In addressing the exploitative nature of the relationship between the Global North and the Global South, there must be some meaningful and practical policy change or paradigm shift at all levels aimed at doing away with the current exploitative situation. Neoliberalism believes that free market is the solution to conflict. For, it will free men from conflicts resulting from struggling over scarce resources. Ironically, looking at the struggle for controlling resources in the Global South, one finds that such rationale does not hold water at all. Free market has motivated many warlords in many countries to start civil wars in order to plunder their countries and sell to the world market regulated by neoliberal unequal policies.

Arguably, the so-called free market is not free. For, the market is free for one party, and it is not free for the other. The freedom of the market must apply equally to both parties in this relationship shall it aim at any meaningful and practical policy change as this volume espouses. Therefore, what the duo must do is to debunk such neoliberal myth of free market by embarking on scientific means of resolving conflict such as addressing the needs of both parties equally and equitably. Mac Ginty and Williams (*Ibid.*) note that free market is but a motivation revolving around economic interests fulfilled by means of corruption, greed and war that makes war a very lucrative undertaking for warlords and their masters in the former. This is because such wars involve untrained young men coupled with availability of weaponry mainly supplied by the Global North. The argument is that banditry, blood diamond and illegal extraction of "blood resources" do pay. Refer to Charles Taylor and the way his militants plundered Liberia and Sierra Leone. Further, Mac Ginty and Williams maintain that free market is an antithesis to market-induced inequality and causation, escalation and maintenance of violent conflict whereby war is obviously the greatest world's industry in the ascendancy of neoliberalism. Collier (2006 cited in Mac Ginty and Williams 2009) posits the "greed thesis, which suggests that the economic motivates are the most reliable indicators of the behaviour of protagonists in the outbreak and continuation of war" (p. 25). The major question one needs to ask here is who produce and sell weapons that warlords use in the Global South? The answer is obvious that the Global North does. To do away with such anomaly in this relationship, the duo needs to renegotiate their terms of relationship based on mutual understanding, equitable and equal footing as opposed to the current "self-help system" (Hauss 2010: 29) that has exacerbated conflict in the Global South.

So, too, apart from causing conflict resulting from struggle for controlling resources in the Global South, neoliberal policies cause environmental degradation due to overexploitation of resources, which, too, causes conflicts in many countries. Chichilnisky (1994) underscores the importance of understanding environment policies tied to the connection between business and environment by posing a question: Why do developed countries tend to specialise in the production and the export of goods that deplete environmental resources such as rain forests? To fine-tune, and address the anomaly resulting from exploitative and unfair relationship between the duo, one driving question should be why is it that the Global South is rich in natural resources–as opposed to the Global North– then the former still is poor? Furthermore, I may argue, why does not the Global North tackle environmental dangers it causes the Global South? Copeland and Taylor (1994) answer the two questions above by citing Baumol and Oates (1988); Pethig (1976); Siebert, Horst, Eichberger, R. Gronych and Pethig (1980); and McGuire (1982) whose investigation disclosed some effects of pollution policy on the pattern of trade between the twosomes.

Moreover, Gilpin (2011) lists down four areas he calls irksome for the Global South to watch carefully. These are the division of the world in exporters of primary products and the exporters of manufactures, adverse factoral terms of trade, and dependence of developing countries on developed for finance and dependence of developing countries on the developed for the engine of their growth. Such an economic setting is not profitable for the Global South. If anything, going on with such setting is as good as doing crazy business that needs an overhaul in order to, fairly treat the duo. An important thing to do is for the former to export technology to the latter with the aim of producing some of technological products and services the former exports to the latter in both halves. Further, no half should be a mere recipient of processed goods while the other half becomes a recipient of raw materials. There should be similarity in export and import as it currently is between the Global North and Asian Tigers.

In fact, the Global North needs to stop its rigidity in dealing with the Global South on which it superimposes its values and norms even when they do not actually work. To do away with such awkward situation that has caused many conflicts in the latter, I would argue that the international community must review, and thereby enter in a new agreement envisaging and enabling a new setting based on justice and equity. Instead of clinging to clientele and paternalistic relationship that neoliberal has always espoused, the new relationship between the two must be built on partnership and exchange of goods and skills. Essentially, this was the spirit of relationship between South and the North before it became colonialism thereafter. Broberg (2011) points at the European Union's relations with the ACP countries revolving around two main pillars namely trade and aid. Such relationship cannot be fair whereby one helps, and another receives help. Such relationship is injurious for the latter and advantageous for the former. Thus, the *modus operandi* of the relationship needs to change so that the two parties can mutually benefit equally. As argued above, meaningful change is possible by considering the basic human needs of both parties.

Practically, the Global South does not need aid but instead, it needs just and equitable exchange of technology, capitals, and cooperation. Ironically, many African countries, for example, spend much money on purchasing weapons from the former (Mhango 2015) instead of spending such money on productive areas such as education, health and investment. The Global North has the technology. Moreover, the Global South has the resources. The two must barter or exchange what they produce. Arguably, this is what the Asian Tigers did to be able to rich where they are now. Another ideal example is South Africa that received a technological boost that saw it outshine other countries in Africa. If this can be replicates in Africa, the results are easy to predict based on such experience. Shall this way of thinking be given a chance; and be allowed to function, permanent peace is attainable in the world.

Therefore, the parties should consider the cost of war economically, socially and politically as opposed to the gains of peace.

Another area of concern in deconstructing; and thereby restructuring the relationship between the duo is the decolonising and restructuring of the international organisations.

Mac Ginty and Williams (2009) argue that essentially "structures of the international system require radical overhaul in order to achieve pacific relationship" (p. 15). The relationship between the former and the latter has no border with the so-called international system. In other words, the international system is synonymous with the West or the Global North. The relationship between the Global North and the Global South is violent in that it fuels and maintains conflicts resulting from struggle for controlling resources the former receives. No doubt, the international organisations such as the United Nations (UN) and other organisations such as the IFIs have played an important role in enhancing exploitation of the Global South by the Global North based on the former's economic models and interests. After forming the IFIs, the Global North embarked on modernisation of the economy that did not affect positively on the citizens in the Global South or in the so-called third world. Since their inception, the IFIs have been serving the Global North by giving lip services to the Global South. Therefore, I can hypothesise that not only the IFIs that need a facelift but the whole UN system. Therefore, the UN, along with the IFIs, needs some reform to suit the needs of the duo in order to enable them to serve both parties equally and fairly based on mutual understanding. Currently, the Global North dominates and monopolises the UN without even looking at the current reality whereby the former decides how it should be ran and what it should do. Stedman (2007) argues that rising powers such as Brazil and South Africa need to have more influence in the UN's Security Council. I would argue that other powers–even if they are not rising–countries such as Angola, Tanzania, the DRC and others with immense natural resources, that are running the economy of the world, deserve recognition based on the strength of the resources they have. This will answer the question why the Global South is poor despite having such immense resources the Global North depends on.

Chapter Five

New Take That the Global South Needs to Embark on

To free itself from North-South exploitative relationship, the Global South needs to embark on rethinking about many concepts such as colonial legacies, human rights and aid, among others, in order to chart a new way forward. Arguably, the latter, even the former, has already gained much experience that can show the two the right thing[s] to do in tackling and possibly lessening or ending conflict, poverty and underdevelopment. As mentioned above, currently, the former is grappling with the wave of illegal immigrants from the latter looking for greener pastures (Arango and Baldwin-Edwards 2014). This poses a great threat to what the former used to take for granted as its God-given standard of living that is now seriously affected. There have been many complaints whereby some of people in the former are openly saying that illegal immigrants are going to destroy their culture the same way illegal immigrants that paved the way for colonialism did in the latter.

Given that the latter has always been on the receiving end, it is upon it to start reevaluating everything pertaining with the relationship with the former. The wave of *illegal immigrants* to the former is likely to be a bargaining chip in seeing to it that former stops exploit the latter. Doing so will create greener pastures illegal immigrants from the latter go for in the former. It is as simple as that. African leaders have become vocal in telling the former to stop exploiting Africa as a solution to illegal immigrant phenomenon. Arezki, Rota-Graziosi & Senbet (2014) quote the former UN-general secretary Kofi Anan saying that "it is unconscionable that some companies, often supported by dishonest officials, are using unethical tax avoidance, transfer pricing and anonymous company ownership to maximise their profits, while millions of Africans go without adequate nutrition, health and education" (p. 1). The duo, too, needs to address this anomaly in their relationship. For, it helps the former to gain even more wealth in the forms of loots from the latter. This is easy to stop shall the international community accept its moral obligation. The latter, consequently, needs to put its house in order so that it can confront the international community on the matter. Importantly, such a move will never bear fruits if countries in the latter take such measures severally but not unitedly.

i) Unreservedly Addressing Colonial Legacy

Although the Global South has always been viewed as a poor party in this relationship which it comparatively is, such poverty has many explanations to its causes of which are colonial legacy and unfair neoliberal policies that kicked in after colonialism so as to perpetrated neocolonialism. As argued above, the current North-South relationship is purely exploitative, hegemonic and colonial, predominantly economically and politically whereby the former exports its values and norms to the latter. To stop this neocolonialism, the international community must unreservedly declare any forms of colonialism, internal and external, a crime against humanity. After declaring colonialism a crime against humanity, there must be enacted some provisions under the international laws forcing all countries that benefited from colonising others to redress the victims of their criminality. Doing so will do away with an essentialised colonisation that makes the latter wantonly believe that it cannot survive without depending on aid from the former. Such essentialist exploitation needs to be deconstructed in order to usher in liberation policies instead of neoliberal gimmicks. The Global South needs to put its acts together, and thereby confront the Global North to register its dissatisfaction resulting from the disservice it has suffered from the former. This is, especially possible after some countries from the Global South are now emerging as powers of the world. The rise of emerging powers in the latter can tip the balance shall they be supported by poor countries from the Global South and work to help it out of poverty and imbalanced relationship with the former. Conditionally, these emerging powers should not strive to become new colonial masters, as the situation seems to imply now wherein China and India are playing the same role the former has always played in preying on others. Hurrell and Sengupta (2012) argue that actually "emerging powers as self-perceived members of the South have laid great emphasis on arguments for fairness" (p. 465). This argument may expand to cover reciprocity and mutuality in dealing with each other and all.

Principally, fairness is an important element that–for a long time–has lacked in the relationship between the pair. Therefore, if countries in the Global South are going to stand with the emerging powers from South, chances of forcing the former to change its exploitative and unfair policies are higher. Again, poor countries of the South need to be careful; and thereby avoid dancing with one devil to end up being in bed with another. Hurrell and Sengupta (*Ibid.*) maintain that "third, emerging powers are a problem not just because of their high growth rates and rapid development but also because of the increasingly central role that they are playing within a global capitalist system." As far as colonisation is concerned, if countries, especially poor ones, in the Global South are not becoming watchful, there are chances of having new colonial masters from within themselves based on economic muscles *vis-à-vis* the new rising powers from the Global South. China has already shown this tendency by exporting its jobless people and attaching strings to aid it offers to poor countries such as requiring them to use Chinese companies in carrying out the projects resulting from Chinese aid. Carmody and Awusu (2007) argue that "for the first time since the era of the slave trade, African trade is arguably re-orienting from the "Global North" to the "Global East" (p. 504). Carmody and Awusu ask if China is "a resource colonialist and anti-imperialist" (p. 505) that poor countries in the latter are now facing. Jiang (2009) equates China with Western countries due to replicating the scramble; and thus new scramble for Africa that has been ongoing for decades with negative ramifications for Africans. This means that the difference between the Global North and emerging economies in the latter is relatively zilch if we clinically interrogate what China has been doing since its rise. Burke (2013) quotes Ian Bremmer, president of the Eurasia Group, as saying that "the Chinese *quid pro quo* typically involves lots of Chinese content, lots of Chinese labour that they're sending over to these countries to work, which hurts local unemployment issues; and of course, the availability of commodities including food to be exported to China. There's sometimes a Faustian bargain in these countries." This is obvious that Africa is getting a bad deal once again from the one who used to be of its allies during the cold war. This shows how neoliberal policies have no permanent and real friends or enemies but profits. Who would think that a socialistic country of yesterday, that preached equality to others, would become a ruthless capitalist overnight? I do not want to blame a lot. Once materialistic evil engulfs anybody, anything can happen even if it means to vend her or his own mother or brothers and sisters. I have evidenced this in Africa where the foreign masters induced and seduced a few local elites to sell their countries as I have indicated above in chapter two aiming at helping Africa to not anymore buy into such bestiality.

Indeed, as mentioned above, Africans in Darfur are now suffering the consequences of China's new scramble for Africa. China has supported Omar Bashir's regime in Khartoum despite facing indictment by the International Criminal Court (ICC) for committing genocide in Darfur. By supporting Bashir, China apart from becoming an accomplice, enacts exactly what the former has always done to the latter. The role of China in Sudan as far as genocide in Darfur is concerned is not different from the one France played in Rwanda. This shows the true face of neoliberal policies that China seems to latch on. Although China has not been ready to discuss human rights and the impacts of ignoring them, it very well knows what it is doing wherever it has sunk its talons.

Apart from human rights, there is the danger of depleting resources in the latter that the emerging powers in the latter are causing. Some resources such as endangered species–especially rhinoceros and elephants–are now on the verge of extinction due to having high a demand in China. Eustace (2012) points at China as a main market where rhino horn is sold into the Asian traditional medicine market where it is used in a cocktail of other substances to cure a range of ailments. This is one of many examples in which China's thirsty for resources is decimating Africa's rare resources such as fish, animals and timbers to mention but a few. As a result, China's status of a rising power seems not to help the Global South.

This is why the latter needs to avoid generalising and uniformly treating countries on its side equally. Every country has its unique challenges, problems and solutions. However, almost all countries in the latter face the same situation as far as relationship with the former is concerned. Most importantly, when analysing the conflict, distinction between emerging powers and poor countries is important. Therefore, when it comes to synchronising the anathema, the latter must not to trust any power even if the said power[s] is emerging from the latter. Exploitation does not know brother or sister. I propound that the latter needs to face the emerging powers to warn them about what they are doing as far as its interest as a bloc are concerned. Being in the same bloc makes no sense if those emerging from it are dancing like those they have always accused of exploiting them.

Furthermore, if the emerging powers are going to use the same neoliberal policies based on Self-helping and self-serving manners and systems, soon, they will become another bloc of neocolonialists to poor countries of the Global South as Jiang (*Ibid.*) has indicated above. So, fairness and evenness that the emerging powers are seeking must, act as double-edged sword cutting both the emerging powers and rich countries in the Global North in dealing with poor countries instead of blaming the Global North only. Evidentially, China, has already shown how dangerous it can be economically. Its deals with poor countries in the Global South tell a different story from what such countries expected of the country they thought; they shared alliance with in dealing with the former. Mac Ginty and Williams (2009) note that China's rapid economic development is likely to potentially contribute to conflict as it is in the case in Sudan above. Therefore, the Global North needs to change its policies towards the Global South in order to counterbalance the rise of China that has never bothered with human rights or rule of law apart from depleting resources in the latter. China needs to look at environment as one of human rights.

Another rising power, Brazil, too, has its share of blames in Amazonian ecological destruction not to mention bullying other plundered countries in Latin America. Arguably, if the rising powers are not well checked, chances are that they will not help the Global

South in either to normalising its relationship with the Global North or walking out of it. Schweller (2011) maintains that evidence shows that, under the rising power conflict model, the rising powers are spoilers. For, they are hell-bent on revising the world order for their interests but not those of the region or the Global South. Whether the emerging powers from the Global South are going to be either actually spoilers or reformers, depends on how poor countries in the Global South will play their cards by utilising their resources smartly and wisely. Again, to reach a win-win relationship between the duo all depends on how they are going to compromise and move forward. The rise of the United States gives us a good example. When the US noted that Western Europe, especially Great Britain was losing its edge economically due to being involved in many wars, it intervened to help to its advantage. This can happen with the current rising powers from the Global South. Therefore, their impacts on the current unfair relationship between the former and the latter will not change anything for poor countries. It is easy to predict what will happen as far as conflicts and economic situations will be. Henderson (1996) maintains that "all countries face the global economic warfare scenario of cutthroat competition, creeping budget deficits, and jobless growth, as well as the other vicious circles" (p. 38). With such cutthroat competition, every country will want to secure its interests even at the expenses of others just as it has been going on in the relationship between the Global North and the Global South.

Due to the population growth globally, the above trend is likely to go on unabated shall the latter decide to choose from the old and new powers. Importantly, the latter must not look at the origin of the power to deal with. Instead, it must suspiciously deal with the duo namely emerging powers from itself and the traditional North. Whoever accepts to do justice, will make a good partner-cum-ally when it comes to deconstructing exploitative relationship. Being a moral wrong even a crime, exploitation as it is without considering the sameness or origin of the one in this deal, is blind. These who lived under capitalistic and socialistic exploitation know, too well, how exploitation knows no ideology, geography or alliance. Exploitation is exploitation, simple. When it comes to exploitation, the one exploiting others brother, father or sister has no border from unrelated person to the person that one abuses or exploits. Exploitation is similar to a bullet shot at a person. Whether the bullet comes from your or enemy's gun is immaterial. What is obvious is the result of what the shot bullet will do if it hits you, death that has never been accepted or welcomed. Therefore, when dealing with exploitation, the victims should trust nobody except equity and justice that they should see and see them done. Choosing whom to deal with is a daunting task for the latter now.

The thirsty for resources has resulted to conflict in the latter. Looking at many conflicts in the Global South, mainly in resource-rich countries, one can argue that the coming of the rising powers into the play will add more fuel to the conflict *vis-a-vis* scramble for resources such as coltan and others. For example, due to its demand and the role it plays in modern machinery such as computers, airplanes and cell phones, coltan or tantalum will always be in high demand. Moreover, due to technological advancement of the economies of the rising powers–as the condition of maintaining economic growth, coltan will overshadow all efforts of resolving the conflict in the DRC. Bleischwitz, Dittrich and Pierdicca (2012) concur noting that the need for tantalum used for high-tech cutters, in air and space technology, and for turbines is expected to grow due to its new applications in ICT, machinery, energy production turbines, energy storage, aircrafts and optical industry. While the Global North or the West has always applied its negative peace in the DRC (Mac Ginty, 2008) nobody knows what the rising powers will use to resolve the said conflict. To normalise the relationship between the former and the latter, the two must direct their efforts to erasing this core-peripheral setting. Moreover, this is only possible through mutual exchanged between the duo whereby the former will exchange its advanced knowledge and technology with the resources available from the latter. This setting is workable. The rise of the Asian Tigers in early the 70s gives a good example. Paldam (2003) notes that the rise came into being after finding the policies that combined the best from the Western (Capitalist) and the Eastern (Communist) economic systems. Although the countries in the Global South do not have the luxury to choose from policies between the new and old powers due to using the same policy template, they still can carefully choose whom to align with under certain conditions that will put the old and new powers in the competition to win the hearts and minds of poor countries. For example, just as the Global North has always done, poor countries in the Global South can use cartels as their business strategy in supplying the duo. If the duo well manages and well plans their relationship, it is likely to put two axis of power into an economic-paradigm shift in dealing with poor countries of the Global South. By so doing, the powers from either the former or the latter, will not fuel conflicts resulting from the drive for controlling resources in the Global South.

ii) Rethink Human Needs and Human Rights

The Global North has always portrayed itself as the guardian of human rights in the world. However, in enforcing human rights–which, in essence, do not make sense if they do not address basic human needs. I have touched on how the Global North toppled the so-called rogue states in the Global South. The pretext given was that the rulers of those states were violating human rights. Again, considering other countries that do the same yet enjoys the protection of the former, creates problems. To do away with such a double standard, human rights and democracy should be applied equally all aiming at protecting and promoting basic human needs for all first. The duo is a new cosmology in which Burrowes (1996) urges that primarily each component of any cosmology must revolve around the satisfaction of human needs. Instead of overthrowing regimes and leave back chaos as it currently is in Iraq and Libya, the international community must use peaceful means such as sanctions and negotiations. I think that consociational democracy is the best model to use in this relationship. Byrne (2001) argues that consociational systems need to be decentralised as stipulated in rigid constitutions with the aim of empowering the people. This is what the Global South needs in its relationship with the Global North and in running its internal business. However, for Africa, the choice is not supposed to be between decentralised or centralised systems but to follow its path of democracy aimed at enhancing it to reach its goals. This will help Africa to do away with conditional democracy from the global North.

Another important issue to practically and systematically address for the North-South relationship is to meet human needs due to the fact that every rights revolves around basic human needs. As indicated above, neglect or unmet basic human needs in the Global South have led to many conflicts, poverty and underdevelopment resulting from uneven and unfair distribution of resources the Global North buys and consumes from the latter. Although the former–under liberal peace, which has failed–has tried to intervene in resolving conflicts in the latter by using aid, its approach does not work. There is no way aid, peacekeeping missions can act as deterrence without addressing basic human needs, and the root causes of the conflict. Christie (1997) argues that there is no way deterrence as means of preventing direct violence can succeed without meeting human needs for security and identity, among others. If anything, many conflicts and internal exploitation among the groups in the latter resulting from the unfair relationship between the former and the latter revolve around insecurity and identity, especially ethnic conflict in which the protagonists such as Hutus and Tutsis in Rwanda, are the good sources of conflict and poverty. This is because their sharp division; not to mention the mistrusts between or among them colonisers from the former created. Byrne *(Ibid.)* argues that the "role of identity is becoming increasingly important to our understanding of ethnic conflict resolution" (p. 329). All this goes back to colonial legacy. Colonisers created fake identities that gave rise to insecurity in many colonies in the Global South. Identity, sometimes, acts as a determinant in ethnic conflicts revolving around either distribution or control of scarce resources. Refer to conflicts in Rwanda, Sri Lanka, Nigeria, and many more. So, for the two to deter conflicts, their relationship must strictly address basic human needs to begin with. Moreover, it is possible to attain human needs through deconstructing liberal policies that have always helped the former to exploit the latter. Instead of superimposing its policies on the latter, the former needs to rethink about its approach toward the latter so that such underlying issues can be resolved in order to avoid more conflicts. Burrowes (*Ibid.*) argues that:

> Security for the people of the south requires the restoration of political process that allow decision about production and distribution of resources to be made by the people themselves (rather than local or foreign elites) in accordance to the needs of participation, distributive justice and control (p. 144).

By empowering the people in deciding how and what they should produce and supply, the Global South will have a say in the world's economic affairs in order to raise its voice and counter exploitation that has been ongoing for a long time. By so doing, the "othering" paradigm will shift from "them" and "us" to "we-ness." And indeed, this will reduce or stamp out conflict resulting from poverty, greed, struggle for controlling resources; and there will be no need anymore–as far as the latter is concerned–for the West to topple governments. Equally, the Global North must stop exporting its proxy wars to the Global South. As we will show in the last chapter on case study two–what has been going on in Syria where two antagonistic powers, the US and Russia, have held the country and the region to ransom wantonly–is still relevant *vis-a-vis* the relationship between the duo. In other words, the Global North and Russia must stop their new imperialistic missions in the Global South. Carpenter (2013) argues that the "regional context for the Syrian conflict is at least as complex as the internal setting, reflecting both a triangular geopolitical contest for dominance" (p. 3). If anything, the way the duo is going to resolve the conflict in Syria will teach us how we can deal with such conflicts resulting from neo-imperialism.

In conclusion, if the duo works on above-proposed measures, chances of having a conflict-free world are higher. First, the Global North has already accumulated enough capital that enables it to function swiftly without necessarily depending on exploiting the Global South. Second, the Global South is at a good stage of development shall its resources benefit its people. Third, if the duo accommodates the proposed exchange of technology, knowledge and resource, both parties will equally benefit from their relationship, and thus, the need of fuelling conflicts resulting from struggle for resource controlling will become meaningless. Arguably, fair, just and mutual cooperation is the cornerstone of development and peace. I, therefore, strongly propose the deconstruction and reconstruction of the current setting for the aim of benefitting both parties to the conflict. Instead of performing the role of supply of raw materials and consumer of processed goods, the Global South will become a competent and equal player just like the Asian Tigers, Japan, China and India so to speak.

As oft-argued above, the relationship between the duo is defective in that it benefits one party as it robs another. Therefore, it needs to be overhauled to see to it that this relationship equally and equitably serves the interests of both parties. Doing so will reduce conflicts resulting from unmet needs and struggle for control of resources in the Global South. The duo has a lot to do to address many shortfalls embedded in this unfair relationship. I would argue that such inequitable relationship that fosters exploitation of the Global South by the Global North is a very fertile for many violent conflicts. So, too, I would argue that neoliberal policies have completely failed to do justice to the Global South despite some gains.

Chapter Six

Part II: Two Case Studies: Africa, the Role of Definition and Divisionism

After exploring the anomalies and problems of the relationship between the Global North and the Global South, I have purposely decided to write the chapter on a case study that aims at showing another ignored or overlooked aspect of how the former exploits the latter, especially intellectually through defining almost everything for the latter. This chapter dwells on the concept of Africa's [under-]development. Is Africa, really, underdeveloped as the former defines it?

As the title shows, there are two case studies. After introducing the first case, it is important to shed some light on the second case study. It is about the role the Global North played in creating and using divide and rule as the strategy that has lived on so as to keep on playing a great role in exploitative rapport between the duo which is the major them of this volume. As you will, divide and rule helped the former to exploit the latter during colonial era and thereafter. This being the situation, we need to address this facet of history in order to diagnose the problems instead of blaming the miseries it is suffering on the latter. Again, as it has been in the entire volume, much concentration has been put on Africa due to the reasons known that it is the most disparaged continent on earth and in the latter. Therefore, let us explore the real situation together hereunder.

Troubling Myth of Africa's [Under-] Development

i) Introduction

In trying to tackle the above heading, I will start with two questions as the foundational hunch and a window into the issue at hand. The questions I ask, therefore is on if Africa is truly and desperately dependent, poor and underdeveloped as its detractors have always ridiculously defined it. What role did divide-and-rule strategy, the Global North used during and after colonial era to fuel violence, usurping power, politics and (anti-)development, predominantly in Africa play in the exploitation of the latter? These questions are very crucial and equivocally overwhelming so to speak. However, the answers to the questions why Africa is underdeveloped and the role divide-and-rule strategy played in exploiting the latter may differ from one person to another, of all; Africa needs to provide not only answers but also accurate answers.

While many academics have tackled the problems resulting from the so-called Africa's underdevelopment and the role divide and rule played, much remain to be seen *vis-à-vis* providing the accurate and pragmatic answers to the duo in order to do away with manmade impasses dogging their relationship. The move to shift Africa out of the Western-defined underdevelopment, academically speaking, needs to start theoretically then pragmatically all based on dynamic human nature. Mawere (2010) argues applying the theory of evolution to pin down the fact that the purpose of life for any human has never been static. Again, if this is the real situation, why has the former vacuously, unfairly categorised and permanently viewed the latter as static while human nature dictates that human life is always dynamic whether consciously or unconsciously? Why do Africa's doomsters and prophets of doom contradict this logically, simple, clear and understandable human nature? Is there any malice against Africa all geared by the quest of exploiting it forever as it has been the archaic and colonial view of it? Arguably, Mawere's argument, apart from being powerful, is true and provocative, especially for those who have always underrated Africa with the aim of relegating it to their manmade underdevelopment. This is where the importance of formulating a definition that reflects the reality of things emanates. Indeed, this is where the quest of questioning Western agendas and its thinkers who formulated the current definition of development is important. This is, especially important for Africans who, in a sense, are the victims of this very categorisation based on colonial criteria as espoused by Western thinkers.

It is, therefore, from this milieu that this chapter seeks to challenge the so-called Africa's underdevelopment. The chapter will show how such a conclusion is, maliciously concocted in order to make Africa believe that it is naturally dependent. In so doing, I question the legality-cum-rationale of those who assign such a tag and role to Africa without underscoring some other vital elements in reaching such a conclusion that, in all honesty, lacks credibility; especially for the victims of such international conspiracy against Africa. Hereunder, I explore some aspects of defining Africa as an underdeveloped continent while it sits on immense resources such as rivers, people, market minerals, gas, oil, fertile land and forests, among others.

ii) Troubling the Predicament of [Under-] Development

Whether Africa is underdeveloped, thus dependent or not, all depends on the definition, lenses and means one uses to reach at such a conclusion. So, too, it depends on who is making such an evaluation. Therefore, in evaluating Africa's underdevelopment, one can get many different answers depending on what is included or excluded in the evaluation. Arguably, the question whether Africa is truly underdeveloped or not is a dichotomous matter—that needs us to look at both sides of the coin—instead of wholesomely making such a myopic and toxic conclusion. For, those who maintain that Africa is comparatively underdeveloped know the reason[s] among which is the one that Rodney (1972) maintains that it is exploitation, but not evolution. Indeed, Africa was made poor—something that has pointlessly gone on up until now—so as to be deemed as underdeveloped.

However, when I critically and honestly interrogate the components, criteria and true meaning of development based on human basic needs (Burton 1990), sometimes, I see very different realities (Yang 2003) that need to affect our conclusions and answers altogether. For, despite sharing needs, human beings have diverse needs all depending on their cultures, time, priorities and, above all, choices. Even the way they make sense of things is, very different. For example, one of the basic human needs is security.

Despite security being a self-explanatory concept, when it comes to how to achieve it, culture plays a very important role. We achieve and understand security differently based on our assumptions and orientations. For example, people from collectivistic societies expect to get the guarantee of their security from the society while their counterparts from the individualistic societies, security is a personal matter as opposed to collectivistic societies in which the same is more societal than personal. Even the way the two perceive security is different. This concept of security applies in order to show how people from two societies above evaluate security and thus, development, very differently. For the member of hunters in Kalahari Desert in Namibia, security means everything that contributes to the survival of the entire group while in the Western societies, security can be guaranteed by having a gun that an individual purchase. For Kalahari hunters, this is nothing but social capital that has its root in African traditional societies. Hence, while security is the quest for all groups, its realisation is completely different. In a group of hunters or collectivistic society, security depends on interdependence while in the latter it depends on one's independence. Likewise, we view development differently whereby in the former moral attachment, social capital, trust, sharing, connectivity and interdependence are guarantees to development just as they are in the realisation of security.

More so, development, for the former, is more a moral issue while in the latter it is a material matter. Therefore, the angle this chapter takes *vis-à-vis* the underdevelopment of Africa will fundamentally be based on its history and the archaic nature of the international system governing development and the *realpolitik* of the current world that tend to ally with individualistic culture as opposed to collectivistic one. The victims of such prejudice of the so-called underdeveloped countries need to question, with all determination, the yardstick others exclusively use to define and assess development among others. The need to question the logic of choosing some components of development while ignoring or excluding others is vital; shall we aspire to treat one another deservedly. The dialogue resulting from such interrogating and negotiating the form the process must take will eventually help us to get a fitting definition for whatever concept[s] we apply in the process of ranking countries almost in everything. There is no way Africa and other countries, categorised as underdeveloped, can get out of the manmade impasse they are in without deconstructing the definitions, rationales and systems by which categories, conclusions and ranks and their rationales. For development or underdevelopment to make sense, all stakeholders need to be involved in the process by deciding the terms and parameters to use in analysing and defining what they would all want to call [under]development. We need to know what people know about these two concepts instead of letting Western think tanks and policymakers decide for all others. As you will see later, I wonder to find that in rating development even materially why untapped resources such as minerals, lakes, rivers, and wildlife receive no considerations. This is a material side. Again, it also baffles to find that nonmaterial assets such as cultural richness and peaceability receive no prominence in development rating. Rogoff (2003) observes that generally and historically development is a cultural process; however, research on it has basically accommodated only researches and theories coming from Western middle-class communities under the current dominant grand narrative that has undeservedly self-appointed to be the diviner of the modern world.

Although some people tend to take the concept of defining things for granted without interrogating them, the definition[s] plays a vital role in conceptualising and thereby getting things rightly or wrongly pinned down. Definition, as a concept, dictates how people understand or misunderstand whatever ideas or things and their definitions. Therefore, it is crucial to interrogate the definitions we use, who defines what, why and how such a thing or concept is defined so. We need to have a sort of negotiation about the definitions we use without privileging some to do this for others. The definition is a roadmap for us to conceptualise whatever concept we come across. Therefore, before accepting the definition[s] we need to subject it to some tests to see if it meets and suits what it defines. As well, when we make a claim that Africa is [under-]developed, we must specify in what ways; and how did we reach such a conclusion[s]. It does not make any sense, especially for the victims of the current paradigm of [under-]development, for example, to say that owning a car or house makes a person more developed than the person who owns a herd of 100 cows is wrong. Development is like beauty that is always in the eyes of the beholder (Mawere 2016). If we need to evaluate development by considering somebody's needs, understanding and culture. This is why African traditional anglers view modern trawls as useless—due to causing environmental harms—compared to their canoes. What many wrongly view as development or advancement and better in the eye of one person may be detrimentally different in the eyes on another.

Furthermore, you can see in the concept of taking care of elderly people between the so-called underdeveloped and developed countries. While it is squarely the duty of their children to look after elderly parents in Africa, for example, it is different in the so-called developed countries where elderly people are provided with almost all material amenities minus spiritual or moral ones while in Africa is vice versa. The two systems of looking after the elderly persons have their, flaws, strength and shortfalls. However, when it comes to assessing which society is doing better than another, modern way of ranking the latter ranks higher than the former. What is evident here is the ignorance of the fact that in the two groups, the former provides less material support but more moral while in the latter it is vice versa. The elderly persons living in an air-conditioned house with all amenities minus visitations or human attachment from their children are materially better but morally worse. So, too, the elderly persons living in a shack with less material support but with abundant social support are morally better but materially worse. In other words, the duo is equal save that in ranking them; many consider the latter as doing better than the former. The bottom line here is simply that we need to negotiate these differences based on both aspects of human needs, culture, desire and whatnots of the person[s] in question instead of generalising everything as it if the lenses from the culture we use are analogous.

When it comes to development, the incorporation and inclusion of human needs and understanding of the needs and concepts are essential. Take for example, two people namely a doctor who gets much money because of his professionalism and the artist who makes much more money than the doctor makes predominantly in the so-called developed world due to his skills. This claim shows how different circumstances can bring material things. However, when it comes to rating countries, art and culture nobody views culture as an asset. Arguably, there is no way a people can be [under] developed in everything; otherwise such a conclusion is arrived by/through what Escobar (2011) refers to as the "'colonisation of reality' in which some representations become dominant; and thereby shape indelibly the way in which reality is imagined and acted upon" (p. 5). This is where the complexity and relativity of development lies. On this note, I propose the inevitable decolonisation of the way the world has been doing things under the current dominant grand narrative in order to do away with the effects of intellectual colonisation and domination. I see the current dominant grand narrative as a culprit for many ills and evils the so-called underdeveloped countries have suffered. He concurs with Rodney (*Ibid.*) arguing that the so-called underdevelopment of Africa is, basically, historical but not real or evolutional. There is no way Africa's former colonial masters could entertain historical factors while they know that doing so will expose their ploy that they would like to have internalised by their victims so as to keep on depending on them pointlessly. In others words, we need to 'decolonise reality' based on today's actuality; and the tools we can use, *inter alia*, is the decolonisation of education (Mhango 2016) due to its toxicity that needs the process of detoxification based on African aspirations and principles but not foreign ones. Berthélemy (2006) maintains that there is no way poor countries can get out of the trap of underdevelopment without necessarily ambitious plans aimed at eradicating illiteracy. When reality is [mis-]construed depending on hidden agenda by the one representing it, chances are that hegemonic views are likely to dominate others just as it has been the case in defining the [under] development of Africa which shows a form of illiteracy itself. It does not make sense to refer a continent with ancient civilisation as underdeveloped while to the contrary young civilisations whose—successes resulted from crimes such as slavery, colonialism and neo-colonialism they committed against those they categorise as underdeveloped–are referred to as developed countries which most of them happen to be in the Global North. Doing so is developmental injustice its victims need to fight. Allowing such tendency, whereby development and underdevelopment are defined and rated by the culprits in the Global North, is so detrimental to the so-called underdeveloped countries in the Global South. It is like allowing a convict to decide to preside over the case involving those he or she offended. The safest way for such a person to be free is to condemn his or her victims. To avoid such criminality is to make sure that brains are decolonised and detoxified in order to function nicely based on realism. The exploitation of the latter has been possible due to the propaganda machinery colonialism has always put in place to safeguard its interests as opposed to those of others in this othering (Khalid 2011) tendency and strategy. As it is in international commerce, the West has always acted as one group against the so-called underdeveloped countries due to this othering tendency championed by neo-liberal policies and neo-colonialism.

In essence, arguably, development or underdevelopment is a relative term. Equally, development is supposed to include many aspects such as history, civilisation, culture, aspirations and achievements in many areas. It does not make any sense, for example, to categorise that the United States of America (USA) as more developed than Egypt, Sudan or Zimbabwe whose civilisations are older than the USA itself as a country. Development is supposed to be dichotomous, linear and perpendicular by nature in order to accommodate various variables of human society. What is more, the job of defining development must result from consensus upon which it is supposed to be inclusive by nature whereby all stakeholders should negotiate the definition they must use based on their understanding, culture, intentions, mores and needs among others. For example, South Africa, under former Apartheid regime, the definition of development viewed it as more economically and technologically advanced than its neighbours such as Zambia and Zimbabwe. However, the latter outdid the former *vis-à-vis* struggles for liberation and human rights. Again, the West, that supported such criminal regime, ignored such aspects simply because it had the wherewithal to define the duo based on its alliance and interests. To define whatever, we want equally, we can apply Self-determination Theory (SDT) that Niemiec and Ryan (2009) define as an understanding of human motivation that requires a consideration of innate psychological needs for competence, autonomy, and relatedness, among others. As you can see, relationship and autonomy appear in tandem. Therefore, in defining and making sense of development, we need to accommodate this natural human drive towards self-preservation in their environment. Niemiec and Ryan make a good observation by emphasising psychological human needs as opposed to physiological ones to indicate how psychological needs are more prominent to the human. However, this should never confuse that human physiological needs are unimportant. They all are. The difference is that in assessing development and underdevelopment, much emphasis must not be on material needs to the extent of, sometimes, ignoring or belittling immaterial needs. Whether this is true or not, depends on how one looks at these two aspects of needs namely psychological and physiological. So, too, it depends on the culture one is coming from. This is obvious that we are talking of qualitative or inner needs than outer needs. Here I am talking of nonmaterial as opposed to material human drives all based on one's choice and motivation of doing so not to forget the motive[s], objective[s] according to one's environment. This is why it is unfair to view a thug as developed simply because he illegally acquired materials from the pauper who is forgiving and law abiding. This chimes in the relationship in question if we critically examine how the West accumulated material wealth by colonising and robbing others. Again, under capitalistic neoliberal policies that are devoid of morality, the global North has the right to be content with his ill-gotten wealth.

There can be development in different aspects and areas *vis-à-vis* a particular country or society. Therefore, it misleads to make generalisations as far as development is concerned as is currently the case whereby some countries that are well off materially are deemed developed even when they are poor in moral and nonmaterial aspects as I will further indicate. Sometimes, you wonder to find a country with many suicides or deaths resulting from obesity in the high ranks in development! Before putting such a country in high ranks of development, we need to know what is causing such traits. To add insult to injury, some of these countries are rich economically. Again, when it comes to rating the levels of development, malnutrition receives consideration while obesity—that results from overfeeding—is not. What is the consequence of the two? I would argue that countries with the absence of suicidal traits need an accolade for doing better than those grappling with the phenomenon do; even if these countries are economically poor. For, however developed countries boast of having advanced medical services, developed countries facing suicidal problem need to think twice due to the fact that suicide is mental health matter that many poor countries do not have. Their culture that prevents suicide is their asset just like any other material assets like knowledge, medication and money.

Economic development should also accommodate justice development. For example, currently, South Africa stands as a highly developed country in Africa. However, the same country has a big gap between the haves and the have-nots compared to Zimbabwe. This makes South Africa an under underdeveloped *vis-a-vis* human equality and economic justice. South Africa's enjoyment of its natural resources revolves around colour whereby the majority indigenous South Africans are poorer than their white minority counterparts are. May and Govender (1998) note that poverty is not confined to any one race group, but is concentrated among blacks, particularly Africans: 61% of Africans and 38% of Coloureds are poor, compared with 5% of Indians and 1% of White (pp. 2-3). The situation is the same in the so-called most advanced nation on earth the US at the same period where systemic bigotry is on the rise thanks to having rigid and archaic system of modern-time apartheid. Dalaker and Naifeh (1997) note that poverty rate for Blacks in 1999 was still about three times the poverty rate for White non-Hispanics (7.7 percent) (v). In terms of economic development, some countries enjoy material development although they are morally underdeveloped or decayed. In addressing the dichotomous nature of development, Weingast (1995) observes the paradoxical nature of the government and notes that the same governments might be strong in protecting economic rights of its people as well as in confiscating properties from their citizens. This is the nature of many governments built on Western philosophy. Such a trend was oblivious in the 2007 US credit crunch where the government spent public money in bailing out lossmaking private companies despite opposition from the citizens who ended up becoming losers simply because the government used its muscles to rob them. Bailout is nothing but corruption based on capitalistic cronyism. Rosas (2006) observes that the hefty costs shouldered by taxpayers and the obvious moral hazard incentives that accompany bank bailouts make it important to understand the conditions under which politicians rescue banks simply because corporates reciprocate by sponsoring politicians during the campaigns. This has been ongoing for many years. Collier and Goderis (2008) concur with Rosas in that in countries ruled by unaccountable regimes, politicians use the resource windfall revenues to bias the outcome of elections or in non-democratic regimes political contests. Essentially, this is the major cause of underdevelopment in the latter that the former has always perpetrated.

Concerning defining corruption by countries or governments, the so-called developed countries escape blemishes from the vice. The reason is obvious that they are the ones who dictate the terms and definition of the vice.

Therefore, they apply and play *holier than thou* that have existed since neoliberal policies swamped the world. In whatever aspect of social science, it is wrong to, generally categorise countries as developed or otherwise by excluding or ignoring some other vital aspects such as the effects of whatever categorisation on human wellbeing. Human beings are not like machines that need only repairs and supply of energy such as electricity or gas. Instead, humans naturally and equally need more than material needs. What differs is the degree of appreciating such things. For example, collectivistic societies from which many countries ranked as underdeveloped put more premiums on moral wellbeing than the individualistic societies whose premium is more on material wellbeing than moral ones. Nancy and Aaron (1998) argue that such societies are not homogenous in that cultures are not homogenous. Thus, individuals from such societies present a very different self-conception depending on independence and interdependence. Such an argument can show how two different societies namely collectivistic and individualistic diversely conceptualise development. For example, for individualistic societies, freedom and security depend on the power an individual has in consumption while the latter freedom is not as important as interdependence whereby the society acts together as opposed to the former where every individual acts alone and independently of others. So, too, in an individualistic society, personal freedom and security have more importance than in the collectivistic society in which the freedom and security of the person depend on and revolve around the wellbeing of other members of the society. Therefore, it holds water to argue that in defining and rating development, the parties must accommodate and reconcile their differences instead of allowing one society to define everything to its advantage that is the detriment to the other. Essentially, such different takes on development and wellbeing has caused unfair situation embedded in the relationship between the two whereby the former has always robbed the latter of its resources for the development of the former. Such a tendency has maintained systemic corruption in which the former benefits while the latter loses. Mehlum, Moene & Torvik (2006) cited in Collier and Goderis (2008) argue that resource rents invite non-productive lobbying and rent seeking; and that the pay-offs from these activities are high in countries with grabber-friendly institutions but low in countries with producer-friendly institutions. If anything, what is required of the two is to deconstruct and overhaul such an unfair system on which the relationship of the two has always latched if not hinged on.

To meet human needs well, the process of defining development must accommodate both material and moral aspects in formulating the definition or categories of advancement, development and underdevelopment in order to avoid using narrow and flaw definitions in addressing the needs of the duo. Luck and d'Inverno (2001) note that there must be the system in which an "object comprises a set of actions and a set of attribute" (p. 12) by which factors every definition must abide by; and thereby accommodate in order to avoid biases. Arguably, in defining anything, this must not be a general rule without any exception. For example, you cannot define the behaviour of the governments that act controversially as indicated above lineally or vertically only without interweaving all aspects of its behaviours aimed at coming up with a balanced and inclusive definition. Such a take invites us to interrogate the development of the developed world and the underdevelopment of underdeveloped countries critically and equally.

You can take a leaf from Africa. While Western countries have almost everything any human needs, the situation is contrary in many African countries. As well, when it comes to, for example, the prevalence of happiness, the so-called underdeveloped countries outshine the so-called developed countries. According to Winterman (2006), the Pacific island nation of Vanuatu was the happiest place on earth, according to a new 'happy planet index.' Further, Winterman notes that while Vanuatu claimed the leading in happiness, the UK was languishing in 108th place, below Libya, Iran, and Palestine. It is a fact that humans need and seek materials in order to live happily. Why then exclude happiness from evaluating the development of any country. There are many more missing things of defining and evaluating the level of [under] development of any country. For example, why should those defining development or otherwise consider the peaceability of countries of the world so as to discourage wars resulting from struggle for controlling resources in poor countries in which governments and warlords seek the opportunity to supply the resources to the West and other rich countries in order to become rich quickly? Researchers found that the causes-cum-secrets behind Vanuatu's happiness were rooted on the culture of the people based on harmonious coexistence and interdependence that lack in the so-called developed countries. Vanuatu's lead turns Western misleading assumption that happiness is about making choice based on economic muscles (Sen 1995) to its head. For the former and the latter to relate and interrelate well, they both equally need to underscore the needs of a society individually and uniquely. This is why the concept of happiness and happiness index kick in; all aimed at showing how many neoliberal definitions of many concepts, chiefly development, underdevelopment and wellbeing are shallower. Naturally, people have different perceptions, priorities and, above all, aspirations. For example, while individualistic-cum-materialistic Western countries consider material wellbeing, collectivistic societies prioritise moral wellbeing before material wellbeing. It baffles to note that a country like the US–with such sharply segregated cities and communities along races–to feature high in the list of the so-called developed countries.

We need to consider non-material things in the logic of development definition because poor countries cannot compete economically under the current regime of economies wherein rich Western countries created an exploitative system that only benefits and serves them. Apart from this, for example, African traditional economy died when neoliberal policies became the policies of the world championed by the so-called International Financial Institutions (IFIs). How can anybody expect Africa to provide sound health services while the West butchered and replaced its Traditional Medicinal Knowledge (TMK)? Africa depends on medicines from abroad after losing its own. The consequences of this are evident in the so-called modern life whereby Africans are dying of obesity–which seriously affects them due to bad habits they copied from Western countries. Refer to the infiltration of MacDonald and other fast foods in the latter. Traditionally, Africans would not become obese because their lifestyle was itself a cure. Caballero (2005) argues that "the high energy demands of manual labour and daily-survival activities make it difficult for people to achieve a net positive energy balance and therefore to gain weight" (p. 1514). Again, the situation has now changed dramatically after African ways of life suffered heavily from Western machinations. Caballero (*Ibid.*) observes that:

> In more urbanised developing countries with a higher GNP, food scarcity may no longer be the driving factor behind energy intake. Instead, the availability of cheap, energy-dense foods (including those

from street vendors and fast-food restaurants) may facilitate the consumption of more calories (p. 1514).

The floods of cheap and fast food are not an accident. As indicated above, Western companies such as MacDonald, Subway, KFC, Chicken Chef and others are now making inroads to Africa to make quick bucks at the expense of Africans. Thanks to corrupt and dependent African leaders and intellectual domination by the West, despite knowing the danger of fast foods, Africa has never done anything. Many Africans are blindly taking fast foods and Western lifestyles as modernity while they actually are not, but toxic. The danger of this trend is even higher than anybody can expect; because Africa has–ever since the introduction of cultural and political colonialism–always copied from the West. Due to this toxic and hedonic relationship, Africa has never produced anything the Global North could copy. Ironically, such is the same that rate world countries in development. Can there be anything good from Africa apart from its resources and consumption market?

The example given above can clearly show how many terms we use tend to be controversial and wanting. Considering this fact, therefore, I argue that Africa's underdevelopment is an inflicted-cum-self-inflicted wound since Africa allowed others to define it; and in so doing, there are many crucial factors on human development that seem to be–either purposely or out of ignorant–left out in the definition of [under] development. Allowing enemies to define the latter's development offers an opportunity to ignore many important aspects that are supposed to be included in the definition of development. Sometimes, I wonder to find that a why referring to a dazzlingly multicultural society like Africa as under or undeveloped. Essentially, this is what colonialism and hegemony are all about. What do you expect when you play in your enemies' hands expecting her or him to [re]define you? It has never made any sense, to me as a thinker, to concur with those who draw a propagandist conclusion that Africa is poor and underdeveloped. How is this possible if Africa sits on hugely vast resources? Again, when you allow somebody else to define you, he or she will define you according to his interests, terms and wishes. Achebe (2000 cited in Healey 2015) puts it that "until the lions [prey] produce their own historian, the story of the hunt will glorify only the hunter" (p. 11). It is sacrilegiously scandalous for Africans to keep on believing that their continent is poor and underdeveloped after over fifty years of shedding colonial chains. You do not need to be an economist to note that the West maltreated Africa almost in every sphere in order to, easily exploit it due to its discords as colonial leavings. The former has reinforced its hegemony on Africans either through ignorance or manipulations carried out by their own governments. Before concurring with any definition, it is important to ask many questions such as what is the definition all about, what agreed-upon criteria have been used and why. Being at home with somebody's definition of you is as good as committing suicide. It is only the dog and other pets that allow human to define them by assigning to them some tags.

As foregoing argued, Africa suffers from twofold causes of the definition of underdevelopment wherein there are some external and internal factors leading to a misleadingly generalised conclusion of Africa's underdevelopment. Thus, it is our aim to address both causes namely external and internal ones. Englebert (2000a, 2000b cited in Nunn 2007) observes that "imposed post-colonial institutions explain a significant proportion of the underdevelopment of the countries of sub-Saharan Africa" (p. 2). This is why the fact that there are some inadequacies in arbitrarily defining Africa based on the imposition makes more sense. It is true; especially if we underscore the fact that Africa's successes and failures have always been defined by the IFIs among others imperialistic tools of reinforcing modern imperialism (Rolfe 2008). Instead of drawing sweeping conclusions on whether Africa is truly poor and underdeveloped or not, we need to underscore the causes and reasons of such a predicament-cum-impasse. Everything that happens must have reasons. As argued above, development is a relative term. So, too, the causes of Africa's predicaments are relative in that some are internal while others are external. Henceforth, it is our duty to trace the causes of Africa's underdevelopment even though the said underdevelopment is controversial. This take is important. For, it aims at avoiding romanticising everything the West has produced as it has been for the so-called modernism as opposed to the traditionalism that has always been romanticised as a magic bullet even where it is an impediment. There is some underdevelopment and development under whatever lens used just like in any mortal society. Importantly, we must consider the causes of poverty, thus underdevelopment in real terms but not on factious ones whereby crucial aspects of the society–that would hugely contribute to defining true development; and thus true ranking–are ignored or purposely excluded. Bertocchi and Canova (2002) note that despite the elimination of "colonial drain", ex-colonies kept on paying for the consequences of their history even after gaining independence. In other words, it is absolutely nonsense to rate any victim country in development without considering the consequences of its history in the first place.

So, too, for whomever that wants to appropriately address the underdevelopment of the latter, mainly for Africa, must primarily address this external factor based on historical and current concocted realities as far as relationship between Africa and its former colonial masters is concerned, especially on defining development. This is crucial; because many so-called developed countries got their development by robbing the so-called underdeveloped and poor countries. Essentially, it takes two to tango. The question we need to ask ourselves is: What has Africa done; and still does to do away with such suffering from historical consequences? As urged above, the first and foremost suitable step out of this impasse, the latter in, is for it to define itself; instead of allowing its exploiters and enemies in the former to define it as it has been since the introduction of colonialism.

Furthermore, the latter needs to ask its former colonial masters to open their closets full of skeletons resulting from the crimes against humanity that they committed to Africa through colonialism and slavery. This is important given that the same culprits–instead of being brought to justice of whatever form under international laws–have been given another opportunity to get away with murder by setting terms of defining who is developed and who is underdeveloped. Africa needs to get its ducks in a row very; very well shall it aspire to get out of the quagmire it is in wantonly.

What makes the latter's situation impossibly untenable is the fact that the former has always sought to impose its formula of development; and make the latter believe it can attain development without underscoring historical realities revolving around former's development. Many thinkers want Africa to follow the same pattern and pathway to development while the real situation on the ground says differently. For example, some thinkers have proposed for Africa to follow the so-called stages of development namely the traditional society, preconditions for take-off, take-off, the drive to maturity and the age of high mass-consumption (Rostow cited in Izuchukwu 2011) without underscoring the fact that many so-called developed countries accumulate the capital by colonising and robbing others. To show how abusive misguidedly this chicanery is, (Lipietz 1987) insultingly compared the so called underdeveloped countries to children to adults (the so-called developed countries of the North representing adults). Who decided who is mature and who is immature based on what? As argued above, how do you equate countries such as Egypt, Ethiopia, Sudan or Zimbabwe to children while they are the oldest civilisations on earth? As indicated above, the final stage of development is the age of high mass-consumption. How can Africa develop by highly consuming massively while all it consumes comes from abroad? I would argue that the Global South need to industrialise based on its home needs before thinking about mass-consumption. Even lions in the wild consume massively since there are massive preys to consume. Telling Africa that it needs to highly consume massively without producing what it produces is as dangerous as telling the lions to massively consume goats or cows. Where will they get the cows without being in conflict with humans?

As if it is not enough, almost all prophets of copycat development preach production as the first means to achieving development. Well, Africa has never stopped producing. However, despite producing sufficiently, Africa suffers from exploitation ever since colonialism whereby its produces siphoned up to neo-colonialism in which price-fixing is rife not to mention conditions attached to the trade regime at the time. The aim of production is to accumulate capital. Again, how can Africa accumulate capital under exploitative international trade regime?

As argued above, there cannot be any notable development for the Global South:

a) By following Western pathway and formula;

b) Without deconstructing, restructuring and reconstituting the current international trade regime that is exploitative and racist by all standards;

c) Without reinvesting in profitable areas such as stopping producing for the external market without addressing home needs. For example, former-colonial masters duped many countries in the Global South making them believe that through producing the so-called cash crops, African countries do not consume, they would accumulate much money. Such a ruse ended up destroying Africa economically even more. For, because African countries do not consume the so-called cash crops, consumers in the West decided how much they must pay while the producers have no say in price setting.

Mhango (2016) calls cash crops "crush crops" because they have never ushered development in except crashing the economies of African countries under the ruse of making money in order to accumulate capital. Accumulating capital is not a bad idea save that it becomes bad when you tell a continent to do the same the way the West did. There are no more countries or world to conquer, colonise and rob currently. This would make sense for the victims of international robbery in which Africa needs redress and then talk about capital accumulation. I do not think African countries can currently accumulate as big capital as Britain or France did when they colonised Africa. Even the hype-touted countries in Asia tigers namely Hong Kong, South Korea, Singapore and Taiwan did not make it through without receiving aid and money by the same countries that looted Africa. Therefore, I can say that one of the major capital accumulation means for countries to develop is the capital that former colonial masters robbed Africa. There is need for those countries that robbed Africa to pay reparation.

Furthermore, Africa needs to cultivate a culture of self-reliance and self-valuing including self-defining. Mhango (2015) underscores the importance of reunifying Africa at the tune of how it was before 1884 when colonial powers partitioned Africa on the Berlin Conference of 1884-85. Arguably, without reuniting Africa, there is no way Africa can make any headways without being frustrated and sabotaged by the current colonial-created superstructure in whatever form be it the IFIs or unequal cooperation. It becomes hard to understand how Africa can get out of the impasse it is in without doing some things such as the reunification and thereby having the same policies and strategies as a single and united entity facing the same enemies and problems altogether. Such anathema-cum-anomaly–that Africa has always faced–interweaves external and internal causes in order to work together in making Africa what it is today whether you term it as underdeveloped or arrested development. Sometimes, it becomes hard to separated external and internal causes of Africa's 'underdevelopment' since the two forces reinforce each other purposely or accidentally. For the sake of clarity, this chapter discusses such factors separately. It is like ketchup wherein is difficult to separate eggs from mushrooms, oysters, mussels, walnuts, or other foods that make ketchup what it is.

iii) Doctrinaire Development

No doubts that some of Africa's quandaries resulting to the so-called its underdevelopment can, *inter alia*, be divided into two categories. The first causes can be attributed to colonial legacies almost in all spheres namely economic, political and social wherein Africa is culturally, geographically, historically and racially discriminated against so as to be easily exploited (Mhango *Ibid*.). Since 1884, when colonial powers from the former divided Africa into small and weak states, its traditional economy became extinct. Africans who used to live in collectivistic society, for the first time, experienced the rules of individualistic ways of life whereby every new country created at the Berlin Conference 1884 started to act solo. In addition, whenever such a country needed partners in whatever encounter, it looked at its colonial masters but not neighbours and sister states. You can see this in the economic and political models African countries employed after acquiring freedoms. All African countries fell into two camps namely the West or East camps that were involved in the Cold War. Even after the end of the cold war, Africa is not out of woods yet. Dunning (2004) argues that occasionally "the end of the Cold War could make threats to withhold development assistance to African states more credible" (p. 412). Thus, Africa seems to suffer even more economic and political setbacks under the unipolarity than it was under the cold war period at which the former Union of Soviet Socialist Republics (USSR) and China used to support some countries in deterring the influence of the West that supported countries on its fold and vice versa. Currently, such aid is no more, however hazardous it was. Goldsmith (2001) refers to this as a 'moral hazard' in which aid has cost Africa greatly. Presently, Africa is under multiparty democracy its former colonial masters superimposed on it. Economically, Africa's economy has always depended on the North in the relationship in which Africa plays the role of natural material supplier and consumer of processed goods from the same countries it supplies its natural or unprocessed resources. To make matter worse, China and Russia, that used to support some African countries simply because they were in their camp, are now scrambling for Africa with the West all aimed at going on enjoying its cheap resources.

As argued above, despite Africa playing the role of raw material supplier and processed goods consumer, is it really underdeveloped or poor? How possible with such abundant resources? Why those defining development do not include untapped resources or vibrant culture that Africa boasts of having? For, development or underdevelopment is the product of socio-economic and political culture of the people or society. Porter (2000) maintains that actually "economic geography in an era of global competition involves a paradox. It is widely recognised that changes in technology and competition have diminished many of the traditional roles of location" (p. 15). This means that traditional roles that global competitions felled based on hegemonic neoliberal policies, guarantee the exclusion of such roles in defining development. Such a take is obviously flaw in that the definition of development revolves around geographic locations wherein the perception is that the West is highly developed in comparison to the East. This take is not empirical due to the arguments above but socially constructed as it aims at reinforcing hegemony and colonial understanding as realities while they actually are not. For, if you look at the so-called Western countries, you find that some are in north others in West. To get away with murder, the now-favoured definition of such countries is the creation of the axis of North-South or West-East if not the First, Second and Third worlds. There cannot permanently be first, second and third world in everything. Somebody can be first in something while another can be second or third and vice versa but not orthodoxly first or last in everything as it is currently.

iv) Wake-up Call for Africa as a Specimen for the Latter

This section intends to act as a wakeup call for African countries to wise up and take their destiny in their hands by becoming self-reliant as they divorce the tendency of dependency as far as real and true development is concerned. The first step for Africa is doing away with the label of an underdeveloped continent. Instead, they must start with cultivating the culture of intellectual self-defining as opposed to allowing others to define Africa. Thereafter, Africa needs to question and interrogate whatever definitions those defining them propounded either about Africa or about world issues. Therefore, this section intends to put a finger on the crux of the matter. Since attaining their political independence, over fifty years ago, African countries have pointlessly, over and above, believed in and lived on aid that rich countries—mostly Western—have extended to them. Most of the African countries have their budgets, elections and other development project always been supported by these countries. To begin with, it is crucial to interrogate if the aid does help economies to grow in economic terms (Rajan and Subramanian 2008) in order to gauge if the economies of such countries have grown because of receiving aid. Additionally, Africa needs to gauge to see what will happen if the manner and trend of offering aid to these countries changes. This is important. It shows how the so-called development, sometimes, maybe elusive for such countries, especially when emphasis is put on material things; and thereby ignore nonmaterial things such as culture, morality and the environment. I do not think that countries renowned for polluting the earth are truly developed compared to those that do not pollute in addressing this development paradigm. Knowing what will happen will help African countries to start thinking about the less travelled way out of their predicaments. Lensink and Morrisey (2000) invoke endogamous theory to show how aid has never brought any development to African countries saying that it even affects growth determinant even on investment. This is obvious due to the fact that even when it comes to assessing, defining and gaging–if there is growth or not–the same donors have an upper hand *vis-à-vis* the modalities of research and the results obtained thereof. You can see this truth on the connection between aid and corruption. Mathiason (2005) and Blanchflower (2008) cited in Mac Ginty and Williams (2009) note with concern that in the year 2007 worldwide overseas development assistance was $103 billion whose big chunk ended up being paid to Western consultants (p. 14). Again, how much does Africa lose in such corruption spearheaded by Western companies? The African Union (AU) Report cited in Ribadu (2009) answers the above question. It notes that corruption drains the region of some $140 billion a year, which is about 25% of the continent's official GDP (p. 2). Ironically, despite Western countries involved in such mega corruption sponsoring such corporations, they never receive the tag of corruption. There is a duality in committing crimes. Here I am talking about Western corporations. What is the fate of African venal rulers such as Joseph Mobutu (former Zaire, now the Democratic Republic of Congo (DRC) Sani Abacha (Nigeria) and Omar Bongo (Gabon) among others? Wrong (2005) discloses that:

> In 1999, the Economist estimated that African leaders had stowed $20bn in Swiss bank accounts. Investigations in Kenya after

President Daniel arap Moi left office indicated that, at the very least, $1bn had been sent overseas by former officials. University of Massachusetts researchers have estimated that from 1970 to 1996, capital flight from 30 sub-Saharan countries totalled $187bn, outstripping those same nations' external debt (p. 1).

It is obvious that countries whose rulers involved in this mega theft were categorised as underdeveloped due to being pauperised. Who is holding, for example, Switzerland with its advanced and big economy whose success results from looted monies from the so-called underdeveloped countries? Ironically, despite being the accessory to the crime, you will hear the same Switzerland offering aid to Africa. Actually, what many Western countries offer to Africa as aid is but the surplus resulting from robbing Africa either, as indicated above, through bogus consultancy or syphoning raw materials. Despite such criminality, modern definition of development views Switzerland as a highly developed country. This is because of the exclusion of the moral aspect that ties it to robbery in defining development.

Additionally, Hickel (2013) notes that:

> Robert Pollin, an economist at the University of Massachusetts, estimates that developing countries have lost roughly $480 billion in potential GDP as a result of structural adjustment. Yet, Western corporations have benefitted tremendously. It has forced open vast new consumer markets; it has made it easier to access cheap labour and raw materials; it has opened up avenues for capital flight and tax avoidance; it has created a lucrative market in foreign debt; and it has facilitated a massive transfer of public resources into private hands (the World Bank alone has privatised more than $2 trillion worth of assets in developing countries).

Due to material drive and cultural and moral exclusionary flimflam in defining and rating countries in development, the figures above never received any consideration. You can see how such huge amounts of money stolen from Africa lack in categorising or rating countries *vis-a-vis* development or underdevelopment. I cannot understand the rationale behind such ignorance and exclusionary tactics the West has always applied on Africa almost in everything sensible and meaningful. What is clear though is the fact that Western countries are maltreating Africa in order to make Africans internalise such anomaly in order to subscribe to the belief that Africans cannot live without depending on aid.

Essentially, what the media report, in the main, depend on how donor countries want it preferably, in many cases, such coverage must favour their verdict even if it is wrong. Hydén (1980) provides an answer that, when it comes to defining development and underdevelopment, Western countries–apart from having an upper hand–are privileged; because they are the birthplace of the school of thought that dominates official debate about the issue in question, namely [under-]development. Whether aid is a causal force or otherwise behind growth to African economies is subject to discussion. There are arguments that [under-]development at an individual country level is always differently positive and negative depending on how the country abides by the conditions donor countries stipulate. Dollar and Easterly (1999) note that "getting down to individual countries, a 1996 report on Uganda argued that any aid reduction 'could be harmful for medium-term growth in Uganda, which requires external inflows…" (p. 4). However, if we consider how Uganda, at the time of realising the report was the darling of the West, chances are that such findings aimed at showing how donor money had performed its miracles to the country. Oloka-Onyango (2004) tells why Uganda in the cited report seems to be an exception to the general rule. He notes that this is because Uganda has always safeguarded US's interests in the GLR. The US does not fail its ally in anything be it legal or illegal, acceptable or unacceptable. Therefore, sometimes, the so-called development or underdevelopment depends on the personality instead of the actuality. Oloka-Onyango goes on lucubrating on how Museveni was able to garner supports from Western bigwigs due to maintaining close ties from Margaret Thatcher through John Major and up to Tony Blair. More on why Museveni became a shining star comes from Hauser (1999) who argues that, essentially "in Uganda, a high level of donor support for the Museveni government has been compatible with the Ugandan government's reluctance to introduce multiparty democracy. Donors have opted for 'dialogue' rather than coercive methods'" (p. 621). Try to compare this with what happened when Gaddafi decided to become a good boy of the West; and what transpired after he did the opposite leading to his toppling; and later demise. Practically, the US–that leads the West in this business of safeguarding their interests in Africa–has neither a permanent friend nor a permanent foe except permanent interests. Easterly (2009) notes that development goals are unfair to Africa due to the strings attached to aid that Africa receives.

In addressing the major question, I will explore the conditions or strings attached to aid and the role aid plays in realising development in Africa, *inter alia*. It is empirical to explore what donors expect to get out the aid extended to African countries; and above all, how the aid is used. Examining the nature, role and intentions of aid becomes important because almost every powerful country has interests in Africa while Africa does not have any interests in these countries. Under such unequal relationship, devoid of inequitable reciprocity, the outcomes are obvious that whoever complies with aid conditions, donors will view such an entity successful however temporarily as it was in the case of Uganda. Regarding having interests to protect in Africa for foreign non-African countries, it is clear the West is not alone. Currently, China and India are seeking leverage in Africa, all aimed at safeguarding their interests, too, at the detriments of Africa. To do so, the duo are extending aid in order to gain leverage by winning hearts and minds of African rulers who are the only ones that decide who should have sphere of influence or not. This is the second scramble for Africa after the first that ushered in colonial rule in Africa. My assumption is that, if there is no equal and equitable reciprocity, donors are likely to benefit while the recipients lose in the name of aid, as it has been the case for Africa. Current example on Tanzania shows how aid has never benefited Africa, among many other African countries. After suffering for a long time in the hands of donors, Tanzania's Government recently urged its people to end donor dependence. This happened when the Millennium Challenge Corporate (MCC), an independent U.S Government foreign aid agency, cancelled aid. Staff (2016) reports that Tanzania won a five-year package of grants in 2008 worth $698 million from the MCC cancelled a second round of grants.

Although I do not condone election fraud Tanzania is accused of to have occurred in Zanzibar, essentially, what Tanzanian government thought it was aid from the MCC seems to have been more verbal than practical just like the project that gave birth to all this namely, the Millennium Development Goals (MDGs). Pronk (2004) claims that the MDGs are not global; and they have become vague or unbalanced as the inducements work on the favour of donors even when their terms are not clearly stated or promises kept.

I can logically argue that donor community wanted to use inducement to have sort of unchecked powers to control Tanzania something that is replicated almost in all Africa countries. For the country that produced tanzanite, gold, and other precious minerals in tonnes, what is $698 million if it manages its resources well? Tanzania–that faced such a denial of already promised aid–produces natural gas; is the home of Lake Victoria, the largest national park Serengeti and many more among resources that the country has. Yet, in categorising and defining economic development of the country, such economic bases miss in the equation. Shekighenda (2016) quotes Tanzania's president, John Pombe Magufuli, as saying that his country was to stand on its own; and it will persevere. This was after the MCC denied his country the monies. If this was not out of anger, many African leaders need to think this way so that they can creatively and responsibly thwart such dependency in order to pull their countries out of wanton beggarliness and thereby define their levels of development based on their own criteria. Ironically, when donor countries default on their promises no punitive measures are taken against them simply because 'blessed is the hand that giveth than the one that taketh' one may argue. So, too, recipients have no authority to question their donors which emanates from colonial legacy. Africa needs to, radically and systematically, change this anomaly-cum-anathema.

More fundamentally, Africa, if indeed wants to become free and prosperous, needs to think out of aid-dependency box; and stop living on handouts while it is sitting on immense untapped resources. I wonder why such huge reserves of minerals and resources are not included in the formula of rating development. Yes, it baffles to find a country that has no resources such as Switzerland–whose economy, *inter alia,* depends on stolen money–ranks higher in development than countries like the DRC with all huge land mass and resources.

Besides defaulting, donors apply various ruses to dupe poor countries. An ideal example is the whole project known as the Heavily Indebted Poor Countries (HIPC) that the World Bank (WB) initiated in 1996 aimed at cancelling debts for some highly indebted countries of which many are in Africa. If you look at HIPC's *modus operandi*, you find that it is more a hoax if not a ruse to lull poor countries into more debts than a serious commitment to alleviate or fight poverty in poor countries. Cohen (2001) notes that:

> Present value calculations, however, do not scale down the service of the debt by the probability that it will be honoured, nor (which almost amounts to the same thing) by the likelihood that the debt will have to be refinanced (either through new loans, explicitly rescheduling or arrears) (p. 9).

Is there any relief that the cancelling of debt brought to African countries or it is just tinkering around the edges? How many countries came out of poverty; thus, out of underdevelopment? Moyo (2009) notes that debt cancellation by adding more debts–not to mention serving the debts–creates; and thereby perpetuates vicious-debt circle for Africa. Such a situation has over and above enhanced corruption and visionless regimes that have ruled Africa for a long time. What do you expect when you sink millions of dollar in such a hole? The DRC, under Mobutu's kleptocratic regime, provides an ideal example of how debts become a burden to many African countries. This does not mean that donor countries do not know this danger. Theirs has always been the rip off in poor countries provided there are guarantees that such countries will pay their debts in the future. Reno (1997 cited in Wright 2008) observes that Mobutu's regime in the former Zaire fell from 17.5% of government spending in 1972 to 2% in 1990, and agricultural spending (mostly subsidies) fell from over 40% of the budget to 11% in 1990. Meanwhile, during that time, the president's share of the budget increased from 30% to 95% (p. 974). While Zaire, now the DRC, was cascading to poverty; hence to underdevelopment, the countries that conspired with Mobutu to rob Zaïre, enjoyed the accolade of being developed. If moral aspect been included in the elements used to rate countries development– it is obvious–such countries would not feature high in development. What such blind rating does is like rating a thug as a richest person on earth without underscoring the fact that the wealth the said thug purports to own belongs to others. As argued above, countries such as Switzerland and other heavens for illicit money are not supposed to be rated without incorporating moral aspect in the whole process. This is the argument Africa and the so-called underdeveloped countries should rise in order to partake of the process of analysing and rating development.

v) **Conclusion**

> *As powerful as history is, and you need to know that history, at some point you have to look to the future and say, 'OK, we didn't get a good deal then, but let's make sure that we're not making excuses for not going forward* Barack Obama cited in Shearlaw (2014).

The quote above reminds the duo of their responsibility. Although Obama, as a leader of the strongest country in the former is trying to justify their crimes, he has a point that the duo needs to sit down and look at things as they are. Again, is it fair for the former to blame the latter for complaining? No sane person can just complain like a newly born baby without any logical reasons. Politics aside, Africa has all rights to complain, as it is for the former that has all blames for the predicament of the latter.

Suffice it to say, whether Africa is underdeveloped or otherwise is like a myth that needs to be troubled and demystified, especially for the Africans whose role in reaching such a conclusion is amiss. As indicated in this discourse, nothing makes sense to many–predominantly those who do not subscribe to such a conclusion. For, many criteria used to define development are wanting. So, too, those who appointed such criteria have ignored so many more important elements that would make sense had they been considered in reaching the conclusion. Therefore, the demystification of the said myth is looming and crucial to be done in order to get a fitting definition resulting from a dialogue on what should be exclude and what should be included and why. Furthermore, there is nobody who can do this job except African academics who need to address the matter academically and courageously. To do away with being referred to as an underdeveloped continent, Africa needs to face those defining and ranking and make sure it has a say in the process in order to be part of it. Africa, like any human society, is the home of the humans and animals wherein humans run it. Therefore, it is an insult to keep on defining Africa as if Africans cannot propound their own definitions of whatever they form part. I can say that, at this point and time, Africa needs to reorganise itself to see to it that it changes the way it has been doing things after the results proved that the ground is tilted; and things have never worked to its favour. Suppose Africa redefines its economy modal based on its needs by producing what it can locally consume before embarking on producing for the external market. It is obvious that Africa does not have guts as Europe in terms of technology development. Again, it still heavily depends on agriculture for consumption and for export; and this takes a big chunk of Africa's agro-outputs. Given that Africa has never had any say in price setting, it needs to produce what it can have a say on and consume altogether first. Many farmers produce cash crops to end up spending a little money they get on purchasing foods of which some are pointlessly imported.

Furthermore, Africa needs to, markedly stop trusting whoever comes to it with whatever from definition to models of production or economy. Importantly, Africa effectively needs to come up with its own economic model and policies in order to get out of elusive and manmade underdevelopment as defined by the West. To begin with, we now know where the confusion-cum-problem of rating Africa as underdeveloped emanates. It is upon the victims to see things in their true colours so that they can do something about it quickly and urgently. Complaining is Africa's right. Again, complaining is not the pretext of staying side and look as if those affected are not victims who have suffered for over five decades. The way towards really and sustainable development lies on Africa's awakening to see to it that it takes its destiny into its hands. Moreover, doing so is nowhere except in taking charge of defining the terms of whatever that it is; Africa is part of. That is it.

Chapter Seven

Case two: Violence, Power, Politics and (Anti-) Development in Africa

i) Introduction

The first instalment about Africa's [under-] development which ties in with the title of this instalment in that they all deal with development. The first one is about underdevelopment while this is about anti-development resulting from the relationship in question. Since the Global North introduced its administrational systems in the Global South, Africa has evidenced many violent conflicts resulting from power struggles across the continent. Soon after acquiring independence, many African countries found themselves facing *coup d'états* not to mention other types of squabbling among local elites scrambling for controlling the reins of power as the automatic means of controlling resources Africa is endowed with. Nothing motivates such greedy local elites as the market in the Global North.

Arguably, African politics in the post-colonial era evidenced many underdevelopments resulting from anti-development nature of power struggles in many countries, especially countries that were under military juntas or corrupt dictators who divided their people along ethnic and ideological lines in order to exploit and rule them easily. In tackling violence, power, politics and anti-development, I explore, *inter alia,* the divide-and-rule strategy that colonial powers employed viciously and perpetually to arrest Africa's development and future. The colonising power heinously entrenched acrimonies and division in African politics and powers based on violence as the major cause of Africa's underdevelopment by Europe (Rodney 1972) all aimed at serving colonial interests through neocolonialism after colonial masters exited Africa temporarily under the ploy of independence. Since African countries got independence and thereafter, European way of doing things, thanks to aping almost everything from the former, has always influenced African politics.

African governments, parliaments and other national institutions are but Europe's typical replicas. The Global South currently has almost all political and institutional settings mainly based on European models as opposed to the ones countries in the South had for many centuries before the arrival of European colonisers in the late eighteenth century when they "officially" put their stamp on world's politics. To underscore how Africa fared before the introduction of colonialism, one needs to ask a question: Were there any political and institutional systems in Africa before? The answer is obvious and simple. There were a lot of them on the African soil, some of which were even at par or above European ones. Dahomey provides an ideal example to show and prove how some African societies were ahead of European ones. Claessen (1987) note that "the Dahomean governmental system, that was used in the ancient Kingdom of Dahomey in modern West Africa was large and complex. Several categories of officials and functionaries can be distinguished" (p. 210) from where, or from whose, if not Europe? Essentially, the art of administration is nothing new to Africa just like any society given that even some animals and insects run their groups through certain types and settings of administration. What makes the current administrational system new is the fact that Africa adopted European systems of administration as its colonial relics and carryovers if not hangovers. Dahomey's example provides a window into how African societies run their affairs and organised themselves before being colonised.

What evidence else is needed to prove such claim? There is much evidence subscribing to the fact that Africa was not as redundant and underdeveloped as many European bigots alleged; and others still maintain. It defies logic for a person or people who sanely portray themselves as civilised in their right frame of mind to argue that Africa was redundant and primitive as far as governing systems are concerned. What does "complex and distinguishable categories" mean if we face it? On how advanced and developed Africa was, I do not want to touch on Egypt, the giant of civilisations of the world. I, therefore, address myself to what brought Africa to a vile situation it is in today. I use only one facet of colonial lies and plots, divide-and-rule, as a strategy colonisers used to explore the four concepts this chapter tackles. I will try as much as I can to avoid venturing outside because there are many ploys that European colonial masters employed to deceive themselves and the world that Africa was devoid of anything to do with civilisation.

However, for matters of clarity, I may venture out a little bit, however, my focal point will be on divide and rule as the harbinger of violence, power struggles, divisive politics and anti-development practices as evidenced in Africa from the colonial era. I must state from the outset that violence, power, politics, and anti-development are the sour fruits of malicious colonialism and its machinations those with colonial mentality and malice against Africa maintained as means of subduing and exploiting Africa perpetually. I will base my argument, as argued prior on divide-and-rule strategy based on ethnopolitical dimensions of African society, continent and country.

Although the parties to conflict are responsible for most of ethnic and ethnopolitical conflicts Africa is currently facing and suffering from, they have all hallmarks of colonial strategy famously known as divide and rule. European colonial monsters—I honestly like to use—instead of masters given that they were nobody's masters except monsters that devoured our continent (Mhango 2015) introduced, and used this strategy aimed at easily weakening, sabotaging and exploiting their former colonies that indirectly went on becoming neo-colonies. However, in many cases, the strategy of divide-and-rule colonisers—who are all from the Global North—used to create and fuel negative ethnicity and ethnopolitical conflicts in many places they colonised, went unnoticed.

In this instalment, I seek to show, and thereby prove, how the divide and rule created many ethnic and ethnoconflicts in the former, especially the ones that Africa is witnessing today. For example, through segregating, pitting one against another, and favouring one against another, European colonial masters created identity conflicts in Africa that have haunted the victims even after colonisers physically left the continent. Carter, Irani and Volkan (2009) identify two major causes of ethnopolitical conflicts namely 1) identity and 2) politics; maintaining that "neither identity nor values are negotiable" (p. 302), principally when they have the baggage resulting from artificiality and negativity attached to them as the former created them.

Undeniably, under divide and rule, colonial masters from the former reinvented their victims based on, *inter alia*, pseudo-physiological and historical features of the groups in order to create new and artificial, as well as, antagonistic entities; that ended up turning each against each another. This is what the inventors and the perpetrators of this heinous systemic crime against humanity that have hanged on up until now envisioned. Burundi and Rwanda, whose ethnic conflicts have been intermittently ongoing since the introduction of colonialism, provide an ideal example. In creating such acrimony, Germany, Belgian and French colonial masters used physiological features such as the heights and the noses to indicate that Tutsis were superior to Hutus which they did maliciously knowing how it was a sheer lie that went on up to 1994 culminating in the genocide that shocked the world. Even when the international community knew prior that genocide would take place in Rwanda, it just ignored such warnings. This proves how the former has maintained divide and rule even after some countries in the former became independent.

Essentially, after divide and rule was introduced in these the countries above wherein the warring communities used to live harmoniously and cooperatively before, natural identities of the these communities were completely altered so as to give rise to artificial and fake ones the victims used to disparage, discriminate against, and exterminate each other wantonly. Unfortunately, given that the victims blindly and gullibly accepted their artificial new identities, they did not venture outside of the box by trying to assuage or terminate such artificiality of their identities. For, even when Germany and Belgian colonial masters lost these two colonies after losing in their wars in Europe, French colonial masters who took over, expanded on this poisonous system thereafter. As if it was not enough, post-colonial governments in these two countries reinforced this identity artificiality and toxicity that, as argued above, culminated to genocide in Rwanda. French colonial masters used the same elements of hatred and deception to fuel divisions among Hutus and Tutsis in two countries even after acquiring independence. McNulty (2000) maintains that:

> France, uniquely in Europe, prides itself on having a global humanitarian mission, and evidence that this "homeland of human rights" was implicated in genocide through its military support until 1994 for the extremist regime in Rwanda shocked many who had applauded the declared pro-democracy, pro-humanitarian stance of President Mitterrand since 1981 (p. 105); also see Kuperus (2016).

Apart from Burundi and Rwanda, the DRC provides an ideal example. As mentioned prior, the former once did the same in the DRC after some neighbouring countries invaded and plundered it. Instead of forcing the invaders to get out of the DRC; and thereby face international laws, the former became the destination for many resources plundered from the DRC. Coltan has always featured high as one of the resources that rich countries get from the DRC. According to the News (2010), coltan is a heat-resistant material that can hold a strong electrical charge, mainly used to make capacitors used in a wide variety of electronic devices, from cell phones, avionics to nuclear reactors. Coltan is, also used in high-heat-resistant steel alloys for applications such as aircraft engines. Due to the role coltan plays in the economies of rich countries and its high demand, many beneficiaries ignore the conflict or just offer lip services to it as it has been since the conflict started in the DRC. Nathan and Sarkar (2011) refer to cell phones as "blood mobile phones"; and they want the international community to declare mobile phones illegal just like it did with the blood diamond that used to fuel wars in Liberia and Sierra Leone. After illegalising and declaring blood diamond, the conflicts in the two countries were resolved and thereby, the suffering these countries faced subsided or ended. Due to the international divide and rule, the West has failed to illegalise coltan as means of putting a stop on the conflict in the DRC. The failure to illegalise and declare coltan illegal and bloody and cell phones blood cell phones shows how the whole world can be blamed on fuelling, and benefiting from the conflict in the DRC. I, therefore, advance that, in a sense, whoever uses cell phones; voluntarily or involuntarily fuels and funds the war in the DRC.

ii) Proxy Recolonisation and Extension of Divide-and-Rule

Because colonial masters changed the shape and manners of colonising their former colonies by recolonising through homemade black colonialists, or call them, stooges who stodgily perfected the art of division, even after theatrically relinquished their colonies, they kept on interfering in the business of these countries. They kept their grip on power by taking sides or reinforcing and perpetrating divisive politics based on power struggles among various artificial communities they created in many countries facing ethnic conflicts. Under such politics, there evolved division along *hoi polloi* and *hoity toity* not to mention the North-South divide. Despite this being contrary to the law and the meaning of independence, colonial masters never received any reprimand or redressed their victims under the international laws that seem to favour the North as opposed to the South. Again, due to the anarchical and unfair nature of the international system, for example, Belgium, Germany and France have never faced any criminal liability for the genocide they authored and fuelled in Rwanda. Such international political racism brings us to the fact that all types of powers, be they political, social or economical in the Global South, especially in Africa, are still artificial and much more are still controlled by the Global North which authored colonialism based on divide and rule. Arguably, before this knife that—to borrow from Chinua Achebe, slit their cord of harmonious coexistence and interdependence in Africa so as to fall apart, two societies in Burundi and Rwanda used to live peacefully cooperating in happiness and grief before the introduction of colonialism that left them perpetually divided and antagonised wantonly. Regarding ethnopolitical conflicts, that colonialism created and fostered, local elites, in many countries in the latter, egoistically and blindly use and fuel them; in order to easily and heinously reach their artificial and short time goals. Wimmer, Cederman and Min (2009) note that such a move is a pretext of protecting or advocating the rights and the wellbeing of "'their peoples' which provides incentives to align political loyalties along ethnic divides" (p. 317) as opposed to their natural harmonious and coexistent relationship based on interdependence and cooperation. Such toxic politics of "our people" versus "their peoples" does not dwell on issues as far as seeking and using socio-political and economic power are concerned.

Worse enough, most of, if not all political parties, in countries facing toxic and negative ethnicity or ethnoconflicts in the Global South, are formed along ethnic lines which many scholars such as Marx, and Durkheim, among others, thought would disappear as societies modernised. Newman (1991) faults the early 1970s scholars who argued that ethnic conflict would subside with the emergence of 'modern' societies as defined and espoused by the former. Again, they got it wrong given that most of such scholars were Europeans who wrongly thought that Africa would follow the same trend Europe followed to reach at what they wrongly refer as modernity. Due to such biased and misguided assumptions Western thinkers propound, there arises a need for African thinkers to revisit the root causes of ethnic conflict based on colonialism. This is the workable mechanism they need to follow instead of wasting time thinking that 'modernity' would solve the problem while it actually has exacerbated it due to allowing exploitative laws and systems to become what is referred to as international institutions. As long as colonial systems regulating African economic, political and social power remain the same, the problem that ethnicity and conflict pose, will grow even bigger. For, if we examine the polities and policies under which Africa convenes elections and forms governments, it can be found that everything revolves along ethnicity almost in all countries facing antagonistic ethnicity such as Burundi, Rwanda, Nigeria, Kenya and the Central Africa Republic (CAR), among others.

Regarding deliberating upon how to form political parties that are used as representative vehicles in forming governments, instead of dwelling on human needs based on justice, equality and parity, groups forming such parties dwell on personalities, particularly "who is ours" and "who is not ours" all based on their fake and superimposed ethnicity and loyalty to the group. In so doing, those ascribing to such machinations, create artificial enemies due to their artificiality in seeing things. Like father, like son. Given that the protagonists, the Global North, maliciously and artificially invented and created, they, too, fall to and follow the same diabolic and misleading pattern by creating obnoxious and artificial enemies among those naturally and practically deemed to be their brothers and sisters as it is in the case of the two examples provided above among others in Africa. Instead of looking in their tool box as far as their future is concerned, the protagonists found themselves entrapped in the impasse so as to fail to underscore the fact that "the future lies in mustering all our energy to design imaginative but viable alternatives" (Max-Neef, Elizalde and Hopenhayn., 1992: 197). Instead of cooperatively and creatively looking for and forging strategies to overcome the impasse the groups ferociously and blindly find themselves in, the parties to the conflict reinforce and internalise everything for their self-destruction due to their acceptance of artificial animosity and negativity based on artificial reasons. The politics of "our-turn-to-eat" (Burgess, Jedwab, Miguel and Morjaria 2010) in Kenya provides an ideal example of how ethnicity can blind and hijack people even if such people are viewed as educated. Instead of doing justice, such politics revolves around ethnical favouritism, vote rigging, and sometimes, results into persecution and violence after merits become nothing. Additionally, arguably, co-ethnicity becomes merits. The situation becomes worse given that most of those running the show are the ones many presume to be elites or enlighten ones. Once such allegiance–based on tunnel and destructive view colonisers maliciously, blindly and artificially created based on bastardised and misrepresented ethnicity–causes fear and stalling which complicate and exacerbate the conflict even more so that all parties to conflict become completely blindly unaware of the human rights and needs of others. Olick and Robbins (1998: 106) cited in Armstrong and Crage (2006) argue that "collective memories are "images of the past" that social groups select, reproduce, and commemorate through "particular sets of practices" (p. 725) that are obviously destructive to the protagonists and productive to their inventors. While toxic ethnicity resulted to genocide in Rwanda, in Kenya, it resulted to the 2007 Post-Election Violence (PEV) (Roberts 2009). Under such ethnical rationale based on the allegiance and alliance to the group, it becomes harder to avoid the politics that author anti-development for the society. When such politics of fear and hatred kicks in, the affected countries experience what happened during the elections in Kenya in 2007-08 whereby over a thousand innocent people lost their lives simply because they were not the members of the community that killed them. Instead of thinking and behaving like Kenyans, people altered and chose the identities they thought would protect them and their interests however wrong and deceptive this was. Such colonial carryovers have affected even our much-touted Western democracy that totally failed to address this problem as it occurred in Kenya, among others.

As regards to the needs of the societies and people, the electorate or the constituency–in such ethnopolitics–does not address issues; instead, it revolves around the "us" versus "them" axis. Local elites use this division to strengthen the in-group solidarity and in fighting as well; all aimed at getting away with the murder by taking the members for a ride. Under such toxic ethnopolitics, elites preach fear and hatred in order to make those they deem to be "their people" to conceive and see the danger their farfetched 'enemies' pose. Essentially, such toxic and negative ethnicity and politics always produce the "politics of fear." In such pointlessly antagonistic politics, it is easy to see how divide and rule plays its role of reinventing and creating fake thinkers and fake beings based on lies and machinations that aim at weakening and subduing group members ready for exploiting them. The victims of divide-and-rule strategy do not see things the way they actually are; but, instead, they use the lenses of fear and suspicion resulting from hatred caused by divisions ensued after the malicious creation of such artificial entities entangled in an artificial conflict whose effects may lead to endemic and permanent negative effects to the protagonists. For the victims of divide and rule to treat others unfair is a fair thing to do. You can see how blind such ethnopolitics cause in Rwanda where the minority Twas, a minority society made of pigmies, was not considered in the preparations for genocide. For Hutu extremists, Twas did not exist and, if they did, they did not matter. When the killings between Hutus and Tutsis started, Twas, just like anybody else, had to flee their country simply because two powerful communities were at each other's neck. Swahili sage has it that wars are always blind.

iii) The role of Parties to Conflicts in Resolving the Conflict

Principally, it is important to carefully, rigorously and open-mindedly examine and explore divide-and-rule and the way various colonial masters maliciously created and employed it in various countries as a vehicle and tool of reaching their heinous goals of colonising, exploiting and running colonies cheaply and easily. Arguably, I seek to adduce some evidence from Africa, and if need be, Asia and Europe, to support the arguments made and solutions prescribed. Therefore, I carefully and honestly explores the strategy of divide and rule from when it was invented—at colonial time—to the aftermath of colonialism in various places in Africa. By so doing, I want to substantiate; and show the legacies and the consequences of the strategy, especially at the modern times when Africa the Global North accuses Africa of not doing its homework timely and rightly. In its attempts to get rid itself of the consequences of such chicanery as colonial powers maliciously enacted, Africa gets it wrong. For, many countries in the South tend to invite and trust the same enemies with the hopes that they can solve their problems not to mention the conflicts while they want to reinforce and advance them to their advantage that is the peril of many countries in the Global South.

It makes more sense to survey, explore, criticise and, in the end, offer some recommendations of whatever nature and undertakings the Global South takes as means of addressing the conflicts all aimed at transforming or resolving them if not positively managing them. Therefore, I offer my recommendations based on the deconstruction and unveiling all flaws and malice behind whatever strategies the colonial masters enacted and reinforced in the minds and psyches of their victims. Such recipes act as the means of avoiding or dealing with ethnic and ethnopolitical conflicts in constructive and innovative ways all aimed at helping those entrapped in them out of them productively. The deconstruction of the strategy of divide and rule is a good measure aimed at stopping the repetition of the mistakes and flaws by maintaining superimposed divisions, fake identities and difference among victims among other things.

So, too, I strongly propose reparations of the victims by their oppressors aimed at helping the duo to deal with the effects of imperialism that followed after colonial masters left their former colonies. Importantly, I cogently urge parties to the conflict to seek what unites them instead of clinging to what divides them. Here history provides a good prospect of resolving the conflict productively based on the opportunities the conflict offers. Methinks and argue that members of such artificially created ethnicities must revisit their past, for example, for Burundi and Rwanda, they must cautiously and judiciously explore how they lived and fared before the introduction of colonialism. Mhango (2016) proposes the deconstruction of the strategy of divide and rule by urging its victims to turn it upside down in order to unite and rule themselves as they like. This discourse, as critical as is, calls such attempts to resolve such ethnic conflict the reversed nature of the problem whereby they can get a solution by reversing everything. Instead of looking forward to get the solution, the victims must look backward in order to move forward. This is logical; given that what transpired amidst them in the past is easy to trace compared to predicting the future that ignores the past of the victims. As argued above, in so doing, the parties to the conflict must seek all nuggets that used to unite them as they put aside anything and everything that fosters or fuels divisions and animosity among them.

Moreover, it is important for the victims to seek their own ways of justices be they restorative, distributive even collective ones. Despite their shortfalls, Gacaca Courts in Rwanda provide an ideal example of how victims can deal with their own conflict conditionally that they do it in a transparent, constructive and goodwill all aimed at getting out of the impasse and moving forward. It is unfortunate that Africa allows those who created and fuelled its many ethnic conflicts to resolve them based on their own type of justice that does not fit and help the victims. The current ethnoconflict in the CAR provides an ideal example. France, CAR's former colonial master that ridiculously created the division in the country is now messing even more by investing and banking on militaristic means instead of rebuilding relationship among the protagonists. In many cases, foreign interventions in conflict in Africa seek to; synchronously help the victims while at the same time protecting the interests of those interfering as opposed to the interests of the victims. Others interfere in the conflict in order to seek leverage or show off internationally as any hegemonic state would like to do. Clark (1998) maintains that, for example, "France has managed to preserve its rank as first regional security provider, although by default, mainly in crisis situations (including in the Ivory Coast, Mali, and the CAR)" (p. 5). Ironically, despite this reality to be all over the place *vis-a-vis* foreign interventions, many African countries (Rwanda excluded) still pin their hopes on them while they actually know that foreign intervention revolves around self-serving and self-promoting at the expenses of the victims. On their part, African thinkers and politicians need to underscore this anomaly; and thereby make sure that they empower their own people instead of depending on foreigners to maintain their power. Such foreign interventions, given that involve foreigners who do not know the history of the victims or those who misrepresented and alter the true history of the victims, do not help anything except reinforcing the divide and rule strategy based on conditionality such interveners set for the victims to be helped.

The DRC provides another ideal example. When Burundi, Rwanda and Uganda supported Laurent Kabila to topple DRC's long-time dictator, Joseph Desire Mobutu, later Mobutu Seseseko, Congolese thought that the trio was helping them to rid them of the parasite while it actually wanted to plunder their resources that attracted opportunists from within and without to take advantage of shaky government after Mobutu fell. As argued above, Burundi, Rwanda, and Uganda helped Kabila and later invaded the DRC in order to plunder the resources. Griggs (1996) argues that "the geostrategic interests of Zairean Tutsis Rwanda Burundi and Uganda were laid bare in October 1996 with the creation of pro-Tutsi controlled 300km strip of eastern Zaire from Uvira to south Goma in North" (p. 70). Now, local Congolese Tutsis invited their colleagues from neighbouring countries renowned for having exploding populations with scarce land and resources. You can see how the card of ethnicity played a great role in the ethnic conflict that ended up becoming an international conflict. Essentially, this Tutsi strip is the result of the demarcation of the country the colonial masters did in 1884 during the scramble for and partition of Africa whose internal effects is the division of some societies in more than one country. Here is very possible see how divided and rule does not only end on people but also on their land. Again, if we consider the relationship between Tutsis and non-Tutsis in the region, chances are that ethnicity has a great role to play in this setting. Jackson (2006) argues that "Secret Council" of Tutsi elders obsessed with the "purity of their race" (p. 109) which in Conflict Resolution Field is called "the chosen ones mentality" still pull strings. Given that colonial masters invented negative and toxic ethnicity to perpetuate exploitation based on superiority (for the exploiters) and inferiority (for exploited) complexes, one can see how toxic such ethnicity can be. Vlassenroot and Huggins (2005) argue that the DRC makes a good target for local opportunists due to the fact that "there are natural resources of much greater value, and much more 'lootable' character, than agricultural or pastoral land" (p.119). This is in itself provides motivation for warlords to put their hands on whatever brings money quickly. Horowitz (1985 cited in Byrne and Irvin 2000) observes that "ethnic conflict is at the centre of politics in divided societies" (ix). The conflict in the DRC also has all hallmarks of divide and rule whereby Tutsis famously known as Banyamulenge have been playing an important role supported by Rwanda and Uganda based on sharing ethnic ties. Also important is the fact that after Kabila toppled Mobutu easily, there was created an assumption-cum-precedent that anybody with a good backing can topple the government and thereof control the reins of power that directly accord him control over resources. In such a greedy and cutthroat situation, whoever that has numbers from 'his people" or allies can come to power and serve himself/herself with his people as it happened to Kabila after taking over.

iv)   Ethnoconflicts and Resources

Due to benefiting from the plundering of the DRC, the international community cares much about its interests even if doing so means trampling on the rights of victims in the DRC. Montague (2002) argues that, after the international community distancing itself, the invaders, and the warlords seized the opportunity of militarising even the economy of the DRC; and thereby became combat economy. Ballentine and Nitzschke (2005) argue that such in the military or combat economy wherein the security apparatus of the state (military, paramilitary groups, police) and rebel groups, as well as, domestic and foreign allows conflict entrepreneurs support and fuel the conflict in order to benefit from it as it has always been since the conflict broke out in the DRC. If we consider the fact that such institutions mentioned above, are under the management of men as it has been in a patriarchal society, gender exploitation becomes higher, especially when rape and sexual exploitation are committed with impunity; because the international community, after distancing itself from the conflict, has always turned the blind eye. Again, toxic ethnicity gives birth to another calamity namely gender violence. Once such indifference becomes the order of the day, chances of gender-related violence to be committed are high. Defeis (2008) notes that "nothing discredits the United Nations more than the continuing sexual abuse of women and girls by soldiers belonging to its international peacekeeping missions" (p. 189). The international community needs to do justice equally and equitably; otherwise, victims view such indifference and complicity as international racism against Africa where the society revolves around gender and division along sex and gender lines.

Currently, the legacy and effects of divide and rule are visible in politics in many affected countries in Africa whereby loyalty to whatever political party or group misleadingly revolves around artificial and all-time-destructive ethnicity. There is "us versus them" divide socially, politically and economically as Carter, Irani and Volkan (2009) argue that access to "land (access to other natural resources, notably oil and water)" acts as a tool of oppression based on ethnicity in many countries mentioned above, *inter alia*. In other words, you do not exist if you do not belong to "us"; and if you do, you are our enemy or a second-class citizen in our country wherein you are automatically an obstacle to our wellbeing and development that cannot we cannot achieve without your underdevelopment under our anti-development lenses. In such a situation and rationale, protagonists do not consciously become aware of the needs and humanity of those they deemed to be their enemies. They think it is the right thing for them to eliminate or maltreat their artificial enemies. So, in such lethargic way of doing things, you deserve to be gotten rid of so that we can thrive and survive. When clear and sane mind prevail, those calling each other enemies are brothers and sisters who used to live like friends and partners in everything before the introduction of such obnoxious and poisonous system in place. Facing such a catch-22, ethnic ruling parties or groups tend to turn their enemies into second-class citizens or inferior ones.

Furthermore, ethnic and ethnopolitical conflicts resulting from divide and rule have since caused many mistrusts and misunderstandings among societies that used to live together harmoniously before the coming of colonialists. Identity-based conflicts occurred and surfaced in many different places under the divide and rule that changed names according to where and who used it. Again, the effects and aims of divide and rule remained the same to all colonised people almost in all places. It resulted to the creation of animosities, artificial identities and differences, among others. In addition, the effects of divide and rule and power struggle in Africa can be observed by applying social cubism theory to show how deeper and wider divide and rule strategy affected the colonised people in various countries and communities as far as ethnopolitical conflicts are concerned. To gauge how much deeper and wider divide and rule, as a colonial strategy, affected the countries or people to whom or to which it worked, social cubism theory applies well. Under social cubism, Byrne and Carter (1996) analyse six facets of the conflict namely demographics, economics, history, political factors, psychocultural factors and religion. Social cubism covers six facets of the society and shows how divide and rule use them to antagonises, divides and exploits the victims.

Colonisers used demographics, almost in all cases, colonial powers favoured the minority by side-lining or totally excluding the majority they exploited and belittled not to mention total exclusion in administering the colony something that forced them to capitulate and live with anger and hatred against the favoured ones. Further, discriminating against the majority covered all areas such as provision of social services such as education and medication. In Rwanda, for example, Tutsis were favoured in the provision of education as it was for Kikuyu in Kenya. Along with demographics, the colonisers used economics as a tool for the minority to exploit and rule the majority through ethnic favouritism. Jobs, in the colonial governments and other privileges, went to the favoured groups something that caused hatred and vengeance as it was the case in Burundi and Rwanda after the two countries got their independence whereby the majority started persecuting the minority. In a sense, the victims became perpetrators and vice versa. Essentially, divide and rule revolves around the hinge of ethnicity whereby the majority suffers exclusion economically, and politically.

Colonisers used the history of the colonised people to pity one against another. For instance, in Rwanda, Tutsis were made to believe that they were regarded as intruders or invaders who settled in Rwanda 900 A.D compared to Hutus who appeared in Rwanda 2000 B.C (Carter 2009). Before the coming in of colonisers, JUSR like other Africans, Hutus and Tutsi generally lived peacefully despite having small-scale conflicts (which are normal in any society) that did not tear them apart as it happened after the coming of colonialism with its divide and rule strategy that left Africa divided and weakened. Evidentially, precolonial African society distinctively contributed to human history through its civilised art of living peaceably (Lonsdale (1981 cited in Schatzberg 2014) in the states of their own making. This shows how solidified and peaceful primordial African society used to be before the introduction of divide and rule that led to many ethnic and ethnopolitical conflicts.

However, in trying to weaken, and cheaply run colonies, colonisers, especially, British invented the divide-and-rule strategy that affected the colonies negatively. Carter, Irani and Volkan (2009) note the strategy of divide and rule, apart from deeply influencing African society, it also promoted European colonialisation. Therefore, the first thing, divide and rule did, was to create antagonism between or among groups based on what they perceived to be their slight and immaterial differences. In so doing, colonisers created artificial identities and differences based on physical or biological looks or historical realities of the groups. As noted above, such artificial reinvention of the groups added new identities to the groups that took them as real while they actually were not. For example, Tutsis in Rwanda, as argued above, believed after undergoing brainwash that they were superior to the Hutus based on the length and shape of their noses. Tutsis took this absolute nonsense to be a true part of their identity thereafter however devious it was. Arguably, the two communities acquired a new and fake identity. Once an identity is established, it is hard to alter; and becomes one of the values of the group. Goffman (2009) in his book, *Notes on the Management of Spoiled Identity* argues that artificial identity creates a select social category. It is recently became clear that, after the 1994 genocide in Rwanda, both groups saw themselves differently in order to start to deconstruct such artificial identity Germany, Belgium and French colonisers created under divide and rule. Currently, Rwanda does not use one's ethnicity to identify him or her. Instead, the authorities refer to Hutus, Tutsis as Rwandans. This is good and the first step of deconstructing toxic ethnicity. However, this approach may work temporarily if we consider what happened in the former Federation of Yugoslavia after the death of Marshal Josip Broz Tito, former president, who abolished ethnicity to end up hitting back after his death. Whether the de-ethnicisation will work or not in Rwanda, it is too early to tell.

Again, Conflict Resolution academics, practitioners and professionals need to keep an eye on Rwanda's experiment on deconstructing ethnicity to see which way it will go in the near future after President Paul Kagame–who is instrumentally behind it–hands power over to another Rwandan as president. The irony with Rwandan experiment however is the fact that, despite deconstructing ethnicity, the authorities, ironically still refers to the victims of genocide as Tutsis which, in essence, is rekindling it. Hutus perceive such categorisation based on ethnicity as collectively a collective condemnation, discrimination and uplifting Tutsis if not reinforcing the vice.

Another important fact is that it takes long time for groups to realise how artificial some of what they perceive to be their identity is. Sometimes, such awakening happens after miseries strike as it is for the case of Rwandan genocide or Kosovo ethnic cleansing.

Moreover, as noted above, in applying divide and rule, colonial masters from the former played one community against another in the latter while favouring the minority as opposed to the majority. Such a strategy worked well where there were some differences or historical animosities such as in the case in point whereby the British used history as the means of dividing the two. To make things worse, under divide and rule, colonial masters have kept quiet whenever their sins surface. Instead, they pretend to go into colonies to resolve conflicts as a way and means of saving face. Colonisers used the acrimony between and among their victims to create future regime that have safeguarded their interests in their ex-colonies. By dividing their colonised people, colonisers were able to get some secrets that enabled them to conquer and tame both groups. Through the antagonism created, groups were ready to betray one another as a strategy of winning colonial favours at the expenses of their enemy groups.

v) How the Former Reinventing New people and Creating Animosity in the Latter

Sometimes, under the noxious divide-and-rule stratagem or indirect rule, colonial masters appointed and supported the favoured community to, vicariously rule the communities that were not favoured. Carter, Irani and Volkan (2009) note that "Germans found it logical for the Tutsis to rule Hutus....they decided to administer Rwanda by indirect rule system" (p. 136). In so doing, Germans started *Tutsification* that culminated in the 1994 Rwandan genocide. Ironically, the international community has always blamed Rwandan genocide on Hutus only instead of Germans who enacted this system, Belgians and French not to mention the Tutsis whom Germans used to rule and exploit the majority Hutus. Germany created animosity and hatred between the two groups as the means of smoothly running the colony at the time it was under Germany colonial rule, and later under Belgian and French colonial rules. Under divide and rule, colonial masters created artificial races with artificial identities that segregated and hated one another for colonisers' easy preying on. After Germany was defeated in the WWII, Rwanda went to Belgian colonial rule that built in the same by exacerbating the rift between the two groups.

In essence, Belgium went on with the same policy of division Germans had created. Carter, Irani and Volkan *(Ibid.)* note that "they (Belgians) perpetuated the Tutsification of Rwanda" (p. 131) in that they favoured the minority Tutsis as opposed to the majority Hutus. Such policy created enmity that it became the root cause of the 1994 genocide. Tutsis were made to believe that they were superior to Hutus and vice versa something that created mistrusts, angst, vengeance and fierce division among the people who used to live together peacefully before the arrival of colonisers. Due to the myopia and self-seeking tendencies, the duo bought into this chicanery aimed at making them forgetting what used to unite them as they concentrated on what now was dividing them.

Arguably, as noted above, colonisers introduced racism based on things such as the length of the nose and the time when one community evolved in the place, they call their countries (Burundi and Rwanda), history, religion and region (Nigeria) among others. Byrne and Carter *(op. cit.)* note that "regardless of which ethnic groups arrived first, both communities have been deeply influenced by the strategy of "divide and rule" promoted during European colonization" (p. 159). Such artificiality and artificial and farfetched reasons worked almost in all countries that have faced ethnoconflicts. After the colonisers left, they made sure that they left divisions abaft so that they could use it to weaken and keep on exploiting their former colonies. If anything, such perpetual exploitation of dividing African into small and weak states during the scramble for, and partition of Africa of 1884, which itself was a geographical and political divide and rule strategy towards the entirely united continent, worked perfectly for the interests of colonialism.

Strategically, many ethnic groups found themselves divided between two or more countries as it was for some African ethnic groups such as Masai (between Kenya and Tanzania), Makonde (among Malawi, Mozambique and Tanzania), Nyasa (between Malawi and Tanzania) and many more, (Mhango 2016). This divide and rule was; and still is used by some African rulers as Acemoglu, Verdier and Robinson (2004) argue that "the logic of the divide-and-rule strategy is to enable a ruler to bribe politically pivotal groups off the equilibrium path, ensuring that he can remain in power against challenges" (p. 164). If anything, divide and rule is one of the tools European colonisers used during; and after colonialism that they left after handing over the colonies to black colonialists. Thanks to divide and rule, Africa has, since independence–played the role of, maintaining the division; and thereby has suffered greatly under black colonialists who used; and still use the same strategy to remain in power. What African black colonialists did is to turn divide and rule upside down and produced rule and divide. So, too, geographical and political divide and rule affected the reunification of Africa which has become impossible due to the fact that many post-colonial African leaders championed it and failed because African countries were, and still are divided even after the colonial masters left over five decades ago.

Similarly, divide and rule, which later became rule and divide, has always been an obstacle against the total unification of Africa. Colonial puppets and cronies such as Mobutu Seseseko (the Democratic Republic of Congo (DRC) Dr. Hastings Kamuzu Banda (Malawi), Jomo Kenyatta (Kenya), Omar Bongo (Gabon), Denis Sassou Ngwesso (Congo) and many more made sure that Africa remains divided so that they could safely remain in power provided that their colonial masters supported and protected their corrupt regimes revolving around ethnicity. Power to such puppets was the means and the end with which they safeguard by dividing their people. Differently from the colonial masters, African colonialists got in power then started dividing their people that helped them to remain in power for long periods. Zimbabwe's former president Robert Mugabe is a recent example of rule and divide perpetrated by African rulers. He used divisive tactics to rule Zimbabwe for over three centuries. First, he divided Zimbabweans between freedom fighters and collaborators. Once this ploy started to lose its wand, he improved it by dividing Zimbabweans along pro-revolution and anti-revolution. Further, he embarked on blatant racism wherein Zimbabweans of European descent were termed foreigners in their own country. By exploiting ideological and colour divides, Mugabe took farms from white farmers and gave them to his cronies by leaving out all those he perceived to his political enemies out. His ploy worked. For, soon after taking land from white, some Zimbabweans even some African leaders supported him viewing him as a true Africanist who stood to assuage colonial evils. Voters, too, supported his policy as the means of surviving in the elections that followed the seizure of land from whites.

The camouflage of divide-and-rule and blaming the victims by sparing the perpetrators worked until 2017 when the army overthrew Mugabe.

Mugabe's divided-and-rule policies now aped by an ultra-nationalist party in South Africa, the Economic Freedom Fighters (EFF) that is campaigning asking South Africans, especially blacks to vote for it so that it can take land from Boers and redistribute it to blacks. Once again, divide and rule is at work. British colonial masters handed the country to the minority Boers after colonising the country for 350 years. When the Boers took the reins of power, they introduced Apartheid policies that left the majority blacks in the cold. To get away with murder, Boers formed a few Bantustans that acted as their puppets. Now that South Africa is free, just like other African countries, some elites such as the EFF are using the same tactic of dividing people aimed at getting in power. This time around, the EFF, like it was for the Zimbabwe African National

Union–Patriotic Front (ZANU-PF), is using racism to achieve its goals (Mhango 2016). Although the South African ruling party, the African National Congress (ANC) is reluctant to buy into racial politics, if voters vote the EFF, whose followership is growing tremendously, chances are the in the near future, the ANC will follow suit in order to survive politically, particularly after committing many errors in power. Although it is early to tell, South Africa without visionary leaders like Mandela, chances for it to go Zimbabwe way are high. The situation is still the same in Namibia where a few white settlers own more land than blacks are. Since its independence, Namibia has been struggling with the land issue as Adams and Howell (2001) note that:

> Malawi has just embarked on a land redistribution programme, which targets large, foreign-owned estates for the resettlement of the landless poor. Land redistribution has been a central plank of land policy in Zimbabwe, Namibia and South Africa since their transition to majority rule (p. 1).

Moreover, divide and rule applied even after independence whereby the then two superpowers, the United States (US) and the Union of Soviet Socialist Republics (USSR) divide other countries based on their influence; and used their allies especially at the United Nations (UN) where their masters used them to pass some issues in which they had interests. For example, due to rendering services to the West during and after the cold war, despite robbing the DRC, Mobutu succeeded to tighten his grip on power up until rebels overthrew him in 1997. Thanks to the support from the West, Mobutu ruled for a long time by using the same trick of playing greedy and myopic local elites against each other topped up with financial and military assistance and support from countries in the former for the exchange of cheaper minerals and resources. Those who do not bother to read the history tend to blame ethnic groups in fighting for power and resources as it currently is in the DRC where many atrocities have been committed. Again, warlords plunder resources that they end up selling them to former colonial masters in the Global North without facing any charges for such conspiracy and crimes against humanity. The blame game has gone on almost in all African countries facing ethnic conflicts. In Nigeria, for example, when Biafra sought to secede, many blamed this action on communism that supported this move. Those who created the mess in Nigeria, the British, were the first to either blame or jump in to resolve the conflict. Thanks to such mentality of blaming those in ethnoconflicts, Post (1968) argues that actually "Nigeria has joined the Congo (Kinshasa) as the sick man of Africa. The high hopes of 1960-62 became the forebodings of 1964-65; now there seems little to feel but sickness of heart at the death of one's friends and despair at the end of a dream" (p. 26). Post is accusing Nigeria of its ethnoconflicts without mentioning the British that created them. This has been the take of the world. It blames the victims alone without including those who invented divide and rule which caused all these conflicts in the latter.

Differently, Post (*Ibid.*) goes on showing how British created all ethnoconflicts Nigeria has ever experienced observing that "when Britain carved out Nigeria for itself it created, in the words of one of the more enlightened colonial experts, 'perhaps the most artificial of the many administrative units created in the course of the European occupation of Africa'" (p. 27).

Post shows (*op. cit.*) the contradiction ethnoconflicts draw even for those who analyse them. He started by blaming Nigeria for its failure that borders it with another failed state of the time, DRC (then Congo Kinshasa before it was renamed Zaire then DRC). Post realises his mistake of hurling insults at, and blames on Nigeria so as to admit that Britain is the one to blame for creating such acrimonious and artificial political entities so as to foster its interests even after attaining independence as it has ever been for many African countries. Aghedo and Osumah (2015) concur with Post. He argues that "the colonial state was largely created to serve the economic interests of the imperialists; helping to ensure law and order and guarantee an environment that enabled the colonialists to expand their interests" (p. 2). Such adherence to law and order would have been impossible without divide and rule. Aghedo and Osumah go far deeper connecting the Boko Haram, an Islamic fundamentalist terrorist group operating currently in Nigeria, Chad and Cameroon, to divide and rule whereby colonial education in Nigeria left out Muslims of colonial education system; and thereby became disgruntled after independence arguing that lack of education, employment and other poverty helped militants to recruits their foot soldiers. Again, considering how Boko Haram insurgence is misconstrued as an Islamic move against Christian and secular government, one may underscore how divide and rule is elusively and safely still entrenched in Nigeria's ethnoconflicts.

Whereas British colonisers used communities against others based on their ethnic history, they expanded the practice by including more elements. Christopher (1988) notes that "the simple Christian-Heathen or English-foreigner dichotomy was replaced by ever more elaborate classifications as governments divided and re-divided populations into discrete groups, on the basis of linguistics, religion, ethnicity and skin colour" (p. 233). Instead of dividing Nigeria along ethnicity, the British divided by religion and region.

One may wonder how British divide and rule created many conflicts in the world today. In the Israel-Palestine conflict, this strategy played an important role that culminated into the protracted conflict that has been going on for many years. How divide and rule played out in Israel-Palestine conflict is obvious as Shlaim (1995) notes that on the one hand:

> The central charge is that Britain armed and secretly encouraged her Arab allies, and especially her client, King Abdullah of Jordan, to invade Palestine upon expiry of the British Mandate and do battle with the Jewish state as soon as it came into the world (p. 293).

Further, Shlaim (*Ibid.*) notes that practically "Britain knew and approved of this secret Hashemite-Zionist agreement to divide up Palestine between themselves, not along the lines of the U.N. partition plan" (p. 297). As if this was not enough, the same Britain, in conjunction with America, has portrayed itself as an international mediator-cum-guarantor whereby its former Prime Minister, Tony Blair, became Middle East envoy for the Quartet, a diplomatic group consisting of the United Nations, the European Union, the United States and Russia. Once again, this shows how lethal divide and rule can be, specifically through the camouflage it takes even today in the Israel-Palestine conflict. Ironically, those who created the conflict are still safe without any blame while the blame goes to their victims. Such manipulations can be seen not only in Israel-Palestine conflict but also in Northern Ireland where Marxists claim that "the capitalist class, both British and local, has artificially fomented the conflict in Northern Ireland" (Whyte (1978) which seems to be ridiculous for those who know the true history of the conflict. As said in the beginning, it is easier to blame victims than the oppressors simply because the oppressors have all the tools of manipulation such as using academics and mass media to defend their positions. Like Post (1968), Whyte (1978) discovers the contradiction of his statement. He presents another view from non-Marxist who argues that actually "Britain based her partition policy on divergences she herself created and fostered among the Irish people" (p. 267) all aimed at subjugating; and thereafter exploiting them. Arguably, if this is the nature of how academics look at ethnoconflicts, chances of the blame game to go on by excluding those who actually enacted the conflicts. Academics need to rewrite the true history of divide and rule and propose that countries that created this strategy and those who benefitted from it must bear responsibility by redressing their victims. This will not only do justice to the victims but it will also create a precedent for others thinking about or planning to do the same in any form to think twice. Likewise, by redressing the victims, the world will be erasing the anomalies and ills resulting from unfair distribution and use of resources and wealth. By addressing the anomalies, the relationship between the Global North and the Global South, the two are able to create a yin-yang bond of interdependency due to the fact that, apart from depending on each other, they still need each other.

vi)   **Assimilation Inhalation and Perpetuation**

Although Britain created and had many more conflicts than other colonisers had due to having many colonies, it was not alone in using divide and rule as a strategy of easily running her colonies. As it has generally been the strategy of the former, French used the same, however, under different names. They called their policy or strategy *assimilation* whereby a few select colonised people enjoyed some privileges such as accommodation in French culture in order to perceive themselves to be more civilised than those their masters excluded. This created division among colonised people. Kumar (2006) questions the legacy such a crime left to the world today, especially assimilation under what was famous known as mission civilisatrice. To make sure that colonised people could not be united; and thereby fight against French colonialism, French colonialists introduced intra-racism to make sure that the victims could not come and think together on their problem. Aglion (1944) notes that "the territories administered by France on the Dark Continent may be divided into two separate and distinct parts: 1) "White Africa which in some quarters the call this "European Africa" and 2) "Black Africa" (p. 78) in that white Africa is the Maghreb and black Africa is Sub-Sahara Africa (SSA); also see Mawere and Mubaya (2016). Aglion goes on arguing that the "administration of territories under protectorate is carried on by the French in an indirect manner" (p. 78). How stereotypical such connotation is? Indirect manner is a crop of so-called thinkers the former has employed in disparaging the latter. Despite such historical injustices, the former still maintains silence as if the victims are not equal human beings even if they have different skin pigments. France needs to come forward and make a formal apology to its victims on top of redressing them. How a sane person can refer to Africa as the Dark Continent while it has more light than the whole world? Africa needs to use such evidence to bring France and the like to justice for the evils they created and perpetrated against it. Like France, Britain that dispatched criminals such as Stanley, the exaggerator in chief that fabricated such insults (Shaw 1994), still enjoys accolades as a civilised and advanced country while in actuality it is but to the contrary. With such negativity, is it true Britain civilised?

Principally, indirect or divided and rule was aimed at using conflicting and opposing Indigenous people to rule others in order to minimise the cost of running colonies. Aglion (*op. cit.*) calls this system "sort of attempt to profit by the national disaster" (p. 79) for colonised nations. By dividing colonised people in the groups, ethnic or colour and region, colonialists created what Byrne and Irvin (2001) call "old historical rivalries, revenge and fear" (p. 78) which resulted in the current ethnopolitical conflicts the Africa is facing and suffering from. For, such "old historical rivalries, revenge and fear" are the means and tools elites in the groups use to maintain the solidarity of the group even by dividing them from their enemies so that they can rule the groups easily, cheaply and safely.

As argued above, divide and rule was given different names however its spirit and intention remained the same, dividing and weakening colonisers so as to easily and perpetually exploit them. Portuguese called it *assimilado* that is assimilation in English and French. De Almeida (2001) shows how the same people were divided into different groups with different identities noting that "Portuguese was for the *assimilados*, Tetum, Timorese local language) was for the *gentios* or heathen" (p. 599). Such artificiality based on linguistic superimposed dissimilarity shows how the same excommunicated some people from each other in order to become foreign and enemies to each other wantonly. Looking at the terms and language used, one can discover that they have their origin from Christianity, which, like any other foreign religions, divided people in order to exploit them. Such miscommunication caused a lot of mistrusts and misunderstandings altogether. Islam, too, did the same by categorising people into believers and infidels.

vii)   Conclusion: What Should Be Done?

In sum, I can argue that divide and rule worked during colonial times, and it still works many years thereafter. Essentially, divide and rule, as a strategy, seems to fit in colonialism as well as in imperialism as the means of dividing people in order to control them easily and for a long time, as it is the case of African countries currently whereby their economies have gone serving and servicing those of their former colonial masters. Even the division between the Global North and the Global South is still the same strategy of divide and rule aimed at creating two different entities with different treatments. However, this division is different from ethnic one that colonialism created and exploited for the perpetual exploitation of the victims of this notorious strategy. You can see even in international politics in which the West or the first world receives different treatment from other worlds it created for the same purpose of bullying and exploiting them.

Therefore, many ethnic and ethnopolitical conflicts that Africa is witnessing today have all hallmarks of colonialism; and the blames must be on colonial masters instead of the victims. Divide and rule created many artificial and fake groups and identities, be they ethnic, political or religious, as it palpably is in social cubism on how divide and rule can apply to all six facets of the doctrine. Social cubism is still relevant today in addressing the consequence, tactics and legacies of divide and rule. This strategy still revolves around the six facets of social cubism among others. What seems to have changed is the fact that when divide and rule was invented, colonised people used to be victims. However, after gaining their freedom, some rulers of independent Africa countries metamorphosed themselves into new colonial masters that used the same strategy to weaken the solidarity of their people that were supposed to oppose them democratically. To make things worse, divide and rule seems to be at work as a double-edged sword in Africa whereby African rulers are using it to divide their people with the aim remaining in power serving their former colonial masters. Currently, there are terrorist groups such as al-Shabaab (Somalia), Boko Haram (Nigeria) and others fighting against other Africans to be able to come to power so that they can run countries under their foreign borrowed *diktats*. This can be termed as religious divide and rule, which is another type of neo-colonialism, Africa needs to fight vigorously and timely before it grows even bigger. It took many years for religious groups seeking political power to surface because during the colonial era, colonial rules suffocated them. Under imperialism, as an extension of colonialism whose success story revolves around divide and rule, religious groups are using the same strategy of dividing Africans in two groups namely Muslims and none to gain popularity and claim territories. Arguably, African politics–in many countries–still revolves around ethnicity as colonial strategy of divide and rule. Refer to what happened in the 2007 general elections whereby the Post-Election Violence (PEV) resulting from ethnicity left hundreds dead. Goldstein and Rotich (2008) note the cause of the PEV–as it is clear before Kenyans. They argue that "following Kenya's independence from Great Britain, much of the best land went to Kenyatta's Kikuyu ethnic group, instead of the groups to whom it belonged before the British arrived" (p. 4). It is interesting to note that in Kenya, British favoured Kikuyus despite being the biggest ethnic group in the country. Again, once we compare Kikuyu with the rest 41 ethnic groups, they become minority.

In Uganda, the current government under Museveni an Ankole faces accusations of favouring President's ethnic group as opposed to other communities. The same applies in the neighbouring Rwanda where the government faces the same accusations of consisting only one community that took power after genocide despite abolishing ethnic identities. Equally, psychoculturally, one may argue that Kikuyus are farmers that prove to be more peaceful than nomads are as animal keepers, who happen to be warriors. Therefore, when British colonisers arrived in Kenya, they used land favours as the means of dividing Kenyans along ethnic lines; and thereby creating hatred and difference that went on even after Kenya became independent in 1963. Kenya's PEV fits in the social cubism (Byrne, Carter and Senehi 2002) analysis whereby economic, history, psychoculture, demographics among others. To resolve ethnoconflicts mentioned above, the world needs to revisit their history so that it can make things right.

I, thus, propose that there must be mechanisms that will force all countries that benefited from colonialism to redress their victims based on the following facets:

1). It can be a lesson for others and it can act as a deterrent;

2). The reparations will empower the victims economically so as to provide some services to their people especially social education on creating awareness about divide and rule and the consequences victims have suffered since it was invented and introduced to many colonies;

3). Declaring colonialism a crime as it was for Apartheid that became illegal after the ANC took over in 1994. All countries that were once colonised, need to come together and pressurise the international community to address this crimes so that, in the end, they can be redressed for the ills colonialism caused to many ex-colonies and;

4). Change the current international system of doing business whereby former colonies are still playing the same role of serving and servicing the economies of Western countries. For the latter to develop, chiefly Africa needs to make its economy serve its interests first. There in no way one can achieve meaningful development without deconstructing the way African economy has operated by just being a producer of primary goods. Instead, such products need an added value.

Importantly, African countries whose colonisation resulted from their trust to the colonisers should stop trusting their oppressors thinking they can bring about change and solutions to their problems as far as violent conflicts are concerned. It is sad and even ridiculous to note that Africans know why they were perpetually colonised, yet, they still trust the same people to solve the conflicts they enacted in order to go on benefiting from exploiting Africa!

Suffice it to say, divide-and-rule strategy colonisers invented and used to rule resulted into many ethnic and ethnopolitical conflicts Africa evidences today. It is time academics, professionals, practitioners and all dealing with conflict resolution to start thinking about linking those who created divide and rule to the effects of ethnic and ethnopolitical. Therefore, doing so may help in avoiding the repetition or re-enactment of the same in the future because colonialism and imperialism change shape and names according to time and situations. Divide and rule is among political gimmicks that make the world unsafe and violent due to its effects and legacies altogether. To live in a peaceful world, the duo needs to address this exploitative colonial and political tool so that the awareness gotten out of it maybe can help victims to think about reconciliation among themselves and deconstructing the *status quo*. We have seen how European colonisers, and later post-colonial rulers in Africa, used the same method to keep on exploiting and ruling the victims of the strategy in various countries cited as examples in this chapter. It is our duty to step in and help in arresting, alleviating, and if possible, put a full stop to it by making our people aware of it. For, going on with it, will not only cause more harm, predominantly to Africa whose development has suffered for many decades but will also negatively affect the former that will be on the receiving end. Thus, aggravating the problem of immigrants running away from suffering in the latter will flood the former. Therefore, keeping this relationship as it currently is may become detrimental for both sides, especially the former that is not used to receiving millions of desperate people from the latter. What logically can any sane person expect out of horse-jokey relationship? This metaphor fits in the relationship between twosomes shall it not be deconstructed and reclaimed to the tune of creating parity based on justice and real situations. The difference in this relationship however, despite the metaphor, is between equal and same human beings who have been treating each other like beasts. Therefore, conflict, poverty and underdevelopment this relationship has pointlessly created are avoidable if the duo decides to deconstruct and reconstruct their relationship based on new needs and realities of today revolving around basic human needs and rights. It is upon stakeholders from both sides to stand together to see to it that justice is done. As argued in this volume, realignment, redress and, above all, changes of the way things worked are the *sine qua non* to success for both parties of the divide in this relationship. By so doing, the world will be able to enjoy and own sustainable justice and peace.

References

"Rationale for Fighting Corruption." *OECD*, 2014.

Acemoglu, D., Verdier, T., & Robinson, J. A. (2004). Kleptocracy And Divide- and- Rule: A Model Of Personal Rule. *Journal of the European Economic Association*, *2*(2- 3), 162-192.

Acquaah, M. (2012). Social networking relationships, firm- specific managerial experience and firm performance in a transition economy: A comparative analysis of family owned and nonfamily firms. *Strategic Management Journal*, *33*(10), 1215-1228.

Adams, M., & Howell, J. (2001). *Redistributive land reform in Southern Africa*. London: Overseas Development Institute.

Agbiboa, D. E. (2012). Between corruption and development: The political economy of state robbery in Nigeria. *Journal of business ethics*, *108*(3), 325-345.

Aghedo, I., & Osumah, O. (2015). Insurgency in Nigeria: A comparative study of Niger delta and boko haram uprisings. *Journal of Asian and African Studies*, *50*(2), 208-222.

Aglion, R. (1944). French Colonial Policy. *World Affairs*, *107*(2), 78-81.

Aidt, T. S., Veiga, F. J., & Veiga, L. G. (2011). Election results and opportunistic policies: A new test of the rational political business cycle model. *Public choice*, *148*(1-2), 21-44.

Akindola, R. B. (2009). Towards a definition of poverty: poor people's perspectives and implications for poverty reduction. *Journal of Developing Societies*, *25*(2), 121-150.

Aleksynska, M., & Havrylchyk, O. (2013). FDI from the south: The role of institutional distance and natural resources. *European Journal of Political Economy*, *29*, 38-53.

Alexander, J. B. (2009). *Africa: Irregular warfare on the dark continent* (No. JSOU-09-5). Joint Special Operations Univ Hurlburt Field Fl.

Ali, A. J. (1992). The Islamic work ethic in Arabia. *The Journal of psychology*, *126*(5), 507-519.

Amin, S. (1991). The issue of democracy in the contemporary Third World. *Socialism and Democracy*, *7*(1), 83-104.

Amin, S. (2011). *Maldevelopment: anatomy of a global failure.* Fahamu/Pambazuka.

Analo, T., & Olingo, A., (2015). Region's Elite Have Stashed Away over $700m in Swiss Bank Accounts" *East African,* 2.

Annan, K. (2005). In Larger Freedom: Decision Time at the UN. *Foreign Affairs,* 63-74.

Arango, J., & Baldwin-Edwards, M. (2014). *Immigrants and the informal economy in Southern Europe.* Routledge.

Arezki, R., Rota-Graziosi, G., & Senbet, L. W. (2014). Natural Resources and Capital Flight: A Role for Policy?.

Armstrong, E. A., & Crage, S. M. (2006). Movements and memory: The making of the Stonewall myth. *American Sociological Review, 71*(5), 724-751.

Atelhe, G. A. (2014). Democracy and national security in Nigeria: A discursive exploration. *Mediterranean Journal of Social Sciences, 5*(4), 495.

Ayoob, M., & Zierler, M. (2005). The unipolar concert: the North-South divide trumps transatlantic differences. *World Policy Journal, 22*(1), 31-42.

Bakker, K. (2007). The "commons" versus the "commodity": Alter- globalization, anti- privatization and the human right to water in the global south. *Antipode, 39*(3), 430-455.

Ballentine, K., & Nitzschke, H. (2005). The political economy of civil war and conflict transformation. *Berghof Research Center for Constructive Conflict Management, Berlin.[http://www. berghof-handbook. net/articles/BHDS3_ BallentineNitzschke230305. pdf].*

Battersby, P., & Siracusa, J. M. (2009). *Globalization and human security.* Rowman & Littlefield Publishers.

Beine, M. A., Docquier, F., & Schiff, M. (2008). Brain Drain and its Determinants: A Major Issue for small states.

Beine, M., Docquier, F., & Rapoport, H. (2008). Brain drain and human capital formation in developing countries: winners and losers. *The Economic Journal, 118*(528), 631-652.

Berthélemy, J. C. (2006, January). Convergence and development traps: how did emerging economies escape the underdevelopment trap. In *Growth and Integration: Annual World Bank Conference on Development Economics* (pp. 127-156).

Bertocchi, G., & Canova, F. (2002). Did colonization matter for growth?: An empirical exploration into the historical causes of Africa's underdevelopment. *European economic review*, *46*(10), 1851-1871.

Beyerlin, U. (2006). Bridging the north-south divide in international environmental law. *ZaöRV*, *66*, 259-296.

Bisschop, L. (2012). Is it all going to waste? Illegal transports of e-waste in a European trade hub. *Crime, law and social change*, *58*(3), 221-249.

Bleischwitz, R., Dittrich, M., and Pierdicca, C. (2012). Coltan from Central Africa, international trade and implications for any certification. *Resources Policy*, *37*(1), 19-29.

Block, S. A. (2002). Political business cycles, democratization, and economic reform: the case of Africa. *Journal of Development economics*, *67*(1), 205-228.

Boateng, B. (2011). *The copyright thing doesn't work here: Adinkra and Kente cloth and intellectual property in Ghana*. U of Minnesota Press.

Bonefeld, W. (2013). Adam Smith and ordoliberalism: on the political form of market liberty. *Review of international studies*, *39*(2), 233-250.

Boshoff, N. (2009). Neo-colonialism and research collaboration in Central Africa. *Scientometrics*, *81*(2), 413.

Boyce, J. K., & Ndikumana, L. (2012). Capital Flight from Sub-Saharan African Countries: Updated Estimates, 1970-2010. *Polit. Econ. Res. Inst. Inst. Res. Rep.*, no.

Broberg, M. (2011). *The EU's legal ties with its former colonies: When old love never dies* (No. 2011: 01). DIIS working paper.

Brooks, D. (2010). *Bobos in paradise: The new upper class and how they got there*. Simon and Schuster.

Burgess, R., Jedwab, R., Miguel, E., & Morjaria, A. (2010). Our turn to eat: The political economy of roads in Kenya. *Manuscript, London, UK: London School of Economics and Political Science*.

Burke, S., (2013). Is China Buying Up Africa? *CNN*, 3.

Burrowes, R. J. (1996). *The Strategy of Nonviolent Defense: A Gandhian Perspective*.

Burton, J. (1990). *Conflict: Human needs theory*. Springer.

Busch, O., & Weigert, B. (2010). Where have all the graduates gone? Internal cross-state migration of graduates in Germany 1984–2004. *The annals of regional science, 44*(3), 559-572.

Bygballe, L. E., Jahre, M., & Swärd, A. (2010). Partnering relationships in construction: A literature review. *Journal of purchasing and supply management, 16*(4), 239-253.

Byrne, S. (2001). Consociational and civic society approaches to peacebuilding in Northern Ireland. *Journal of Peace Research, 38*(3), 327-352.

Byrne, S. (2010). *Economic assistance and conflict transformation: Peacebuilding in Northern Ireland.* Routledge.

Byrne, S., & Irvin, C. L. (2000). *Reconcilable differences: Turning points in ethnopolitical conflict.* West Hartford, CT: Kumarian Press.

Byrne, S., Carter, N., Senehi, J., Byrne, Q. S., & Model, T. A. M. (2002). Introduction to social cubism. *ILSA Journal of International & Comparative Law.*

Caballero, B. (2005). A nutrition paradox—underweight and obesity in developing countries. *n engl j med, 352*(15), 1514-1516.

Campbell, K. M., Patel, N., & Singh, V. J. (2008). *The Power of Balance: America in Asia.* Center for a New American Security.

Caraveli, H. (2016). Global imbalances and EU core-periphery division: Institutional framework and theoretical interpretations. *World Review of Political Economy, 7*(1), 29-55.

Cardoso, F. H. (2009). New paths: Globalization in historical perspective. *Studies in Comparative International Development, 44*(4), 296-317.

Carmody, P. R., & Owusu, F. Y. (2007). Competing hegemons? Chinese versus American geo-economic strategies in Africa. *Political Geography, 26*(5), 504-524.

Carpenter, T. G. (2013). Tangled web: The Syrian civil war and its implications. *Mediterranean Quarterly, 24*(1), 1-11.

Carter, J. (2009). Lessons to ponder: Insights and advice from the front lines. *Regional and ethnic conflicts: Perspectives from the front lines,* 301-330.

Carter, J., Irani, G., & Volkan, V. D. (2015). *Regional and ethnic conflicts: Perspectives from the front lines.* Routledge.

Cheru, F., & Obi, C. (2010). *The rise of China and India in Africa: Challenges, opportunities and critical interventions.* Zed Books/Nordiska Afrikainstitutet.

Chichilnisky, G. (2006). Global Property Rights: The Kyoto Protocol and the Knowledge Revolution.

Chiu, C. M., Hsu, M. H., & Wang, E. T. (2006). Understanding knowledge sharing in virtual communities: An integration of social capital and social cognitive theories. *Decision support systems*, *42*(3), 1872-1888.

Christie, D. J. (1997). Reducing direct and structural violence: The human needs theory. *Peace and Conflict: Journal of Peace Psychology*, *3*(4), 315.

Christopher, A. J. (1988). 'Divide and Rule': The Impress of British Separation Policies. *Area*, 233-240.

Cilliers, J. (2009). Climate change, population pressure and conflict in Africa. *Institute for Security Studies Papers,2009*(178), 20.

Claessen, H. J. (1987). Kings, chiefs and officials: The political organization of Dahomey and Buganda compared. *The Journal of Legal Pluralism and Unofficial Law*, *19*(25-26), 203-241.

Clark, J. F. (1998). Foreign intervention in the civil war of the Congo Republic. *African Issues*, *26*(1), 31-36.

Cohen, D. (2001). The HIPC initiative: true and false promises. *International Finance*, *4*(3), 363-380.

Coleman, L. (2007). The Gendered Violence of Development: Imaginative Geographies of Exclusion in the Imposition of Neo- liberal Capitalism. *The British Journal of Politics & International Relations*, *9*(2), 204-219.

Collier, P. (2002). Social capital and poverty: a microeconomic perspective. *The role of social capital in development: An empirical assessment*, 19-41.

Collier, P., & Goderis, B. (2008). Commodity prices, growth, and the natural resource curse: Reconciling a conundrum.

Copeland, B. R., & Taylor, M. S. (1994). North-South trade and the environment. *The quarterly journal of Economics*, *109*(3), 755-787.

Coroado, H. & Brock, J., (2015). Angolans Resentful as China Tightens Tts Grip. *Reuters*, July (9).

Curtis, R., Terry, K., Dank, M., Dombrowski, K., & Khan, B. (2008). Commercial sexual exploitation of children in New York City, volume one: The CSEC population in New York City: Size, characteristics and needs. *Center for Court Innovation, 56.*

Dalaker, J., & Naifeh, M. (1998). Poverty in the United States, 1997, US Bureau of the Census, Current Population Reports, Series P60-201. *Washington, DC: US Government Printing Office.*

Danilovic, V. (2007). Deterring International Terrorism and Rogue States: US National Security Policy after 9/11. *Perspectives on Politics, 5*(4), 869-870.

Davenport, C. (2015). Nations approve landmark climate accord in Paris. *The New York Times, 12.*

David, C. Faith, (2011), '. The Hawala System'*Global Security Studies, Winter, 2*(1), 23.

De Almeida, M. V. (2001). Epilogue of empire: East Timor and the Portuguese postcolonial catharsis. *Identities Global Studies in Culture and Power, 8*(4), 583-605.

De Waal, A. (2014). When kleptocracy becomes insolvent: Brute causes of the civil war in South Sudan. *African Affairs, 113*(452), 347-369.

Defeis, E. F. (2008). UN peacekeepers and sexual abuse and exploitation: An end to impunity. *Wash. U. Global Stud. L. Rev., 7,* 185.

Derham, M. (2002). Undemocratic democracy: Venezuela and the distorting of history. *Bulletin of Latin American Research, 21*(2), 270-289.

Diamond, L., & Mosbacher, J. (2013). Petroleum to the People: Africa's Coming Resource Curse-and How to Avoid It. *Foreign Aff., 92,* 86.

Ding, S. (2008). To build a "harmonious world": China's soft power wielding in the global south. *Journal of Chinese Political Science, 13*(2), 193-213.

Djankov, S., Montalvo, J. G., & Reynal-Querol, M. (2008). The curse of aid. *Journal of economic growth, 13*(3), 169-194.

Dollar, D., & Easterly, W. (1999). The search for the key: aid, investment and policies in Africa. *Journal of African Economies, 8*(4), 546-577.

Dunning, T. (2004). Conditioning the effects of aid: Cold War politics, donor credibility, and democracy in Africa. *International organization, 58*(2), 409-423.

Easterly, W. (2009). How the millennium development goals are unfair to Africa. *World development, 37*(1), 26-35.

Escobar, A. (2011). *Encountering development: The making and unmaking of the Third World*. Princeton University Press.

Eustace, M. (2012). Rhino poaching: what is the solution. *Business Day, 20*.

Evans, A. (2011). Resource scarcity, climate change and the risk of violent conflict.

Ezema, I. J. (2010). Globalisation, information revolution and cultural imperialism in Africa. *Information, society and justice journal, 3*(1), 11-22.

Farley, M. (2006). Prostitution, trafficking, and cultural amnesia: What we must not know in order to keep the business of sexual exploitation running smoothly. *Yale JL & Feminism, 18*, 109.

Farmer, P. E., Nizeye, B., Stulac, S., & Keshavjee, S. (2006). Structural violence and clinical medicine. *PLoS medicine, 3*(10), e449.

Fleck, R. K., & Kilby, C. (2010). Changing aid regimes? US foreign aid from the Cold War to the War on Terror. *Journal of Development Economics, 91*(2), 185-197.

Galdamez, E. (2016). *Commercial Sexual Exploitation of Children (CSEC): A community awareness training for the Willowbrook community members: A grant proposal project*. California State University, Long Beach.

Gausset, Q. (2001). AIDS and cultural practices in Africa: the case of the Tonga (Zambia). *Social Science & Medicine, 52*(4), 509-518.

Giljum, S., & Eisenmenger, N. (2004). North-South trade and the distribution of environmental goods and burdens: a biophysical perspective. *The Journal of Environment & Development, 13*(1), 73-100.

Gilpin, R. (2011). *Global political economy: Understanding the international economic order*. Princeton University Press.

Gilpin, R. (2016). *The political economy of international relations*. Princeton University Press.

Goffman, E., (2009). *Stigma: Notes on the Management of Spoiled Identity.* Simon and Schuster.

Goldsmith, A. A. (2001). Foreign aid and statehood in Africa. *International organization, 55*(1), 123-148.

Goldstein, J., & Rotich, J. (2008). Digitally networked technology in Kenya's 2007–2008 post-election crisis. *Berkman Center Research Publication, 9,* 1-10.

Gore, A. (2006). *An inconvenient truth: The planetary emergency of global warming and what we can do about it.* Rodale.

Gorsevski, V., Kasischke, E., Dempewolf, J., Loboda, T., & Grossmann, F. (2012). Analysis of the Impacts of armed conflict on the Eastern Afromontane forest region on the South Sudan—Uganda border using multitemporal Landsat imagery. *Remote Sensing of Environment, 118,* 10-20.

Graburn, N. H. (1983). Tourism and prostitution. *Annals of Tourism Research, 10*(3), 437-443.

Griggs, R. (1996). The Great Lakes Conflict and Spatial Designs for Peace: A Neorealist Analysis. *Boundary and Security Bulletin, 4,* 68-78.

Harvey, D. (2007). Neoliberalism and the City. *Studies in Social Justice, 1*(1), 2.

Hauser, E. (1999). Ugandan relations with Western donors in the 1990s: what impact on democratisation?. *The Journal of Modern African Studies, 37*(4), 621-641.

Hauss, C. (2010). *International Conflict Resolution 2nd Ed.* A&C Black.

Healey, J. G. (2015). The Experience of Small Christian Communities (SCCs) in Eastern Africa.

Heeks, R. (2001). *Understanding e-governance for development.* Manchester: Institute for Development Policy and Management.

Henderson, H. (1996). *Building a win-win world: Life beyond global economic warfare.* Berrett-Koehler Publishers.

Hickel, J. (2013) The Donors' Dilemma'-Aid in Reverse: How Poor Countries Develop Rich Countries, *Global Policy, 12.*

Hollyer, J. R., Rosendorff, B. P., & Vreeland, J. R. (2011). Democracy and transparency. *The Journal of Politics, 73*(4), 1191-1205.

Hulme, D., Hanlon, J., & Barrientos, A. (2012). *Just give money to the poor: The development revolution from the global South*. Kumarian Press.

Hurrell, A., & Sengupta, S. (2012). Emerging powers, North–South relations and global climate politics. *International Affairs, 88*(3), 463-484.

Hydén, G. (1980). *Beyond Ujamaa in Tanzania: underdevelopment and an uncaptured peasantry*. Univ of California Press.

Iheukwumere, E. O., & Iheukwumere, C. A. (2003). Colonial rapacity and political corruption: roots of African underdevelopment and misery. *Chicago-Kent Journal of International and Comparative Law, 3*(1), 4.

Izuchukwu, O. (2011). Analysis of the contribution of agricultural sector on the Nigerian economic development. *World review of business research, 1*(1), 191-200.

Jackson, S. (2006). Sons of which soil? The language and politics of autochthony in Eastern DR Congo. *African studies review, 49*(2), 95-124.

Jaffee, D., Kloppenburg, J. R., & Monroy, M. B. (2004). Bringing the "moral charge" home: Fair trade within the North and within the South. *Rural sociology, 69*(2), 169-196.

Jeffreys, S. (2008). *The industrial vagina: The political economy of the global sex trade*. Routledge.

Jiang, W. (2009). Fuelling the dragon: China's rise and its energy and resources extraction in Africa. *The China Quarterly, 199*, 585-609.

Jobson, R. (2010). Afrocentricity and Commodity Fetishism: Cultural Objectification and the" New" African Diaspora. *Penn McNair Research Journal, 2*(1), 3.

Juma, C. (2015). Afro-Chinese Cooperation. *Africa and China: How Africans and Their Governments are Shaping Relations with China*, 171.

Karsten, L., & Illa, H. (2005). Ubuntu as a key African management concept: contextual background and practical insights for knowledge application. *Journal of Managerial Psychology, 20*(7), 607-620.

Kay, C. (2010). *Latin American theories of development and underdevelopment* (Vol. 102). Routledge.

Keating, M., Hooghe, L., & Tatham, M. (2006). Bypassing the nation-state?. *European Union: Power and policy-making*, London.

Keller, W. W., & Nolan, J. E. (1997). The arms trade: business as usual?. *Foreign Policy*, 113-125.

Khalid, M. (2011). Gender, Orientalism and Representations of the 'Other'in the War on Terror. *Global Change, Peace & Security*, *23*(1), 15-29.

Kibicho, W. (2016). *Sex tourism in Africa: Kenya's booming industry*. Routledge.

Kim, G. (2017). Between Hybridity and Hegemony in K-Pop's Global Popularity: A Case of Girls' Generation's American Debut. *International Journal of Communication (19328036)*, *11*.

Kimani, J. W. (2009). Hi-tech yet highly toxic: electronic and E-waste. *Journal of Language, Technology & Entrepreneurship in Africa*, *1*(2), 46-61.

Komter, A. (2007). Gifts and social relations: The mechanisms of reciprocity. *International Sociology*, *22*(1), 93-107.

Krugman, P. (1979). A model of innovation, technology transfer, and the world distribution of income. *Journal of political economy*, *87*(2), 253-266.

Kumar, K. (2006). English and French national identity: comparisons and contrasts. *Nations and Nationalism*, *12*(3), 413-432.

Kuperus, C. C. C. (2016). *France's involvement in the construction of the Rwandan genocide* (Bachelor's thesis).

Lall, S. (1975). Is 'dependence'a useful concept in analysing underdevelopment?. *World Development*, *3*(11-12), 799-810.

Landsberg, C. (2006). South Africa's Global Strategy and Status. *Johannesburg, Friedrich Ebert Stiftung New powers for global change*.

Larji, N. (2007). The resource curse revised: Conflict and Coltan in the Congo. *Harvard International Review*, *29*(3), 34.

Lazarus, J. (2010, September). Neo-Liberal State Building and Western „Democracy Promotion: " the Case of Georgia. In *7th Pan European Conference on International Relations*.

Lebovic, J. H. (2007). *Deterring international terrorism and rogue states: US national security policy after 9/11*. Routledge.

Lederach, J. P. (1995). *Preparing for peace: Conflict transformation across cultures*. Syracuse University Press.

Lensink, R., & Morrissey, O. (2000). Aid instability as a measure of uncertainty and the positive impact of aid on growth. *The Journal of Development Studies, 36*(3), 31-49.

Lerner, A. M., & Eakin, H. (2011). An obsolete dichotomy? Rethinking the rural–urban interface in terms of food security and production in the global south. *The Geographical Journal,177*(4), 311-320.

Lewis, C., & Reading-Smith, M. (2008). False pretenses. *The Center for Public Integrity, 23*.

Lijphart, A. (1975). The Northern Ireland Problem; Cases, Theories, and Solutions. *British Journal of Political Science,5*(1), 83-106.

Lipietz, A. (1987). *Mirages and miracles* (Vol. 21). London: Verso.

Luck, M., & d'Inverno, M. (2001). A conceptual framework for agent definition and development. *The Computer Journal,44*(1), 1-20.

Lundsgaarde, E., Breunig, C., & Prakash, A. (2007). Trade versus aid: donor generosity in an era of globalization. *Policy sciences, 40*(2), 157-179.

Luo, Y. (2007). *Guanxi and business* (Vol. 5). World Scientific.

Mac Ginty, R. M., & Williams, A. (2009). Conflict and development.*Abingdon: Routledge. Luckham, R., Ahmed, I., Muggah, R. and White, S.(2001) Conflict and*.

Magnus Theisen, O. (2008). Blood and soil? Resource scarcity and internal armed conflict revisited. *Journal of Peace Research, 45*(6), 801-818.

Mamdani, M., & Bangser, M. (2004). Poor people's experiences of health services in Tanzania: a literature review.*Reproductive Health Matters, 12*(24), 138-153.

Marchal, R. (1998). France and Africa: the emergence of essential reforms?. *International Affairs, 74*(2), 355-372.

Mark, C. R. (2005, April). Israel: US foreign assistance. Library of Congress Washington Dc Congressional Research Service.

Matsuyama, K. (2000). A ricardian model with a continuum of goods under nonhomothetic preferences: Demand complementarities, income distribution, and north-south trade. *Journal of political Economy*, *108*(6), 1093-1120.

Matunhu, J. (2011). A critique of modernization and dependency theories in Africa: Critical assessment.

Mawere, M. (2010). On pursuit of the purpose of life: the Shona metaphysical perspective. *Journal of Pan African Studies*, *3*(6), 269-284.

Mawere, M., & Marongwe, N. (Eds.). (2016). *Myths of Peace and Democracy? Towards Building Pillars of Hope, Unity and Transformation in Africa*. Langaa RPCIG.

Mawere, M., & Mubaya, T. R. (2016). *African philosophy and thought systems: A search for a culture and philosophy of belonging*. Langaa Rpcig.

Mawere, M., & Mwanaka, T. R. (Eds.). (2015). *Democracy, Good Governance and Development in Africa*. Langaa RPCIG.

Max-Neef, M., Elizalde, A., & Hopenhayn, M. (1992). Development and human needs. *Real-life economics: Understanding wealth creation*, 197-213.

May, J., & Govender, J. (1998). Poverty and inequality in South Africa. *Indicator South Africa*, *15*, 53-58.

McGowan, P. J. (1976). Economic dependence and economic performance in black Africa. *The Journal of Modern African Studies*, *14*(1), 25-40.

McMichael, P. (2005). Global development and the corporate food regime. In *New directions in the sociology of global development* (pp. 265-299). Emerald Group Publishing Limited.

McNulty, M. (2000). French arms, war and genocide in Rwanda. *Crime, law and social change*, *33*(1-2), 105-129.

Mearsheimer, J. J., & Walt, S. M. (2006). The Israel lobby and US foreign policy. *Middle East Policy*, *13*(3), 29-87.

Mearsheimer, J. J., & Walt, S. M. (2007). *The Israel lobby and US foreign policy* (No. 11). Macmillan.

Meehan, J., & Wright, G. H. (2012). The origins of power in buyer–seller relationships. *Industrial Marketing Management*, *41*(4), 669-679.

Mehlum, H., Moene, K., & Torvik, R. (2006). Institutions and the resource curse. *The economic journal*, *116*(508), 1-20.

Mhango, N. N. (2015). *Africa Reunite or Perish*. Langaa RPCIG.

Mhango, N. N. (2016). *Africa's Best and Worst Presidents: How Neocolonialism and Imperialism Maintained Venal Rules in Africa*. Langaa RPCIG.

Mhango, N. N. (2017). Chapter Nine History, Culture, Religion and [under-] Development in Africa. *Africa at the Crossroads: Theorising Fundamentalisms in the 21st Century, 223*.

Mhango, N. N. (2018). *How Africa Developed Europe: Deconstructing the His-story of Africa, Excavating Untold Truth and What Ought to Be Done and Known*. Langaa RPCIG.

Milmo, C. (2009). Dumped in Africa: Britain's toxic waste. *The Independent*.

Montague, D. (2002). Stolen goods: Coltan and conflict in the Democratic Republic of Congo. *Sais Review, 22*(1), 103-118.

Moore, M. (2001). Political Underdevelopment: What causes 'bad governance'. *Public Management Review, 3*(3), 385-418.

Moyo, D. (2009). Why foreign aid is hurting Africa. *The wall street journal, 11*.

Müller, E., Schluep, M., Widmer, R., Gottschalk, F., & Böni, H. (2009, September). Assessment of e-waste flows: a probabilistic approach to quantify e-waste based on world ICT and development indicators. In *R'09 World Congress* (pp. 14-16). Davos Switzerland.

Nails, D. (2006). The trial and death of Socrates. *A companion to Socrates, 5*.

Nancy, Y. W., & Aaron, C. A. (1998). Personal taste and family face: Luxury consumption in Confucian and Western societies. *Psychology & Marketing, 15*(5), 423-441.

Narman, A. (2014). *Development as theory and practice: current perspectives on development and development co-operation* (No. 1). Routledge.

Nathan, D., & Sarkar, S. (2011). Blood on your mobile phone? Capturing the gains for artisanal miners, poor workers and women.

Ndikumana, L., & Boyce, J. K. (2008). New estimates of capital flight from sub-Saharan African countries: Linkages with external borrowing and policy options.

Ndulu, B. J. (2004). Human capital flight: Stratification, globalization, and the challenges to tertiary education in Africa. *Journal of Higher Education in Africa/Revue de l'enseignement supérieur en Afrique*, 57-91.

Newman, S. (1991). Does modernization breed ethnic political conflict?. *World Politics*, *43*(3), 451-478.

News, C., (2010). Coltan: a new blood mineral. *CBC*, *12*.

Ngambi, H. (2011). RARE leadership: An alternative leadership approach for Africa. *International Journal of African Renaissance Studies-Multi-, Inter-and Transdisciplinarity*, *6*(1), 6-23.

Ngugi, B., (2016). Kenya Overtakes SA as Biggest Investor in African Countries. *Daily Nation*, 7.

Niemiec, C. P., & Ryan, R. M. (2009). Autonomy, competence, and relatedness in the classroom: Applying self-determination theory to educational practice. *School Field*, *7*(2), 133-144.

Nkrumah, K. (1966). Neo-Colonialism: The Last Stage of Imperialism. 1965. *New York: International*.

Nnorom, I. C., & Osibanjo, O. (2008). Electronic waste (e-waste): Material flows and management practices in Nigeria. *Waste Management*, *28*(8), 1472-1479.

Norton, E. (2012). Illiberal Democrats versus Undemocratic Liberals: The Struggle Over the Future of Thailand's Fragile Democracy. *Asian Journal of Political Science*, *20*(1), 46-69.

Noxolo, P., Raghuram, P., & Madge, C. (2012). Unsettling responsibility: postcolonial interventions. *Transactions of the Institute of British Geographers*, *37*(3), 418-429.

Nunn, N. (2007). Historical legacies: A model linking Africa's past to its current underdevelopment. *Journal of development economics*, *83*(1), 157-175.

Nyerere, J. K. (1977). The Plea of The Poor: New Economic Order NeededFor the World Community. *New Directions*, *5*(1), 8.

Oliveira, F. C. B. (2011). O projeto das Antropologias Mundiais diante dos desafios da alteridade no mundo globalizado. *Revista ANTHROPOLÓGICAS*, *18*(1).

Oloka-Onyango, J. (2004). " New-Breed" Leadership, Conflict, and Reconstruction in the Great Lakes Region of Africa: A

Sociopolitical Biography of Uganda's Yoweri Kaguta Museveni. *Africa Today*, *50*(3), 29-52.

Paldam, M. (2003). Economic freedom and the success of the Asian tigers: an essay on controversy. *European Journal of Political Economy*, *19*(3), 453-477.Parks, Bradley C., and J. Timmons Roberts. "Inequality and the Global Climate Regime: Breaking the North-South Impasse." *Cambridge Review of International Affairs 21.4* (2008): 621-648.

Peck, J., & Tickell, A. (2002). Neoliberalizing Space Antipode 34.3 380-404. Peters, John D. *(1999). Speaking Into the Air: A History of the Idea of Communication.*

Peet, R., 2009. *Unholy trinity: the IMF, World Bank and WTO.* Zed Books Ltd..

Persak, N., & Vermeulen, G. (Eds.). (2014). *Reframing Prostitution: From Discourse to Description, from Moralisation to Normalisation?.* Maklu.

Peterman, A., Palermo, T., & Bredenkamp, C. (2011). Estimates and determinants of sexual violence against women in the Democratic Republic of Congo. *American Journal of Public Health*, *101*(6), 1060-1067.

Petrocelli, M., Piquero, A. R., & Smith, M. R. (2003). Conflict theory and racial profiling: An empirical analysis of police traffic stop data. *Journal of Criminal Justice*, *31*(1), 1-11.

Pieterse, J. N. (2015). *Globalization and culture: Global mélange.* Rowman & Littlefield.

Pirotte, G., Pleyers, G., & Poncelet, M. (2006). Fair-trade coffee in Nicaragua and Tanzania: a comparison. *Development in practice*, *16*(5), 441-451.

Ploetner, O., & Ehret, M. (2006). From relationships to partnerships—new forms of cooperation between buyer and seller. *Industrial Marketing Management*, *35*(1), 4-9.

Pop, V., & Legorano, G., (2015). European, African Leaders Seek Compromise on Migrants. *Wall Street Journal*, 11.

Porter, M. E. (2000). Location, competition, and economic development: Local clusters in a global economy. *Economic development quarterly*, *14*(1), 15-34.

Post, K. W. (1968). Is there a case for Biafra?. *International Affairs (Royal Institute of International Affairs 1944-)*, *44*(1), 26-39.

Pricketl, R. (2000). THE GHROILE.

Pronk, J. (2004). Collateral damage or calculated default? The Millennium Development Goals and the politics of globalisation. In *Globalisation, Poverty and Conflict* (pp. 9-33). Springer, Dordrecht.

QUiLiConi, C. (2006). US–Latin American Trade Relations: Path to the Future or Dead End Street?. *BsAs, Flacso ed.*Shank, M., & Schirch, L. (2008). Strategic arts- based peacebuilding. *Peace & Change*, *33*(2), 217-242.

Rajan, R. G., & Subramanian, A. (2008). Aid and growth: What does the cross-country evidence really show?. *The Review of economics and Statistics*, *90*(4), 643-665.

Ravenhill, J. (2010). *Collective clientelism*. Columbia University Press.

Raynolds, L. T. (2000). Re-embedding global agriculture: The international organic and fair trade movements. *Agriculture and human values*, *17*(3), 297-309.

Reisman, W. M. (2007). Acting Before Victims Become Victims: Preventing and Arresting Mass Murder. *Case W. Res. J. Int'l L.*, *40*, 57.

Ribadu, N. (2009). Capital loss and corruption: the example of Nigeria. *Testimony before the House Financial Services Committee*, *19*.

Richmond, O. P. (2008). *Peace in international relations* (p. 112). London: Routledge.,

Roberts, M. J. (2009). Conflict analysis of the 2007 post-election violence in Kenya. *Managing Conflicts in Africa's Democratic Transitions*, 141-55.

Robinson, J. A., Torvik, R., & Verdier, T. (2006). Political foundations of the resource curse. *Journal of development Economics*, *79*(2), 447-468.

Rodney, W. (1972). *How europe underdeveloped africa* (Vol. 239). London.

Rodney, W. (2010). How Europe underdeveloped Africa.*Perspectives on Africa*. Blackwell, Malden, MA, 439-449.

Rogoff, B. (2003). *The cultural nature of human development*. Oxford University Press.

Rolfe, R. E. (2008). On the World Bank as an agent of economic imperialism.

Rosas, G. (2006). Bagehot or bailout? An analysis of government responses to banking crises. *American Journal of Political Science*, *50*(1), 175-191.

Rosenberg, N., Birdzell, L. E., & Mitchell, G. W. (1986). *How the West grew rich* (pp. 113-143). Mumbai: Popular Prakashan.

Rueschemeyer, D., Stephens, E. H., & Stephens, J. D. (1992). *Capitalist development and democracy* (p. 75057). Polity: Cambridge.

Santomé, J. T. (2007). Performance indicators as a strategy for counter-reformist change in educational policy. *Journal for Critical Education Policy Studies*, *5*(2), 529-562.

Schabas, W. A. (2000). Problems of International Codification- Were the atrocities in Cambodia and Kosovo Genocide. *New Eng. L. Rev.*, *35*, 287.

Schatzberg, M. G. (2014). Transformation and Struggle: Space in Africa. In *The Politics of Governance* (pp. 37-63). Routledge. Toye, J., Harrigan, J., & Mosley, P. (2013). *Aid and Power-Vol 1: The World Bank and Policy Based Lending*. Routledge.

Schmitz, C. L., Matyók, T., Sloan, L. M., & James, C. (2012). The relationship between social work and environmental sustainability: Implications for interdisciplinary practice. *International Journal of Social Welfare*, *21*(3), 278-286.

Schweller, R. (2011). Emerging powers in an age of disorder. *Global governance*, *17*(3), 285-297.

Scott, J., & Marshall, G. (Eds.). (2009). *A dictionary of sociology*. Oxford University Press, USA.

Selby, J., & Hoffmann, C. (2014). Beyond scarcity: rethinking water, climate change and conflict in the Sudans. *Global Environmental Change*, *29*, 360-370.

Sen, A. (1995). Environmental evaluation and social choice: contingent valuation and the market analogy. *The Japanese economic review*, *46*(1), 23-37.

Sharp, J. M. (2015). US foreign aid to Israel. *Current Politics and Economics of the Middle East*, *6*(3), 445.

Shaw, M. (1994). Tennyson's Dark Continent. *Victorian Poetry*, *32*(2), 157-169.

Shaxson, N. (2007). Oil, corruption and the resource curse. *International Affairs, 83*(6), 1123-1140.

Shaxson, N. (2012). *Treasure islands: Tax havens and the men who stole the world*. Random House.

Shearlaw, M., (2014). 'Africa Should Stop Blaming History for Its Economic Problems'. –Is Obama Right? *Guardian*, 7.

Shekighenda, L., (2016). Govt for self-reliance as MCC cancels assistance. *Guardian*, 4.

Sheppard, E., & Nagar, R. (2004). From east–west to north–south. *Antipode, 36*(4), 557-563.

Shlaim, A. (1995). The debate about 1948. *International Journal of Middle East Studies, 27*(3), 287-304.

Silver, B. J., & Arrighi, G. (2005). 22 Workers North and South. *The global resistance reader*, 273.

Silverstein, K. (2011). Teodorin's world. *Foreign Policy*, (185), 54.

Simon, D. (2014). Development revisited. *Development as Theory and Practice: current perspectives on development and development co-operation*, (1), 17.

Smith, H. E. (2012). Property as the Law of Things. *Harvard Law Review, 125*(7), 1691-1726.

Smith-Spark, L., (2014) China officials bought illegal ivory in Tanzania, activists claim. *CNN*, 11.

Sogge, D. (2007). *Angola: empowerment of the few*. FRIDE.

Solo-Trillo, E. (2013). Guinea Ecuatorial: un presente eterno. *Journal of Conflictology, 4*(2).

Songstad, N. G., Rekdal, O. B., Massay, D. A., & Blystad, A. (2011). Perceived unfairness in working conditions: the case of public health services in Tanzania. *BMC Health Services Research, 11*(1), 34.

Srinivasan, S. (2007). No democracy without justice: Political freedom in Amartya Sen's capability approach. *Journal of Human Development, 8*(3), 457-480.

Staff, R., (2015). Germany to Spend Up to 16 Billion Euros on Refugees Next Year. *Reuters*, 10.

Staff, R., (2016). "U.S. Agency Freezes $473 Million Aid to Tanzania over Zanzibar Election." *Reuters*, 3.

Staub, E. (2003). Notes on cultures of violence, cultures of caring and peace, and the fulfillment of basic human needs. *Political psychology, 24*(1), 1-21.

Staub, E. (2006). Reconciliation after genocide, mass killing, or intractable conflict: Understanding the roots of violence, psychological recovery, and steps toward a general theory. *Political psychology, 27*(6), 867-894.

Stedman, S. J. (2007). UN transformation in an era of soft balancing. *International Affairs, 83*(5), 933-944.

Stein, E. (2001). International integration and democracy: No love at first sight. *American Journal of International Law, 95*(3), 489-534.

Sun, Y., (2014). China's Aid to Africa: Monster or Messiah?" *Brookings,* February (7).

Sutherland, E. (2011). Coltan, the Congo and your cell phone.

Taylor, I. (2010). *The international relations of sub-Saharan Africa.* Bloomsbury Publishing USA.

Tikkamäki, K. (2013, June). Communities of Learning at Work—Making the Invisible Visible. In *Conference on Researching Work and Learning, Stirling, Scotland* (pp. 19-21).

Timmons Roberts, J., & Parks, B. C. (2007). Fueling injustice: globalization, ecologically unequal exchange and climate change. *Globalizations, 4*(2), 193-210.

Tjosvold, D. (2006). Defining conflict and making choices about its management: Lighting the dark side of organizational life. *International Journal of Conflict Management, 17*(2), 87-95.

Toye, J. (2007). Poverty reduction. *Development in practice, 17*(4-5), 505-510.

Tranos, E., & Nijkamp, P. (2013). The death of distance revisited: Cyber- place, physical and relational proximities. *Journal of Regional Science, 53*(5), 855-873.

Uvin, P. (2001). Reading the Rwandan genocide. *International Studies Review, 3*(3), 75-99.

Van der Ploeg, F. (2011). Natural resources: curse or blessing?. *Journal of Economic Literature, 49*(2), 366-420.

Victoor, A. (2011). *An Other Woman's Rape: Abjection and Objection in Representations of War Rape Victims in the DRC* (Doctoral dissertation).

Vlassenroot, K., & Huggins, C. (2005). Land, migration and conflict in eastern DRC. *From the ground up: land rights, conflict and peace in sub-Saharan Africa*, 115-194.

Vreeland, J. R. (2003). *The IMF and economic development*. Cambridge University Press.

Walker, R. (1987). Consensual approaches to the definition of poverty: towards an alternative methodology. *Journal of Social Policy*, *16*(2), 213-226.

Waltz, K. N. (2010). *Theory of international politics*. Waveland Press.

Wan, Chin-Sheng & Chiou,. W., (2006). Psychological Motives and Online Games Addiction: A Test of Flow Theory and Humanistic Needs Theory for Taiwanese Adolescents. *CyberPsychology & Behavior* 9 (3)- 317-324.

Webb, E. A. (2012). Power in Weakness: Feminist Reclamations of the Suffering of Christ. *Religious Studies Review*, *38*(4), 199-205.

Weingast, B. R. (1995). The economic role of political institutions: Market-preserving federalism and economic development. *Journal of Law, Economics, & Organization*, 1-31.

Werema: Balozi wa Uswisi Nchini Amekosa Adabu!. 2014 (Swiss Ambassador Lacks Respect) *Mwananchi*, 1.

West, A. (2014). Ubuntu and business ethics: Problems, perspectives and prospects. *Journal of business Ethics*, *121*(1), 47-61.

White, P. A. (2005). The power PC theory and causal powers: Comment on Cheng (1997) and Novick and Cheng (2004).

Whitehead, D. M. (2015). Gerard, Emmanuel, and Bruce Kuklick. 2015. Death in the Congo: Murdering Patrice Lumumba. *Africa Today*, *62*(2), 134-137.

Whyte, J. (1978). Interpretations of the Northern Ireland problem: An appraisal. *Economic and Social Review*, *9*(4), 257.

Wimmer, A., Cederman, L. E., & Min, B. (2009). Ethnic politics and armed conflict: A configurational analysis of a new global data set. *American Sociological Review*, *74*(2), 316-337.

Winterman, D., (2006). "What's So Great about Living in Vanuatu?" *BBC*, 7.

Wood, G. (2004). Business and politics in a criminal state: the case of Equatorial Guinea. *African Affairs*, *103*(413), 547-567.

Wright, J. (2008). To invest or insure? How authoritarian time horizons impact foreign aid effectiveness. *Comparative Political Studies*, *41*(7), 971-1000.

Wrong, M. (2005). When the Money goes west. *New Statesman March*, *14*, 2005.

Yang, K. S. (2003). Beyond Maslow's culture-bound linear theory: a preliminary statement of the double-Y model of basic human needs. In *Nebraska Symposium on Motivation. Nebraska Symposium on Motivation* (Vol. 49, pp. 175-255).

Zambian Miners Kill Chinese Manager During Pay Protest. 2012 *BBC*, 8.

Zartman, I. W. (2010). *Preventing identity conflicts leading to genocide and mass killings*. International Peace Institute.

Zartman, I. W. (2013). Mediation roles for large small countries. *Canadian Foreign Policy Journal*, *19*(1), 13-25.

Printed in the United States
By Bookmasters